CHRISTOPHER MARLOWE'S

DOCTOR FAUSTUS

CHRISTOPHER MARLOWE'S

DOCTOR FAUSTUS

A 1604–VERSION EDITION

edited by
Michael Keefer

broadview press

Cataloguing in Publication Data

Marlowe, Christopher, 1564-1593
    Doctor Faustus: A 1604-version edition

ISBN 0-921149-56-5 (bound)   ISBN 0-921149-59-X (pbk.)

I. Keefer, Michael H. II. Title.

        PR2664.A2K43   1991   822'.3   C90-093410-7

Cover: An Astrological Disputation, from Robert Flood, *Tomi secundi tractatus primi sectio secunda, De technica microcosmi historia* (Oppenheim, c. 1620)

Broadview Press

In Canada: Post Office Box 1243, Peterborough, Ontario, K9J 7H5

In the United States: 269 Portage Road, Lewiston, NY, 14092, USA

In the UK: c/o Drake Marketing Services, Market Place, Deddington, Oxfordshire, OX15 OSF

printed in Canada

CONTENTS

to E.K., with love, and to the memory of T.C.K.

PREFACE

Marlowe's *Doctor Faustus* survived the Elizabethan age in two quite distinct versions, the earliest extant editions of which, printed in 1604 and 1616, differ in length by more than six hundred lines. The modern-spelling text offered here is based on the more authentic and dramatically superior 1604 version of the play, while also incorporating readings from parallel scenes in the 1616 text in places where the 1604 text and its early reprints are clearly deficient.

All but a few of the many editions of *Doctor Faustus* produced between the early 1930s and the late 1970s used the longer 1616 or B text as copy-text, and although the view that this was the more original version of the play was decisively overturned more than fifteen years ago, new editions relying on the 1604 or A text have only begun to appear during the past half-dozen years. The first such edition, that of David Ormerod and Christopher Wortham (1985), has since been followed by Roma Gill's new modern- and old-spelling editions (1989, 1990). While I have diverged in various ways from the work of these and earlier editors, I am nonetheless indebted to them—sometimes most deeply so at those points where I have most strenuously disagreed with their conclusions.

The present text of *Doctor Faustus* is shorter, harsher, more focused and more disturbing than that version of the play which readers and play-goers have for much of this century been taught to regard as Marlowe's. It also differs from previous A-version texts for, on the basis of a fresh analysis of the relations between the two substantive texts, I have departed from previous editorial practice by restoring two displaced comic scenes to their proper places, thus eliminating a discontinuity which appears in both the 1604 and the 1616 quartos.

The present edition differs in other respects as well from earlier editions of this play. The career of the historical Dr. Faustus and the manner in which his legend took shape are of greater relevance to Marlowe's play than has often been supposed. In my introduction I have therefore both drawn upon and supplemented the work of scholars like Frank Baron who have made available a new understanding of the historical Faustus and of the originary contexts of his legend. Marlowe was aware of these contexts; we need to be as well, if we wish to understand how this play reshapes and subverts an originally homiletic narrative.

My introduction also seeks to make visible certain links between recent developments in textual scholarship and in literary interpretation. The reversal of editorial opinion with regard to the two versions of *Doctor Faustus* has been accompanied by reversals in the interpretation of this play, and these parallel developments have in turn been part of a broader shift in the paradigms both of interpretation and of textual criticism which has taken place during the past two decades. An awareness of these connections can help one to see how intimately related textual decisions are to critical and ideological orientations—in the present edition as much as in previous ones.

Recent studies of *Doctor Faustus* and of the legend which it dramatizes point to the importance of a contextualized understanding of the play. I have therefore supplemented the play-text with four appendices. These are offered with the aim of bringing into focus the relations between *Doctor Faustus* and the ideological currents which it interrogates, as well as those by which the play was subsequently deformed. Appendix 1 contains those scenes in the 1616 text which deviate from the earlier version, and which, as part of a post-Marlovian re-visioning of the play, turn it back towards the moralistic, homiletic mode of Marlowe's principal source, a prose chapbook commonly referred to as the English Faustbook. Excerpts from that text, *The History of the damnable life and deserved death of Doctor John Faustus*, appear in Appendix 2.

The writings of Henricus Cornelius Agrippa and Jean Calvin excerpted in Appendices 3 and 4 cannot properly be described as "sources" for Marlowe's play. However, they do form an important part of its context—in the root sense of *contextus*, as things inextricably woven into its texture. The names of Agrippa and of Faustus had already been linked by polemicists against Renaissance magic; and in expressing his desire to be "as cunning as Agrippa was" (I.i.118), Marlowe's Faustus alerts us to the parodic echoes of Agrippa's two best-known books, *Of the Vanity and Uncertainty of Arts and Sciences* and *Of Occult Philosophy*, which resonate through his first soliloquy. Calvin's theology, which in Marlowe's lifetime had become the ruling orthodoxy of the Elizabethan Anglican church, is present throughout the play in a more pervasive manner—as the limiting doctrine against which Faustus rebels and by which, paradoxically, he is constituted.

Spelling and punctuation have been modernized in the text of *Doctor Faustus* and in the four appendices (as well as in quotations from Renaissance texts in the notes); in the introduction old spelling is retained, except with regard to u/v and i/j. The name of Faustus's attendant spirit is given in this A-version text as "Mephastophilis," that being the form which occurs most frequently in the A text; I have used the spelling "Mephostophilis," which is the normal B-text form, only when discussing that text, as well as in Appendix 1. In those parts of my introduction which discuss the distinctive features of the A and B texts I have identified quotations by means of their line numbers in W.W. Greg's parallel-text edition as well as their act, scene and line numbers in the present edition; elsewhere quotations are keyed to the present edition alone.

In editing the play-text I have had recourse to the single surviving copies of the 1604 and 1616 editions held by the Bodleian Library and the British Library respectively, and also (for the sake of convenience) to the Scolar Press facsimile of these unique copies. The excerpts from the English Faustbook have been edited from the unique copy of the 1592 edition in the British Library. In Appendix 3, occasional errors in the Elizabethan translation of Agrippa's *De vanitate* have been corrected by reference to the first Latin edition of 1530; my translations of passages from *De occulta philosophia* were made from the first complete edition of 1533. And in modernizing the punctuation in Thomas Norton's translation of Calvin's *Institutes*, I have referred both to the McNeill-Battles translation of the 1559 Latin text and to Jean-Daniel Benoit's edition of the 1560 French text.

During the preparation of this edition I have benefited from the kind co-operation of librarians in the Bibliothèque municipale de Dijon, the Warburg Institute, the British Library, the Bodleian Library, the University of Sussex Library, and the Bibliothèque de l'Université Sainte-Anne. I am grateful also to the editors of the *Journal of English and Germanic Philology*, *The Dalhousie Review*,

University of Toronto Quarterly, Renaissance Quarterly, and *Mosaic* for permission to draw upon articles of mine on *Doctor Faustus* and related subjects which have appeared in these journals.

I owe special thanks to Tony Nuttall (whose presence and example in the early stages of my work were decisive), as well as to Don Beecher, Andreas Buss, Jonathan Dollimore, and James Quinlan; to the Social Sciences and Humanities Research Council of Canada, which in 1988-89 liberated me from my teaching duties with a generous research grant and research time stipend; to the University of Sussex, which during that year gave me a most stimulating environment in which to work; and—most of all—to Janice Kulyk Keefer,

Ma douce Hélène, non, mais bien ma douce haleine:
Seule je te choisi, seule aussi tu me plais.

INTRODUCTION

1. The rationale for a new edition of Doctor Faustus.

(a) Narratives of textual transmission

Marlowe's *Doctor Faustus* exists in two distinct versions, represented by the quartos of 1604 and 1616 and their reprints. This fact confronts textual critics, before they can confidently propose one or the other version as the basis of a new edition, with the task of establishing a plausible narrative of the play's early textual history. By what paths did the play come to assume two such divergent forms, and what reasons are there for valuing one or the other as the more authentic?

The more obvious differences between the 1604 or A text and the 1616 or B text can be quickly summarized: the two texts are closely parallel in Acts One and Two, diverge widely in Acts Three and Four, and converge again for much of Act Five. Although the B text is longer overall by 614 lines of print, its first two acts, surprisingly perhaps, are shorter than A's by some 70 lines. (Some at least of the difference is due to cuts in these acts: a total of eighteen lines of indisputably Marlovian verse are missing in B, as well as thirteen lines of prose that can on good grounds be attributed to Marlowe.) The episodes in the papal, imperial, and ducal courts which make up the greater part of Acts Three and Four are expanded in B to more than twice the length they occupy in A, and the B text's Act Five contains further additions: the "desperate lunacy" (B: V.ii.11) of Faustus in his last hours is witnessed by Lucifer, Belzebub and Mephostophilis; his last soliloquy is preceded by moralizing speeches from Mephostophilis and the Good and Bad Angels; and his death is followed by a short scene in which the scholars discover his mangled limbs.

Both A and B are in different respects inadequate. B is a systematically censored and heavily revised text, while in A's comic scenes there is also evidence of revision: two such scenes (II.ii and III.ii in the present edition) are displaced in the 1604 quarto, and the second of these has two distinct endings. A lacks fourteen lines of the chorus to Act Three; in B the entire chorus to Act Four is missing. Certain passages in A are demonstrably secondary—the result, it would appear, of memorial transmission, traces of which can also, however, be detected in B. Finally, two scenes (II.i and II.iii in this edition) are run together in A, despite indications of the passage of time which make it evident that they should be separated by another scene. In B the scene which should come between them is likewise displaced, but the two scenes are held apart by the bizarre expedient of printing between them eleven lines, copied from the A text, which are all that that text preserves of the chorus to Act Three. (A conjectural explanation of this shared gap in the two substantive quartos will be found in section 7 below.)

For all its deficiencies, the A text represents a relatively more authentic version of the play: the detectable revisions in its comic scenes date most probably from the mid-1590s, while the distinctive features of B can with some assurance be dated to the years 1602 (the additions to Acts Three to Five) and 1606 (the censorship of the play). Moreover, A is a tauter, more coherent and more troubling text: the additions in B, which account for more than half the length of that text, are for the most part unskilful and tedious; and in turning the play back towards the homiletic style of the English Faustbook which was Marlowe's principal source, they incorporate a view of the protagonist and of his predicament which differs from that of the Marlovian scenes common to both versions of the play.

In its essentials, then, the narrative of textual transmission which underlies the present edition is a simple one. (I offer here the merest outline: supporting evidence will be found in sections 6 and 7 below.) Written most probably not long before Marlowe's death in 1593, *Doctor Faustus* was exposed to a process of piecemeal theatrical revision during the period from September 1594 until October 1597 in which it formed part of the repertory of the Lord Admiral's Men (also known as the Earl of Nottingham's company). The play was entered in the Stationers' Register by Thomas Bushell in January 1601, and printed by him in 1604. This printed text is evidently of theatrical provenance: its stage directions, its lack of act and scene divisions, and the evidence in it of memorial rather than purely scribal transmission all indicate as much. As it stands, the 1604 quarto is not a satisfactory performance text: the notion that its displaced comic scenes were ever performed in the order in which they were printed is grossly implausible. But A is probably not far removed from what audiences at the Rose would have seen performed during the mid-1590s.

Further changes to the text resulted in the creation of a second, quite different version of the play. The Admiral's Men decided in 1602 to revive *Doctor Faustus*, and in November of that year commissioned William Birde and Samuel Rowley to alter and expand it: the result was something close to what appears in modern B-version editions such as that of Fredson Bowers. Four years later, the Act of Abuses (1606) imposed heavy fines for profane references to God in stage plays: it was doubtless at this time that all such references, along with some of Faustus's more notable blasphemies, were cut from the B text of *Doctor Faustus*. The person who made these cuts may also have been responsible for a number of other alterations which effectively dampen the Calvinist overtones of the play, although these ideologically motivated revisions could very well have been the work of Birde and Rowley in 1602. Some further changes suggestive of editorial activity — revisions or deletions of obscure words or passages, for the most part — appear to have been made at the time the B text was printed in 1616. This quarto, then, is close to what was being performed between 1606 and 1616 — although, like A, it has at least one feature (the clumsily filled gap between the fifth and sixth scenes of B) that can hardly have figured in any performance of the play.

The foregoing narrative of textual transmission is also a story about the containment of subversion by orthodoxy. The historical Dr. Faustus was a blatant transgressor both in religious and in sexual terms; the legend of his pact with the devil, his transgressive escapades and his final agony of despair which developed during the decades following his death in the late 1530s reaffirmed a Protestant version of that Christian orthodoxy against which he had rebelled. Marlowe, himself a similarly transgressive figure as well as a one-time theological student, gave this legend a subversive twist. Without substantially altering its sequence of apostasy, despair and damna-

tion, he foregrounded the issue of human autonomy, stripped away
the layers of moralistic commentary which in the Faustbooks mask
the ethical problems raised by the doctrine of predestination, and
made the story into an expression of the most intimate fear of sixteenth-century Protestants: that of predestined damnation to eternal
torment. A legend which had buttressed Lutheran orthodoxy in Germany thus became a means of interrogating the quite similar Calvinistic orthodoxy of late sixteenth-century England.

Operating within the limits of a censorship which suppressed any
overt challenge to official doctrine but left room for strategies of
indirection or insinuation (Patterson 17), Marlowe's *Doctor Faustus*
does not invite its audience to imagine any secure alternative to the
orthodoxy which it questions. Indeed, it seems unlikely that Marlowe
possessed such an alternative himself. The violent blasphemies attributed to him by his contemporaries suggest, rather, a stance like
that adopted by George Chapman when in his *Hymnus in Noctem*
(1594) he calls on Night, the "Type, and nurse of death," to raise
his soul

> to that perseverance,
That in my torture, she all earths may sing,
And force to tremble in her trumpeting
Heavens christall temples....
> (Chapman 20; lines 5, 16-19)

I do not mean to suggest that *Doctor Faustus* directly validates
oppositional heroics of this kind: Marlowe perhaps had a more lucid
sense than Chapman of what torture can do to people. It is as a
statement of dramatic effect rather than as a thematic summary that
these lines are applicable to the play. Faustus's brief pretence of
"manly fortitude" (I.iii.85) is shown in an ironic light, and he dies
in a state of terror, self-loathing and despair. Yet his perseverance
in despair is as distinct a sign of divine reprobation as Calvin held
perseverance in grace to be one of divine election, and the insistent
suggestions of the A text that his repeated inability to will his own
salvation is due to the workings of another will, anterior to his and
subjecting him to its determinations, make Faustus's "torture" deeply unsettling. A Calvinistic orthodoxy may appear to win out at the
end of this play, but it does so at the cost of being exposed, in the
moment of its triumph, as intolerable.

Introduction

In the B text this effect is blunted. The revisions and additions of 1602 revert to the moralistic manner of the Faustbooks; and the questions which the A text raises about the nature of the God who presides over Faustus's damnation are obscured in the parallel passages of B by the censor's cuts and alterations. The result is a text which lends itself to interpretation as a more or less orthodox morality play.

Strangely enough, this pattern of an orthodox effacement of Marlowe's heterodoxy has been repeated during the present century, under the aegis of the "scientific" New Bibliography. Late nineteenth-century editors of Marlowe were unanimous in regarding the A version of the play as the more authentic. One such editor, the freethinker Havelock Ellis, identified the author of *Doctor Faustus* as a kindred spirit, a man whose "thirst for emancipation" was expressed in "acute and audacious utterances" (so Ellis characterized the violent blasphemies attributed to Marlowe by his contemporaries) which, he blandly remarked, correspond closely to the views of "students of science and of the Bible in our own days" (Ellis xxxi, 430-1). Although few other late nineteenth and early twentieth-century interpreters of the play expressed themselves in so deliberately provocative a manner, most of them would have agreed with Una Ellis-Fermor's opinion that, like the "bitter attacks on Christians" in *Tamburlaine*, "the picture of catastrophe and confusion in *Faustus*" was evidence of what she called "the perversion of [Marlowe's] mind under the influence of contemporary scholarism and theological dogma" (Ellis-Fermor 66). Her opinion that Faustus, at least in the early scenes of the play, is very much a Marlovian self-portrait was also widely shared.

During the 1930s and 1940s a reaction against this view of the play gathered strength, one which involved a simultaneous recognition of the ironic distance between Marlowe and his protagonist, a suppression of those other ironies by means of which the play problematizes its own Christian framework, and an assertion—based upon the new methods then entering textual criticism—that the playwright's intentions are best preserved in the B version of *Doctor Faustus*. Leo Kirschbaum, for example, defined the play as "a quasi-morality in which is clearly set forth the hierarchy of moral values which enforces and encloses the play, which the characters in the play accept, which the playwright advances and accepts in his prologue and epilogue, which — hence — the audience must understand and accept" (Kirschbaum 1943: 229). Three years later his application of these presuppositions to the textual evidence generated the conclusion that the A text is a memorially corrupted "bad quarto," while B "on the whole...accurately and faithfully reproduces the play which Marlowe wrote, either by himself or with a collaborator" (Kirschbaum 1946: 294). The hermeneutical circle is thus closed: the assumption that the play is an unproblematically orthodox Christian document shapes the textual analysis by which the B text is authenticated; the B text in turn validates interpretations of the play as orthodox. And in 1950, Kirschbaum's arguments were repeated, in a more sophisticated and vastly expanded form, in W.W. Greg's magisterial parallel-text edition of *Doctor Faustus*.

Many of those critics who relied upon the B-version editions of Boas (1932), Greg (1950), Jump (1962), Kirschbaum (1962), Ribner (1963), Gill (1965, 1971), Barnet (1968), Steane (1969), Bowers (1973), or Pendry and Maxwell (1976), did indeed tend to interpret *Doctor Faustus* as an unproblematically orthodox text. Other interpreters, however, resisted this view of the play, even when the influence of Greg's textual analysis was at its height. C.L. Barber (to name only the most important such critic) was exemplary in making the A text the basis of his explorations of the ambivalences and duplicities of this play. A renewed sifting of the textual evidence — by Fredson Bowers, Constance Brown Kuriyama, Michael Warren, D.J. Lake and Roma Gill, among others — has since amply justified this stance. Moreover, the insights of Barber have been ably supplemented by critics like Edward Snow, Jonathan Dollimore, Alan Sinfield and Simon Shepherd, thanks to whom a fuller understanding of this play's discursive contexts and of its disturbingly transgressive force has become widely available.

(b) Master-narratives of textual criticism

It remains the case, however, that recent developments in the field of textual criticism have yet to be adequately reflected in editorial work on *Doctor Faustus*. The preference of editors during much of this century for the secondary, but more or less orthodox B text might with good reason be ascribed to the generally very conservative orientation of the academic literary institution. Yet since this preference was also shaped by two of the most distinguished textual scholars of this century—W.W. Greg, a founder of what became known as the New Bibliography, and Fredson Bowers, an equally distinguished textual theorist who, while demolishing Greg's arguments for the primacy of the B text nonetheless maintained that only a B-version edition could be bibliographically adequate (Bowers 2. 142-45)—it may also be worth considering the extent to which their work on this play was governed by some larger narrative implicit in their understanding of textual criticism.

An oddly Neoplatonic note can be detected in certain of their utterances: in, for example, Greg's famous distinction between the "substantial" and "accidental" features of a text ("Copy-Text" 43), which might be taken to imply a scholastic separation of the 'essential thing' from its historically specific materiality. Bowers, taking up this distinction, described the "accidentals" of a text as "the system of spelling, punctuation, capitalization, and word-division that *clothes* the words," and spoke of the need "to strip the *veil* of print from a text by analyzing the characteristics of identified compositors" ("Editing" 167, 87; emphasis added). What is veiled in these metaphors is apparently not the text's material 'body,' but rather a kind of trans-historical essence. As the human soul is clothed by the body, so the immaterial substantial text is veiled by its accidents: in each case the second, inessential term is made to bear the burden of corporeality—and also, it might seem, of historicity. Although an element of abstraction is unavoidable in textual analysis, this is perhaps an unnecessarily loaded way of talking about the processes that give rise to textual variants.

But Neoplatonic metaphors such as these may be no more than offshoots of an implicit master-narrative that has arguably shaped the empirical narratives of the last several generations of textual critics. This master-narrative displaces into textual terms the Neoplatonic story of the soul's descent from an originary unity to a state of materiality, multiplicity and error, and its purifying reascent to the One. Now, of course, it is the play-text which descends from its authorial originator into a confused world of theatrical alterations, memorial corruption, copyists' errors and compositorial distortion—the dark world, in textual jargon, of the Bad Quarto—from which it is to be led back to a state of primordial unity by the labors of the editor. Donald Pizer has in terms rather like these caricatured the view, which he attributes to Greg and his successors, that "a text emerges from its author's imagination trailing clouds of glory. Then, shades of the prison-house of unauthorized, ill-advised, and self-censored change close down upon it." The editor's role in this quasi-religious allegory is almost a priestly one: confronting the corrupt published text, "he cleans it of its worldliness and restores it to its original purity" (Pizer 147).

No one would quarrel with the project of restoring a text to what has been called its "originary textual moment," as opposed to "secondary moments of textual production and reproduction" (McGann 1985: 192-93). But how is that state to be determined? The master-narrative I have identified conflates the project of restoration with a Romantic conception of authorship, thus obscuring "the dynamic social relations which always exist in literary production — the dialectic between the historically located individual author and the historically developing institutions of literary production" (McGann 1983: 81). Textual critics have commonly presupposed an autonomous author whose intentions were authoritatively expressed in the lost manuscript which it has been their goal (within the limits of possibility) to reconstruct. But where did the authority of Elizabethan play-texts really reside? As Stephen Orgel has remarked, theatrical companies often commissioned a play, stipulated its subject, apportioned sections of the plot to different playwrights, and then revised the resulting text — from which it follows that "the very notion of 'the author's original manuscript' is in such cases a figment" (Orgel 3).

An assumption that the lost original must have been the expression of a single set of authorial intentions provides one explanation for the neglect during the postwar period of the evidence for authorial revision in such plays as Shakespeare's *King Lear*. The notion that the unitary original hypothesized by modern editors never existed, that *King Lear* may be not a single but a plural object, and that its two equally authorial versions are quite reliably represented by the Quarto and Folio texts, seems to have been institutionally unthinkable until the late 1970s, although it has since been generally accepted. A similar assumption about authorship appears to underlie one influential objection to the A version of *Doctor Faustus*. In its comic scenes especially, the 1604 quarto bears traces of oral transmission and actors' gag, which have been taken to indicate that the corresponding scenes in the 1616 quarto must be closer to an original text composed in part by Marlowe, but generally under his direction (Kirschbaum 1946: 277-84; Greg 26, 33-39; for more judicious analyses, see Pettitt 1988a and b, and Hjort 272-75). Simon Shepherd has observed in this regard that editorial decisions about interpolations and variants often rest on assumptions about literary decorum which involve an "undervaluing of performance work" (Shepherd 70-1). Yet only quite recently has the possibility that some of the original comic action was contributed by actors, and that the corresponding 1616 scenes are a later revision received serious consideration (Gill 1990: xviii-xxi).

Modern receptions of *Doctor Faustus* have been distorted in other ways as well by the master-narrative of textual criticism. The presupposition of autonomous authorship encouraged a corresponding de-historicizing of this play—a neglect of institutional and ideological contexts, or of what one might call the 'worldliness' of the play-text and its originators. This erasure of historical differences made it fatally easy for textual critics to fall into the error of remaking Marlowe's putative intentions in the image and likeness of their own. As I have already suggested, the result, in the case of Leo Kirschbaum's and W.W. Greg's enormously influential analyses of the two versions of *Doctor Faustus*, was a closed hermeneutical circle. Their own ideological prejudices—their commitment to a de-historicized Christian orthodoxy, explicitly used by Greg as a textual criterion—led them to authenticate the 1616 text, which in turn legitimized the 'orthodox' moralistic interpretations that had informed their initial preference for it over the more disturbing 1604 text. But Kirschbaum's prejudices are readily exposed; and recent studies have made it evident that the "professed objectivity" of Greg's arguments for the priority of B and the memorial corruption of A is likewise "quite spurious" (Warren 124).

Harold Bloom remarks acerbically that "There has been a fashion, in modern scholarly criticism, to baptize Marlowe's imagination, so that a writer of tragic caricatures has been converted into an orthodox moralist. The vanity of scholarship has few more curious monuments than this Christianized Marlowe" (Bloom 1). It seems clear that much of the impetus for this distortion of Marlowe came from the work of textual scholars. For, as Ormerod and Wortham have observed, arguments which Greg presented as "tentative and provisional became prescriptive to his followers" — with the consequence, in their view, that "a generation of scholarly interpretive writing on *Doctor Faustus* has been debased by widespread recourse to the B-version" (Ormerod and Wortham xxiv).

But might it not be argued that an element of fashion is involved both in polemics against conventional textual criticism and in the current swing among editors of *Doctor Faustus* towards the A version of the play? There is indeed a fairly obvious connection between the New Bibliography's emphasis upon autonomous authorship and the New Critical dogma of textual autonomy — as also between the reign of the New Criticism and the period during which Greg's analysis of *Doctor Faustus* enjoyed a more or less unchallenged dominance (Keefer 1987: 505-08). No less evidently, the historically inflected work of textual critics like Jerome McGann draws upon recent work in hermeneutics and in poststructuralist and cultural materialist literary theory. But to speak of this difference in terms of changing fashions would be to divert attention from the actual arguments of Greg, the attempt of Bowers in the early 1970s to supplement or supplant them, and the subsequent criticisms made of both scholars — as well as from the underlying shift in the paradigms of literary studies which has altered our sense of what constitutes an adequate textual argument.

Yet in a certain sense the editorial history of *Doctor Faustus* positively invites discussion in terms of fashion. Even though the textual evidence available to them was far from unambiguous, editors in the late nineteenth and early twentieth centuries printed the A version with increasing confidence; and the B-version editors of the mid-twentieth century more closely resemble George Bernard Shaw's description of a cavalry charge ("first one comes; then two or three close behind him; and then all the rest in a lump"). Boas's lonely challenge to the authority of the A version (1932) was followed by Greg's editions in 1950, and then in the 1960s and 1970s by nine others — several of whose editors, however, expressed serious reservations about the text they were offering. The A-version remained marginally available during most of this period, thanks largely to the editions of Kocher (1950) and Wright and LaMar (1959). But now another charge, led by Ormerod's and Wortham's 1985 edition of the A text and Roma Gill's recent A-version editions, appears to be gathering momentum. Some of these editions—most notably those of Boas, Greg, Bowers, Ormerod and Wortham, and Gill—clearly result from sustained independent analysis of the textual problem. Others, however, provide ample support for an analogy with Thomas Kuhn's view of intellectual history, according to which paradigm shifts are followed by periods of 'normal science' characterized by the rule of more or less unchallenged axioms—or, one might say, of fashion.

The present edition does not aspire to be fashionable in this or any other sense. The text offered here is an attempted reconstitution of the play as it might have been performed in the mid-1590s. I make no claims as to how closely this text may resemble Marlowe's original manuscript, both because any statements about the contents of that lost document can only be conjectural, and also because there is good reason to believe that the original performance text was not Marlowe's work alone, but embodied the collaborative efforts of actors. Yet while rejecting the Romantic conception of autonomous authorship that has been an integral part of traditional textual criticism, I would at the same time argue that the tendency of some recent textual critics to dismiss authorial agency altogether in favor of a concern with a text's "effective-history" or *Wirkungsgeschichte* is misguided. Anne Mette Hjort has written, with an eye to this play, that "All of the different scribal emendations, all of the changes made by actors, all of the various appropriations, become an integral and unalienable part of the work's *meaning*—for the appropriations of a 'work' and any emendations that these might involve only make manifest the ways in which the work can combine with specific intentional horizons to produce meaning" (Hjort 274). These words suggest an incomplete awareness of the extent to which censorship and revision (itself arguably ideologically motivated) result in a process of textual change which is as much a matter of deliberate erasure as it is of misremembering, accretion and reinscription. For while the meaning of a text is indeed interactively reconstituted within the contexts of its reception, it remains the case that any attempt at a properly historical understanding requires us to distinguish among the various reinscriptions of the textual palimpsest. Moreover, any adequate sense of a text's 'effective-history' must include some awareness of its prehistory and of what one might call its originary intentional horizon—and the most obvious name for what connects these with its subsequent history is "author."

Whether we think of Christopher Marlowe as a discursively constituted subject or in more traditional terms, the other historical traces he left are sufficiently distinct and strange to make his authorship of most of *Doctor Faustus* an important fact. I thus do not find helpful Stephen Orgel's comment that in the texts of this play "the author has become a curiously imprecise, intermittent and shifting figure, even on the title-page," where he is referred to "in the 1604 first quarto as 'Ch. Marl.', and in the 1616 quarto as 'Ch. Marklin'" (Orgel 6). First, because the latter name was in fact printed as "Ch. Mar.": as close inspection reveals, the last four letters on the title-page of the sole surviving copy of the 1616 quarto have been added with a pen. And secondly, because I think that Marlowe's intentions in this play are perhaps less elusive than has sometimes been supposed: their printed 'signature,' though abbreviated even in the 1604 text, may in a similar manner be recoverable from beneath the reinscriptions of revisers, of censors, and of textual critics.

2. Christopher Marlowe

Born in 1564, in Canterbury, the son of a shoemaker, Christopher Marlowe was killed—or possibly murdered—twenty-nine years later in Deptford, near London. One way of understanding his life is as a sequence of interactions among three institutions: the church, the state, and the theater.

Nothing is known about Marlowe's early education. But at Christmas in 1578 he became a scholar at the King's School, which still occupies the old priory buildings in the precincts of Canterbury Cathedral; and in December 1580 he entered Corpus Christi College, Cambridge, where his way was paid by one of the scholarships established five years previously by the will of Archbishop Matthew Parker. These scholarships were normally of three years' duration, but could be renewed for a further three years by students who intended to take holy orders (Bakeless i. 49). Yet after a full six years as a Parker scholar – he received his B.A. early in 1584, and (in very unusual circumstances) his M.A. in July 1587 – Marlowe moved into an association with the theater rather than the church, possibly taking with him some sense of what it meant to be, in Faustus's words, "a divine in show" (I.i.3).

By the time of his departure from Cambridge he was already active as a poet: his translations of *All Ovid's Elegies* and *Lucan's First Book*, along with the play *Dido Queen of Carthage*, are all thought to have been written before 1587; and Robert Greene's remarks in the preface to *Perimedes the Blacksmith* (1588) about "daring God out of heaven with that Atheist *Tamburlan*," and about "such mad and scoffing poets, that have propheticall spirits as bred of *Merlins* race," indicate that both parts of *Tamburlaine* were performed before the end of 1587 (Leech 4). (Greene's pun on Marlowe's name becomes more obvious if one knows that "Marlin" and "Marlen" figure among the variant forms of this name in the Cambridge records.)

While still a student Marlowe supplemented his scholarship money by working as an undercover agent of the state. The books which in June 1599 the Bishop of London and the Archbishop of Canterbury ordered to be publicly burned included a selection from his translation of Ovid, which had been printed together with Davies' epigrams (Gill 1987: 7). But it was for reasons quite unconnected with his writings that in the spring of 1587 Cambridge University proposed to deny Marlowe his M.A. degree. During this period, as Marlowe has Henry III say in *The Massacre at Paris* (c. 1591-92), "a sort of English priests" were drawn "to the seminary at Rheims / To hatch forth treason 'gainst their natural Queen" (xxi, 101-3). The reference is to English converts to Catholicism, many of them graduates of Oxford or Cambridge, who were trained at Rheims to return as missionaries – and who, since the papacy was effectively at war with Queen Elizabeth, were regarded by her government as traitors. One of Marlowe's contemporaries at the King's School, "a most terrible puritan" who was placed in charge of Roman Catholic prisoners in the Tower of London and promptly converted by one of them, followed this path (Urry 49). The Cambridge authorities must have suspected Marlowe of similar intentions, for on June 29, 1587, Her Majesty's Privy Council, no less, intervened on his behalf:

> Whereas it was reported that Christopher Morley was determined to have gone beyond the seas to Reames and there to remaine Their Lordships thought good to certefie that he had no such intent but that in all his accons [actions] he had behauved him selfe orderlie and discreetelie wherebie he had done her majestie good service, and deserved to be rewarded for his faithfull dealinge: Their Lordships' request was that the rumor thereof should be allaied by all possible meanes, and that he should be furthered in the degree he was to take this next Commencement: Because it was not her majestie's pleasure that anie one emploied as he had been in matters touching the benefitt of his Countrie should be defamed by those that are ignorant in th'affaires he went about. (Bakeless i. 77)

What these affairs were remains uncertain. During some at least of the absences attested to by the Buttery Book of Corpus Christi College, Marlowe may have carried secret dispatches to and from English diplomats in the Low Countries (Bakeless i. 71-5, 83-4). The rumors of his intended defection, however, suggest that he was assigned the task of infiltrating recusant groups and spying on them. Continued employment of one or both kinds would explain his presence at Flushing on the Isle of Walcheren in January 1592, where he was denounced by one Richard Baines, a Cambridge M.A. who had defected to Rheims in 1578, but in 1583 turned again and entered Sir Francis Walsingham's secret service. Baines and Marlowe accused one another of counterfeiting money and of intending to go over to the Spaniards or to Rome; Marlowe was arrested by Sir Robert Sidney, the governor of Flushing, and sent back to England, where it would seem the accusations against him were dismissed (Kuriyama 1988a: 346-57).

The dating of Marlowe's plays is largely a matter for conjecture. But by this time, already famous for his *Tamburlaine* plays, he had probably also written *Edward II* and *The Massacre at Paris*, and possibly *Doctor Faustus* as well. It has been suggested that Richard Baines may have contributed in a small way to the conception of that sardonic masterpiece *The Jew of Malta*: Marlowe may have known that when Baines apostasized for the second time, he confessed to have contemplated (quite in the manner of Barabas) wiping out the entire religious community of the English College at Rheims by poisoning its water supply (Kuriyama 1988a: 346-7). During the last year of his life Marlowe wrote *Doctor Faustus* (if a late date be accepted for that play), and also that delicious poem *Hero and Leander*, for which we may be indebted to the fact that an outbreak of plague had led to the closing of the theaters.

Marlowe's friends and acquaintances were not predominantly of the Baines type: they included the poets Thomas Watson, Matthew Roydon and Thomas Kyd, and the mathematician Thomas Harriot; moreover, at the time of his arrest in Flushing Marlowe claimed familiarity with the Earl of Northumberland and with Lord Strange, patron of the company which staged his plays. He was also a member of Sir Walter Ralegh's circle, and enjoyed the patronage of Thomas Walsingham, a nephew of Queen Elizabeth's Principal Secretary, Sir Francis Walsingham (Urry 70-3).

Harriot, Ralegh and Northumberland were all suspected of holding heterodox opinions; Marlowe, with none of their discretion, trumpeted his abroad. Robert Greene, who in 1588 had sneered at the success of *Tamburlaine*, pointed the finger at its author in his deathbed tract, *A Groatsworth of Wit bought with a Million of Repentance* (1592):

> Wonder not [...], thou famous gracer of Tragedians, that
> *Greene*, who hath said with thee (like the foole in his heart),
> There is no God, should now give glorie unto his greatnes:
> for penetrating is his power, his hand lyes heavie upon me,
> hee hath spoken unto me with a voice of thunder, and I
> have felt he is a God that can punish enemies. Why should
> thy excellent wit, his gift, bee so blinded, that thou shouldst
> give no glorie to the giver? Is it pestilent Machivilian pollicy
> that thou hast studied? O peevish follie! [....] The brocher
> of this Diabolicall Atheisme is dead, and in his life had
> never the felicitie hee aymed at: but as he began in craft,
> lived in feare, and ended in despaire. [....] and wilt thou my
> friend be his disciple? Looke but to me, by him perswaded
> to that libertie, and thou shalt find it an infernall bondage.
> I knowe the least of my demerits merit this miserable death,

but wilfull striving against knowne truth, exceedeth all the terrors of my soule. (Maclure 30)

Fine rhetoric perhaps, but "these were dangerous words to have printed against anyone in 1592" (Leech 5).

The association of Machiavellian "policy" with "atheism," while obvious enough as a response to certain motifs in Marlowe's plays, seems appropriate in a manner of which Greene may have been unaware. The former theological student attacked in this passage had undergone a prolonged immersion in the hard paradoxes of Calvinism, many of which have to do with the inscrutable hidden will of a God whose basic motive, as disclosed by his Genevan prophet, is not unlike that of the princes studied by Machiavelli: the promulgation of his own glory (Calvin III.xxi.1; III.xxiv.12; III.xxiv.14). Marlowe had probably also read Machiavelli; more importantly, he had witnessed his precepts in action and knew that "such as love [him] guard [him] from their tongues" (*Jew of Malta*, Prologue 6). While yet a student he had been inducted, in the service of his monarch and the defence of true religion, into a murky world of deceit, betrayal and role-playing, where the pretence of converting to the enemy's beliefs may have taught him how easily interchangeable they were with the ones he was being paid to defend. The name of Lightborne in *Edward II*, and his dissembling expressions of concern (reminiscent, perhaps, of the handling of the Babington conspirators by Marlowe's acquaintance Robert Poley), might be taken to suggest that the poet recognized the similarly demonic character of those contemporary servants of the state whose double role was to incite subversion and to stand as its accuser. But the experience of acting in a demonic role is scarcely conducive to faith in the benevolence of that sovereign will (whether earthly or divine) whose agent one has been.

The subversive opinions which Robert Greene (and subsequently also Thomas Kyd and Richard Baines) accused Marlowe of holding were thus arguably conditioned by what he had witnessed as an agent of the state in its war against political and religious subversion. In this light it may seem significant that the key words of Greene's charge against Marlowe were turned in a very different direction by one Richard Chomley, who knew Marlowe and had been "imployed by some of her Majesties prevy Counsaile for the apprehension of

Papistes, and other daungerous men": Chomley reportedly spoke "all evill of the Counsell; saying that they are all Athiestes and Machiavillians" (Boas 1940: 253-4). A similar judgment may be implicit in John Penry's account of the manner in which he was treated in 1587 by Archbishop Whitgift in the Court of High Commission. Penry was "threatned very bloodily, and reviled upon in a most unchristian sorte," although he had broken no law, and indeed not even been indicted. But "ere you depart the court," Whitgift told him, "we will finde sufficient matter to emprison you..." (Penry xii-xiii).

As these examples may suggest, the notion of atheism was strongly marked in this period by the asymmetries of power. "Atheism" — an attribute of others, almost never of oneself — was commonly deduced as a logical consequence of disaffection from the state church, or of a critical awareness of the manner in which religion served, in Marlowe's supposed words, "to keep men in awe" (Maclure 37). Richard Chomley's accusation is thus paradoxical, for whatever Privy Councillors may have thought or said in private, they had a vested interest in suppressing any public demystification of religious authority. Marlowe, as an oppositional voice, was an "atheist"; they could not be, except at the cost of ceasing to exercise power.

If "atheism" was thus more distinctly a social category than one of private belief, the question of whether Marlowe was an atheist in the precise modern sense is correspondingly of less interest than are the sidelong ironies by means of which he expressed his disaffiliation from Christianity. In *2 Tamburlaine*, for example, having previously offered a consistently naturalistic elemental explanation of his hero's invincibility and eventual physical burn-out, Marlowe has the onset of Tamburlaine's fatal illness follow by a mere sixteen lines his burning of the Koran and his challenge to its Prophet: the religious reader or play-goer who would insist on a swift punishment for blasphemy is thus thrown into the arms of Mahomet. A darker humor is apparent in Marlowe's representation of the murder of Peter Ramus, who was regarded by some as a Protestant martyr. The philosopher begs the Duke of Guise for time in which to "purge" himself, but then digresses into an arid polemic against "one Sheckius," who had contested his view of Aristotle. Ramus's last words —

"eternal God" — are uttered not in prayer, but as the climax to a denunciation of "the blockish Sorbonnists" (*Massacre at Paris* ix. 40-52). Equally to the point is the pious resolution provided by the last two lines of *The Jew of Malta* — "So, march away, and let due praise be given / Neither to fate nor fortune, but to heaven" (V.v.122-3) — which, in context, is the most blatant piece of Machiavellian hypocrisy in the entire play.

Given that the theatricality of power was a commonplace of the period, it seems peculiarly appropriate that Marlowe's sardonic representations and interrogations of power took theatrical form. Calvin, whose theology largely shaped that of the Anglican church, and who labored to clear from any imputation of evil a God whose will determines every act of "the divel & al the rout of the wicked" (I.xvii.11; fol. 66), also described the world as a theater in which we are set as spectators of the works of God (I.vi.2). A related sense of the theatricality of sovereign power appears in Elizabeth's statement to the House of Commons that "we Princes [...] are set on stages..."; and there is a momentary awareness of the ethical cost of this display in the remark of her spymaster Sir Francis Walsingham: "I hold them happiest in this government that may be rather lookers-on than actors" (Shepherd xvii). Marlowe, who was employed rather in the cellarage or the tiring-house of Elizabethan politics, was able to view at close range and from an unaccustomed angle the processes of political and religious legitimation implied by these theatrical metaphors. And when it came to writing for an actual stage, he developed a whole range of rhetorical and dramatic effects which interrupt, parody or mock the theatrics of legitimation.

In addition, though, Marlowe appears in his conversation, "in table talk or otherwise" (Maclure 35), to have striven more openly against "known truth" — or against what one might now call the hegemonic ideologies of the day. As a direct consequence of his indiscretions, he was made, after his violent death, into a prominent exhibit in another kind of theater: the puritan clergyman Thomas Beard, author-translator of a miscellany of moral exempla entitled *The Theatre of Gods Judgements* (1597), wrote of this "Poet of scurrilitie" that "hee even cursed and blasphemed to his last gaspe, and togither with his breath an oath flew out of his mouth" (Maclure 41-42).

Marlowe's death may itself have been a consequence of what Thomas Kyd called his "monstruous opinions" (Maclure 35). On March 19, 1593, a warrant was issued for the arrest of Richard Chomley, who in addition to planning treason at the head of a band of sixty "resolute murdering myndes" is said (in an undated document) to believe "that one Marlowe is able to shewe more sounde reasons for Atheisme then any devine in Englande is able to geve to prove devinitie & that Marloe tolde him that hee hath read the Atheist lecture to Sr Walter Raliegh & others" (Boas 1940: 255). On May 12, Thomas Kyd was arrested and imprisoned on suspicion of involvement in posting "divers lewd and mutinous libells" within the city of London; under torture, he named Marlowe as the owner of heretical papers found in his chambers, and denounced him as an atheist. Six days later the Privy Council issued a warrant for Marlowe's arrest, and on May 20 ordered him "to give his daily attendaunce on their Lordships untill he shalbe lycensed to the contrary" (Boas 1940: 242-4).

On May 30, Marlowe spent the last day of his life in the company of three very shadowy figures. One of them, Robert Poley, a confidential messenger, informer and double agent, has been described as "the very genius of the Elizabethan underworld," a man whose life exudes "an evil odour of fraud, crime and double dealing" (Urry 68); his major accomplishment had been the entrapment and betrayal of the Babington conspirators in 1586 (Bakeless i. 171-80). Another, Nicholas Skeres, appears to have moved from a life of theft and burglary into the lower reaches of the secret service, where he was involved in the Babington plot and subsequently used as a messenger by Sir Francis Walsingham (Bakeless i. 180-82; Urry 87-8). Although there is no evidence that the third, Ingram Frizer, was involved in espionage, he was in the employ of Thomas Walsingham, himself a secret agent as well as Marlowe's patron.

According to the testimony accepted by the coroner's inquest, Marlowe quarreled with Frizer over "le recknynge" for the eight meals the men had consumed; attacking him from behind, he was killed by Frizer in self-defence. Frizer was pardoned for the killing on June 28; on the following day, with the assistance of Nicholas Skeres and the apparent connivance of Thomas Walsingham, he set about cheating a witless young gentleman whom he had already defrauded to the tune of thirty pounds out of a second much larger sum (Bakeless i. 155-68). Robert Poley, in the meantime, continued to attend to the Queen's business. According to a warrant of payment signed on June 12 by the Queen's Vicechamberlain, he had left the royal court at Croydon on May 8, carrying "lettres in poste for her Majesties speciall and secret afaires [...] to the towne of the Hage in Hollande," and reported back to the royal palace of Nonesuch "with lettres of aunswere" on June 8. This warrant very conveniently specifies that Poley had been "in her majesties service all the aforesaid tyme" (Boas 1940: 267) — a formula which would silence awkward questions about his detour in Deptford on the return journey.

Although what is known of Marlowe's companions has raised suspicions that he was murdered, his own aggressiveness — a family trait, it would seem — lends some plausibility to the official story. John Marlowe, his father, appears from archival evidence to have been "rowdy, quarrelsome, awkward, improvident, busy, self-assertive" (Urry 28), qualities which reappear in amplified form among his children. Anne, one of Christopher's younger sisters, was cited in 1603 by the churchwardens of her parish as "a malicious contencious uncharitable person...a scowlde, comon swearer, a blasphemer of the name of god;" in 1626, by then a widow of fifty-five, she skirmished with one William Prowde "armed with staff and dagger, and in May of the following year assaulted the same William with sword and knife" (Urry 34). Christopher was himself involved in more than one affray of this kind. In September 1589 he was attacked in Hog Lane in Shoreditch by one William Bradley, who after duelling with him turned his attention to Thomas Watson, and was killed. In May 1592 Marlowe was bound over to keep the peace by two constables of Shoreditch whom he had evidently threatened; and in September of the same year, in Canterbury, he assaulted one William Corkine with a stick and dagger (Urry 62-8). To this may be added Thomas Kyd's statements, in two letters written after Marlowe's death, that he "was intemperate & of a cruel hart," and known for his "rashnes in attempting soden pryvie injuries to men" (Maclure 33, 36). Kyd's evidence, however, is tainted: he had been tortured; he no doubt knew how Marlowe was said to have died; and he was desperately seeking to ingratiate himself with the authorities.

The eagerness with which Kyd's interrogators pursued his statements about Marlowe's blasphemies is a reminder that the two poets were arrested at the height of Archbishop Whitgift's violent campaign against religious dissidence. Two leading nonconformists, John Greenwood (whom Marlowe had known at Cambridge) and Henry Barrow, had been hanged in April 1593 (Urry 81). John Penry, another Cambridge contemporary who shared their views and who was suspected of having helped to produce the Marprelate tracts, was executed on May 29, the day before Marlowe's death. In the drafts of Penry's appeals to Lord Burghley one hears a half-strangled outcry against tyranny:

> Wear it not my Lord for the hope of a better lyf, yt wear better for us to bee Queen Elizabethes beastes then hir subjectes [...]. For weer wee hir beastes going under hir mark the proudest prelate in the land durst not attempt to tak us unto ther owne handes. [....]

> Shall I not have justic? Will it hurt England to grant mee justic? [....] I ame an inocent, it profiteth mee not [...].

> Are wee a free people under our naturall princ, or are we held for slaves and bond-servantes under some cruell and unjust tyrant[?] (Penry 59, 60-1, 68)

But Penry would have been as horrified as his persecutors by the ribald blasphemies attributed to Marlowe by Thomas Kyd, and, independently, by Richard Baines. Kyd, reflecting back to 1591 or earlier, wrote that "it was his custom when I knewe him first & as I hear saie he contynewd it in table talk or otherwise to jest at the devine scriptures gybe at praiers, & strive in argument to frustrate & confute what hath byn spoke or wrytt by prophets & such holie men." The first instance Kyd offers of Marlowe's blasphemies, though muted in transmission by his own fear, is also the boldest: "He wold report St John to be our saviour Christes Alexis I cover it with reverence and trembling that is that Christ did love him with an extraordinary love" (Maclure 35). Baines, who was not himself under suspicion, writes more directly and more coarsely:

> He affirmeth that Moyses was but a jugler & that one Heriots [Harriot] being Sir W Raleighs man Can do more then he. [....]

That the first beginning of Religioun was only to keep men in awe. [....]

That Christ was a bastard and his mother dishonest.

That he was the sonne of a Carpenter, and that if the Jewes among whome he was borne did Crucify him theie best knew him and whence he Came. [....]

That if he were put to write a new Religion, he would undertake both a more Exellent and Admirable methode and that all the new testament is filthily written.

That the woman of Samaria & her sister were whores & that Christ knew them dishonestly.

That St John the Evangelist was bedfellow to Christ and leaned alwaies in his bosom, that he used him as the sinners of Sodoma.

That all they that love not Tobacco & Boies were fooles. [...] (Maclure 36-37)

Marlowe's challenge was political as well as religious, as is evident from such statements as that the apostle Paul was "a timerous fellow in bidding men to be subject to magistrates against his Conscience," that he himself had "as good Right to Coine as the Queen of England," and that (said Baines) he had given "Contrarieties oute of the Scripture [...] to some great men who in Convenient time shalbe named." Baines concludes that "all men in Cristianity ought to indevor that the mouth of so dangerous a member may be stopped" (Maclure 37-8). Appropriately enough, the author of this pious recommendation was a minister of the Church of England as well as a spy: Baines had purchased the benefice of Waltham in Lincolnshire in 1587, and remained rector of that parish until at least 1607 (Kuriyama 1988b: 9).

The extent to which these traces of Marlowe's passage should be allowed to affect interpretations of his writings is bound to remain a matter for debate. But it can be said that he stands out among Elizabethan poets as an extremist — as one, that is, who in giving voice to the discursive extremes of his era never appears to suggest with any conviction the possibility of a center in which they might meet and be reconciled. The comparative scarcity in his plays of the analogies to natural processes favoured by other Elizabethan writers, and his preference for imagery drawn from the elemental, the astronomical, or the spiritual and daemonic levels of the cosmos (rather than from the level of organic nature, where his contemporaries found a reservoir of social and behavioral norms): these are signs of 'extremism' — which is also to say of a divorce from the commonplaces of natural morality and natural law. Marlowe's characters thus move through a polarized, decentered world of warring elements, glittering artifacts, and fetichized objects of desire, "heaven and earth the bounds of [their] delight" (*Dido*, I.i.32). In the lapidary ironies of *Hero and Leander* Marlowe is the most exaggeratedly civilized poet of the age — and, in the savageries of *Tamburlaine*, its most superbly barbaric one. And just as his individual texts deny their audience or readers the security of a moral center or of a fixed interpretive stance, so also Marlowe's *oeuvre* as a whole resists any attempt to compose at its heart the image of a consistent creative intelligence — unless it be that of the homoerotic outlaw and blasphemer who stares insolently at us from the files of the Elizabethan thought police.

3. The Historical Doctor Faustus, c.1466-c.1537.

Given the obviously legendary or mythic quality both of Marlowe's play and of its principal source, the prose *Historie of the damnable life, and deserved death of Doctor John Faustus*, the fact that a historical Doctor Faustus can be identified with some clarity may come as a surprise. But there was such a person; and like Christopher Marlowe, he was a trangressor both of sexual and of ideological codes.

In 1483 a young man from the nearby village of Helmstadt enrolled at the University of Heidelberg in the nominalist *via moderna* of the arts faculty; his name appears variously in the university records as Georgius Helmstetter, Jorio or Jeorius de Helmstat, Georio de Helmstadt, and Jeorius Helmstadt. He received his bachelor's degree within less than the prescribed minimum of a year-and-a-half of study, but took longer than most students to earn the master's degree, which he was granted only in 1487 — having been held back, most probably, by a requirement that a *magister artium* be at least twenty or twenty-one years old. Born, therefore, in 1466 or 1467, he was a near contemporary of Giovanni Pico della Mirandola (1463-94) and of Erasmus (1466 or 1469-1536). The fact that he was one of only two students in a class of sixty-seven who gave no indication of a family name or patronymic is suggestive: he may, like Erasmus, have been illegitimate. If, as the university statutes required, he taught for two years in the faculty of arts as a Master of Arts, he would have remained at Heidelberg until at least the summer of 1489 (Baron 1978: 16-18).

In addition to the scholastic learning of the nominalist *via moderna* to which he was exposed in his formal course of studies, Georgius of Helmstadt would also have encountered at Heidelberg both the speculative (which is to say occultist) and the philological sides of the new humanist learning. During the 1480s, the city was home to a number of distinguished humanists, who tended to ally themselves with the exponents of the *via moderna*. According to Heiko Oberman, who has studied this convergence of interests, one consequence of the modernists' rejection of the universal terms deployed by Aquinas and the other theologians of the *via antiqua* was "a craving to experience and apprehend the world free from the tutelage of faith" — a craving, however, which soon "proved irreconcilable with the platonically inspired humanist propensity for a *sancta philosophia*" (Oberman 38). In the interim, though, there seems to have been a period in the late fifteenth century during which young German scholars trained in the *via moderna* were able to find a substitute for the theological speculations challenged by nominalism in that syncretic compendium of Hermetic theosophy, Neoplatonic theurgy and Christian Cabala which interested speculative humanists.

The proper title of this Heidelberg graduate was Magister (a doctoral degree was obtainable only in the disciplines of law, medicine, and theology). But by the convention of the time he would have been able, outside academic circles, to call himself Doctor (Baron 1982: 17). It seems very likely that he did so — and that this was the same man whose career as a magician, beginning some fifteen years later, made the name of Doctor Faustus notorious throughout Germany.

In 1507, the humanist Johannes Trithemius, himself a graduate of Heidelberg, and a magician as well as an abbot, described with contempt the activities of a man who announced himself as "Magister georgius sabellicus faustus junior, fons necromanticorum, astrologus, magus secundus chyromanticus agromanticus pyromanticus in hydra arte secundus" — "Magister Georgius Sabellicus, the younger Faustus, chief of necromancers, astrologer, the second magus, palmist, diviner by earth and fire, second in the art of divination by water" (Baron 1978: 96; cf. Tille 2, PM 84). "Sabellicus" appears to be not a Latinized family name, but rather a cognomen adopted in the manner of Renaissance humanists. In company with the apparent modesty of "in hydra arte secundus," it suggests an allusion to Numa Pompilius, the second king of Rome, who came from the land of the Sabines or Sabellici, and who, as founder of the city's religious rites and the supposed first practitioner of hydromancy, could be regarded as a pagan prophet (Baron 1978: 32). "Faustus" seems also to be a humanist cognomen, chosen for its meaning ("auspicious"), and as alluding to one or more of the earlier bearers of the name — most probably the Manichaean bishop with whom St. Augustine debated, or the Faustus who in a widely-read patristic text, the pseudo-Clementine *Recognitions*, is associated with the Gnostic heresiarch and magician Simon Magus (Wentersdorf, Richardson). What this magician's family name may have been we do not know: there are no traces of a Magister Georgius Faust or Faustus in German university records of this period. (The closest candidate is a Johannes Faust von Symmern who received a bachelor's degree from Heidelberg in 1509.)

In 1513 another distinguished humanist, Conrad Mutianus Rufus, wrote of the arrival in Erfurt of a chiromancer named "Georgius Faustus, Helmitheus Hedebergensis, merus ostentator et fatuus" — "a mere braggart and fool," who babbled at an inn and was marvelled at by the ignorant (PM 87-88). The text seems corrupt: Mutianus may have written "Hemitheus Hedelbergensis" ("the demi-god of Heidelberg"), or possibly "Helmsteten[sis] Hedelbergensis" ("from Helmstadt near Heidelberg"). But "Helmitheus" may be, rather, a literary allusion: in the pseudo-Clementine *Recognitions*, as first printed in 1504, a statement to the effect that Pyrrha and Erymetheus were the parents of Helen and Prometheus becomes the garbled claim that Pyrrha and Prometheus were the parents of "Helmitheus" (Richardson 141-42).

Later notices support the identification of the student from Helmstadt with the magician Doctor Faustus. In July 1528 Kilian Leib, prior of Rebdorf in Bavaria, recorded that on the fifth of June "Georgius faustus helmstetensis" had said "that when the sun and Jupiter are in the same constellation prophets are born (presumably such as he)"; and on June 17 of the same year, a soothsayer who called himself "Dr. Jörg Faustus von Heidelberg" was told by the council of the city of Ingolstadt, some ten miles from Rebdorf, "to spend his penny elsewhere, and he pledged himself not to take vengeance on or make fools of the authorities for this order" (PM 89-90).

As his expulsion from Ingolstadt may suggest, Georgius Faustus enjoyed a somewhat unsavoury reputation. He was, according to Trithemius, a braggart, a blasphemer, and a pederast. He apparently boasted in 1506 that if the writings and doctrines of Plato and Aristotle were wholly lost and forgotten, he "would be able to restore them all with increased beauty," just as the prophet Ezra had restored the lost books of the Law (cf. 2 Esdras 14: 20-26). He claimed, moreover, "that the miracles of Christ the Saviour were not so wonderful, that he himself could do all the things that Christ had done, as often and whenever he wished." And Trithemius asserts that when in 1507 Faustus was appointed schoolmaster in Kreuznach, he promptly indulged "in the most abominable kind of fornication with the boys," and fled to escape punishment (Baron 1978: 96-97; Tille 1-3; PM 83-86).

Such indiscretions as these did not prevent Faustus from being hired in 1520 to cast the horoscope of the Bishop of Bamberg (PM 88-89), or from being consulted in 1536 by a close associate of Erasmus's to predict the fortunes of an expedition to the New World (PM 95-96; Baron 1978: 48-66). He seems, however, to have been regarded by some with suspicion. In May 1532 the city council of Nuremberg refused a safe-conduct to "Doctor Faustus, the great sodomite and necromancer" (PM 90). And in 1539, not long after Faustus's death, a contemporary wrote of this self-proclaimed "philosopher of philosophers" that "The number of those who complained to me that they were cheated by him was very great. Now his promises were great.... But his deeds, as I hear, were very petty and fraudulent" (PM 94-95).

4. The Legend of Faustus.

Conspicuously absent from the accounts of Doctor Faustus written during his lifetime is any suggestion that he had a pact with the devil, an attendant spirit, powers of flight, the ability to devour a cartload of hay, detachable legs, or an affair with Helen of Troy. Yet within some fifty years of his death a legend which included all of these features, and which in addition recounted in lurid detail the lamentations and terrors of his final hours, was in print as the *Historia von D. Johann Fausten* (1587).

This book is evidently Lutheran in inspiration: its demonology, some of its episodes and many of its turns of phrase are lifted from Martin Luther's writings and table-talk (Baron 1978: 70-82; 1982: 67-74). Thus, for example, when in 1537 the conversation at Luther's table turned to Faustus, "who called the devil his brother-in-law," Luther told a string of carnivalesque anecdotes—about a sorcerer who devoured a peasant together with his horse and wagon, a monk who offered another peasant a penny for all the hay he could eat and then consumed half a wagon-load before being beaten off, and a man who made it seem that his leg had been pulled off by his Jewish creditor and thus frightened him away (*WATr* no. 3601). These stories reappear in the *Historia* as exploits of Faustus himself; so also does Luther's tale of a magician (identified in one report of the conversation as the abbot Trithemius) who entertained the Emperor Maximilian by having demons take on the forms of Alexander the Great and other monarchs (*WATr* no. 4450).

Perhaps more significantly, Luther was convinced that all magicians have a pact with the devil. In 1537 he told a story illustrating this belief—which was confirmed for him during the same year by a student at Wittenberg who confessed to have foresworn his faith in Christ and promised himself to "another master" (*WATr* no. 3618A-B, 3739). Fifteen years later, recounting this same incident, Philipp Melancthon added the detail of a written pact with the devil; and in 1585 Augustin Lercheimer, who had studied under

Melancthon, combined this story, in a book which was drawn upon by the authors of the *Historia*, with the first published reference to Faustus's demonic pact (Baron 1985: 535-6).

If Luther thus contributed to the Faustus legend's first canonical form, he also presided indirectly over the launching of the legend, both in his table talk and, more distinctly, in the stories he helped to spread when his most persistent radical opponent, Andreas Bodenstein von Karlstadt, died in Basel on Christmas Eve, 1541. In early 1542 Luther and his correspondents in Basel and elsewhere claimed successively that Karlstadt had left behind him a noisome spirit, and that his death had been caused not by the plague but by his terror when the devil materialized to carry him off (*WABr* ix. 621-2, x. 12-14, 24-30, 49). The same motifs of a noisome spirit and of a death at the devil's hands reappear as organizing features of the first clearly legendary account of Doctor Faustus, which was published in 1548 by Johannes Gast, a Protestant clergyman of Basel. The claim that Cornelius Agrippa's dog was a devil had appeared in print two years earlier; Gast writes that Faustus's dog, and his horse as well, were devils (Nauert 327; PM 98).

Further elaborations of the legend were produced by a succession of Lutheran writers, among them Philipp Melancthon, Johannes Manlius and Johannes Wier. Melancthon's references to Faustus in lectures he delivered at Wittenberg during the 1550s are of particular interest for what they suggest about the antecedents and the ideological motivation of the legend. In the first such reference, alluding to an episode in the apocryphal *Acts of Peter and Paul* which had been retold in the *Golden Legend*, Melancthon links Faustus to the heresiarch Simon Magus: "There [in the presence of Nero] Simon Magus tried to fly to heaven, but Peter prayed that he might fall. I believe that the Apostles had great struggles although not all are recorded. Faustus also tried this at Venice. But he was sorely dashed to the ground" (PM 99). In another lecture, reported by Manlius, Melancthon says again that Faustus attempted in Venice to fly to heaven—but this time claims that he himself was acquainted with the man, and provides details (wholly fictive in nature) of his birthplace and education. The Christian name of Faustus has become "Ioannes"; and it now appears that, unlike Simon Magus, he survived his abortive flight. For Melancthon goes on to give a circumstantial account of his death at the devil's hands in a village in the Duchy of Württemberg. As though to confirm that Faustus was a servant of Satan, he adds that during his life he "had with him a dog which was a devil, just as that scoundrel who wrote *De vanitate artium*" — Cornelius Agrippa — "likewise had a dog that ran about with him and was a devil." After telling how Faustus twice escaped arrest, presumably with demonic aid, Melancthon concludes by refuting the boast of this same "Faustus magus, a most filthy beast and a sewer of many devils," that all of the Emperor Charles V's victories in Italy had been won by his magic. "This," he says severely, "was an utter lie. I mention this for the sake of the young, so that they may not readily give ear to such vain men" (PM 101-3).

Melancthon's comparisons of Faustus to Simon Magus are highly suggestive. Like several of his first-century contemporaries, this Samaritan magician professed to be God; and he led a long and vigorous afterlife — both in the refutations of his Gnostic teachings by patristic writers such as Justin Martyr, Irenaeus, Hippolytus and Tertullian, and also in the polemical accounts of his debates and magical contests with the apostles which appear in the canonical book of Acts, in the apocryphal *Acts of Peter* (2nd century), the *Acts of Peter and Paul* (c. 7th century), and the pseudo-Clementine *Recognitions* (4th century). Apostate, antichrist and agent of the devil, Simon also gave visible form to his heresies: he cohabited with a woman whom his followers knew variously as Helena, Minerva, or Luna. Appropriating a motif from the apocryphal Wisdom literature, he claimed she was his own divine First Thought. The evil archons whom she had absent-mindedly engendered, and who created the world, imprisoned her within it in a series of human forms, among them that of Helen of Troy; but Simon had now descended to save her and all who believed in him (Irenaeus I. 23).

The reappearance of Helen in the *Historia* of 1587 is one sign of the Faustus legend's affiliation to the patristic accounts of Simon of Samaria. But Simon and Faustus have more in common than this. Both could be described (to borrow a phrase from Hart Crane's poem "For the Marriage of Faustus and Helen") as "bent axle[s] of devotion" — in the sense that their transgressions against orthodoxy were recuperated by the legends which formed around them in such a way as to legitimize that orthodoxy.

The role of Simon Magus in the legitimation of orthodoxy is evident in the pseudo-Clementine *Recognitions*, where St. Peter explains human history in terms of a sequence of pairs appointed by God: the first of each pair to manifest himself is an emissary of evil, the second an emissary of the true prophecy (III. 59). Thus Cain was followed by Abel, Esau by Jacob, Pharaoh's magicians by Moses, "the tempter" by the Son of Man, and Simon Magus by Peter himself (III. 61). It follows that the prior appearance of Simon Magus is one proof of the authenticity of the apostle who struggles against and overcomes his heresies.

During the 1530s Martin Luther developed a view of his own function which is clearly indebted to this pseudo-Clementine master-narrative. Convinced that he occupied in his time "the role occupied by the true prophet or apostle in the biblical accounts" (Edwards 113), he understood his struggles both with the papacy and with radical opponents as a repetition of earlier struggles—between Cain and Abel, the Babylonians and Abraham, Ishmael and Isaac, Esau and Jacob, and the apostles and their competitors (Edwards 114-15; Headley 64-66, 233). In his annotations on Matthew (1538), Luther speaks of Satan's perpetual invention of new calumnies, and (alluding to his own radical opponents), of those "cunning and pestilential men" among his contemporaries who have served Satan in this respect, but who are confuted by the Holy Spirit. He promptly identifies the same pattern in the age of Jesus and the apostles: "Thus Christ always conquered the cleverest contrivances of the Pharisees, Peter those of his magician Simon, and Paul those of his Pseudo-apostles" (*WA* xxxviii. 501).

Melancthon's construction of a parallel between Simon Magus, who by his very presence testified to the apostolic mission of St. Peter and St. Paul, and "Faustus magus," as he calls him, may thus lead one to suspect that he is hinting, with all due modesty, at a similar guarantee through demonic opposition of his own and Luther's quasi-apostolic role. Such a suspicion is strengthened by Melancthon's claim to have known Faustus not just by reputation but in person—and by a story about an encounter between them which was current in Wittenberg. A travesty of this story was printed in 1581 by a Catholic writer who tells how the large faith of Melancthon's small wife prevented Faustus from making a sausage fly out of her kitchen (Baron 1985: 534). Four years later the story itself appeared in a book written by Augustin Lercheimer, a graduate of Wittenberg in the 1540s and a protegé of Melancthon's who himself made an important contribution to the development of the Faustus legend.

In the first edition of his *Christlich Bedencken und Erinnerung von Zauberey* (*Christian Synopsis of Magic*, 1585) Lercheimer transmitted several stories about Faustus (or Faust, as he calls him) which were quickly reworked by the authors of the *Historia* (Baron 1985: 521-42). From one of these we learn that while Faust was in Wittenberg, "he came at times to the house of Philipp [Melancthon]," of all people, where he received both hospitality and admonitions. Resenting the latter, he told his host one day as they descended to dinner that he would make all the pots in his kitchen fly up through the chimney. To which Melancthon replied, with less than his usual eloquence, "Dass soltu wol lassen, ich sch[e]isse dir in deine kunst" (Baron 1985: 532) — "You'd better lay off; I shit on your art!" And the sorcerer did lay off, for (as Lercheimer added in 1597, in the third edition of his book) "the devil was unable to rob the kitchen of this holy man" (PM 122). This kitchen debate reproduces in miniature the rhetorical and magical contests between St. Peter and Simon Magus in the *Recognitions* and the apocryphal Acts; in reading it one may be reminded that the first Christian to encounter and triumph over Simon Magus was none other than the apostle Philip (Acts 8: 5-13).

Oddly enough, in the third edition from which I have already quoted, Lercheimer denounces the *Historia* as containing things that are "trivial, false and nasty," and as a libel both upon the university with which it associates Faust and also upon "Luther, Melancthon, and others of sainted memory" (PM 121). Although his own story links the sorcerer more intimately with the Lutheran leadership than does anything in the *Historia*, he was clearly upset that anyone should imagine Faust to have been a product of Wittenberg.

And yet there are echoes of Luther's and Melancthon's logic of legitimation in the *Historia* as well. Lercheimer followed his story about Melancthon's ability to resist Faust's devilish tricks with one about an elderly neighbour's attempt to convert the sorcerer. The two together seem to have inspired the story of the Old Man's in-

tervention with Faustus in chapters 52 and 53 of the *Historia* —
where, although Philipp Melancthon has disappeared, a trace of him
remains in the Old Man's exhortation to remember how St. Philip's
preaching converted Simon the supposed god to faith in Christ (ch.
52, p. 102). It is left to the reader to remember how promptly Simon
Magus lapsed from this faith — as Faustus likewise does in this same
chapter.

If Faustus could in this peculiar sense be at once a precursor,
an enemy and a guarantor of the Lutheran faith, so also could Cornelius Agrippa, to whom Melancthon likened him. In 1522 the
reformer Capito reported to Agrippa a conversation with an admirer
who had claimed that "what Luther sees now, [Agrippa] saw long
ago" (Agrippa 1970: ii. 729-30). There is some truth to this: Agrippa
had been involved in controversies with the theologians of the men-
dicant orders since 1509. But his stance in these matters was quite
unlike Luther's eight or ten years later, and although Agrippa was
active in disseminating the early writings of Luther, he never fully
sided with him. The apparently Lutheran tone of parts of *De vanitate*
is deceptive: in this book Agrippa is actually advancing the same
magical notions of spiritual rebirth and deification, derived from
Hermetic and Cabalistic sources, that animate his *De occulta
philosophia* (Keefer 1988: 620-39). Agrippa was a well-known ex-
ponent of what Frances Yates termed the Hermetic-Cabalistic tradition. This tradition, to which Georgius Faustus was more
peripherally attached, both preceded Luther and encouraged radical
evangelical opposition to his doctrines.

During the decades immediately preceding the Reformation the
newly available and supposedly ancient texts of Hermes Trismegistus
and the Kabbalists, which it was thought could contribute to a restoration of the pristine verities of Christianity, aroused considerable
excitement. In the careers of such humanists as Jacques Lefèvre
d'Étaples and Johannes Reuchlin, who by 1521 were being attacked
along with Erasmus as precursors of Luther (Herminjard i. 64), a
linkage between reforming impulses and Hermetic-Cabalistic interests is evident. However, the occultist tradition's emphasis on
spiritual autonomy and on a deification achieved through spiritual
rebirth was diametrically opposed to Luther's biblical exclusivism
and his rejection of free-will; while this tradition helped to create a

favorable climate for the reception of his early writings, it subsequently contributed to radical reforming tendencies which outflanked or subverted the positions of the magisterial reformers.

Thus the Hermetist and alchemist Theophrastus Paracelsus, who in 1525 sided with the Tyrolese peasants and miners in their abortive revolution, shared "a physical, almost a magical view of baptism" with another radical doctor, Michael Servetus, who in his *Restitutio Christianismi* (1553) echoed Cabalistic speculations and quoted Hermes Trismegistus (Williams 318, 611). Cornelius Agrippa himself had links with radical reforming tendencies (Zambelli), and a paraphrase of his *De vanitate* was published in 1534 by the spiritualist reformer Sebastian Franck (Williams 460). Four decades later Valentin Weigel made use of Hermes and Paracelsus in his attacks upon Lutheranism, and declared Hermes and the Neoplatonist Proclus to have understood spiritual rebirth better than the "high theologians" (Ozment 218-19). One may then suspect that the recurrent emphasis upon deification among the radical reformers—I am thinking of Schwenckfeld's understanding of the eucharist as a reception of Christ's celestial or mystical flesh and hence as a movement towards deification, of Servetus's similar understanding of adult baptism as a transforming illumination and regeneration, and of their shared view of faith as a deificatory sanctification (Williams 112, 311-16, 335)—was in part derived from Hermetic-Cabalistic sources. To the extent that this was so, radical reformers were giving expression to the same impulses that prompted Cornelius Agrippa's representation of Christ in *De vanitate* as the "deifying Wisdom," *sapientia Deificans* (Agrippa 1970: ii. 314).

The Hermetic-Cabalistic tradition encouraged more extreme forms of prophetic and magical delusion as well. Faustus, whose blasphemies Johannes Trithemius reported in 1507, was still claiming two decades later to be a prophet (PM 89). Trithemius also wrote about the visit of a similarly boastful Italian magician, Joannes Mercurius de Corigio, to the court of Louis XII of France in 1501. From other sources (among them his own writings) it is clear that this magician announced himself as a wonder-working Hermetic-Christian redeemer; Trithemius's apparent suppression of this aspect of his claims raises the possibility that he also knew more about Faustus's Hermetic-Cabalistic affiliations than he was willing to reveal (Keefer 1989: 85-86).

These magicians seem in a curious way to have been haunted by the demonic figure of Simon Magus. I have commented above on Faustus's possible indebtedness to the pseudo-Clementine *Recognitions*. Joannes Mercurius, who claimed to be Enoch, Hermes, Christ and Apollonius of Tyana, called his wife Helena Maria (McDaniel 218): while the second name may imply that he thought of her as the spouse of the Holy Spirit, the first suggests that he also identified himself with Simon Magus. Although Cornelius Agrippa never made such claims as these, he does suggest a connection between the heresies of Simon Magus and his own *De occulta philosophia*, and elsewhere conflates the doctrines of Hermes with what appears to be a reference to the Standing One, as Simon called himself (*De occ. phil.* III. 44; *De van.* cap. 48; see Keefer 1988: 643-9).

This conflation seems apt, for the writings attributed to Hermes in fact date from the same period as the Gnostic heresies, with which they have much in common. Renaissance Hermetism and Cabalism were thus reviving tendencies which, many centuries previously, the legend of Simon Magus had been used by orthodox Christians to combat. Martin Luther's appropriation of that legend's logic of legitimation helps to explain why an analogous legend was developed by his followers.

In the course of the Faustus legend's narrative exfoliation, the anti-Catholic overtones which had been present in its earliest forms became more pronounced, and the legend acquired, in inverse form, many of the features of the popular genre of saints' lives — a genre which it also helped to displace (Allen 13-41). At the same time, the carnivalesque elements evident in Luther's anecdotes about magicians were taken up and amplified. But whatever it contained of anti-Catholic polemic or of folktale, the legend remained a repressive narrative — one which sought to legitimize Protestant orthodoxy through a terrifying representation of the wages of transgression. It is no coincidence that the period between 1560 and the late 1580s, during which the legend received its full narrative elaboration, also saw the first major outbreak of witch-hunts in Western Europe — an outbreak in which, with the vehement approval of orthodox intellectuals, thousands of people, most of them women, were imprisoned, tortured and judicially murdered.

5. *Marlowe's* Doctor Faustus: *Sources and Context*

The free English translation of the Lutheran *Historia* which was printed in 1592 has been commonly represented as the sole source of *The Tragical History of Doctor Faustus*. However, there are grounds for asserting that Marlowe was not merely adapting EFB for the stage, but was also actively reshaping the legend—and, I would suggest, subtly undermining its repressive orthodoxy—through an exploration of its historical and ideological roots.

Faustus's desire to be "as cunning as Agrippa was" (I.i. 118) provides one clue as to the manner in which motifs from other texts are woven into this play. Agrippa's rhetorical demolition of all the orthodox forms of knowledge in *De vanitate* was suspected, despite the evangelical orientation of that book, of having been designed to prepare readers for the magical doctrines espoused in *De occulta philosophia*: although in *De vanitate* he was (in his translator's words) "Professinge Divinitee," he was thought to be doing so hypocritically (cf. Thevet ii. fol. 544r-v). This is very much the pattern of Faustus's first speech. Announcing his intention to be "a divine in show" (I.i.3), he launches into a sophistical survey of the academic disciplines, of which there is no hint in EFB, and then into a rapturous praise of magic, which is paralleled in *De occulta philosophia* but not in the Faustbooks. By the time he mentions Agrippa, Faustus is thus already emulating him, if in a parodic manner.

The Hermetic-Cabalistic notion of spiritual rebirth and deification which figures in both of Agrippa's best-known works (Keefer 1988: 620-39) is also ironically echoed in this play. Faustus initially declares: "A sound magician is a mighty god: / Here tire, my brains, to get a deity!" He thus announces a project of a self-begotten rebirth into divine form which would deliver him into "a world of profit and delight, / Of power, of honor, of omnipotence" (I.i.63-64, 54-55). In his last soliloquy, however, he wishes futilely that he might evade eternal punishment by being "chang'd / Unto some brutish beast" (V.ii.100-1), and he calls upon the stars that reigned at his nativity to

> draw up Faustus like a foggy mist
> Into the entrails of yon laboring cloud,
> That when you vomit forth into the air
> My limbs may issue from your smoky mouths,
> So that my soul may but ascend to heaven.
> (V.ii.85-89)

In what can be read as a violently physical reversal of spiritual rebirth, Faustus proposes an abject surrender of bodily integrity in exchange for the salvation of his soul: having once aspired to "rend the clouds" (I.i.60), he now begs for physical dissolution in their entrails, for resorption into a dismembering womb, followed by regurgitation and dispersal.

It would appear that Marlowe saw a connection between Renaissance occultist traditions and the Simonian resonances of the legend. When Faustus cries out, "Sweet Helen, make me immortal with a kiss; / Her lips suck forth my soul, see where it flies!" (V.i.93-94), his playful attribution to his demonic paramour of the power to confer one at least of the attributes of a god is also, it would seem, an allusion to the Cabalist idea that the human soul "can be ravished by God in a mystical union referred to [...] as 'the death of the kiss'" (Mebane 127; cf. Yates 99). This blasphemous conceit is linked to Marlowe's evident awareness of the patristic legend of Simon Magus. For while in the *Historia* and EFB Helen is a straightforwardly erotic figure, his Faustus transforms her, like Simon's Helena, into a parodic image of the figure of divine Wisdom. In the words of Solomon, Wisdom "is the brightnesse of the everlasting light, the undefiled mirrour of the Majesty of God, and the image of his goodnesse. [....] For shee is more beautifull then the Sun, and above all the order of the starres, and the light is not to be compared unto her. [....] I have loved her, and sought her from my youth: I desired to marry her, such love had I unto her beauty" (Wisdom of Solomon 7: 26, 29; 8: 2 [Geneva Bible]). Faustus's echo of this passage is unmistakable:

> O, thou art fairer than the evening air
> Clad in the beauty of a thousand stars;

Brighter art thou than flaming Jupiter
When he appear'd to hapless Semele,
More lovely than the monarch of the sky
In wanton Arethusa's azur'd arms,
And none but thou shalt be my paramour.
(V.i.104-10)

If in these respects Marlowe supplemented what he found in
EFB with motifs from other sources which he recognized as belonging to the legend's informing context, what can be said of that other
context within which the play was first written and produced? Christopher Ricks evokes an intimately corporeal as well as social aspect
of this originary context with his reminder that, like its early audiences, *Doctor Faustus* is environed by the hellish terrors of the plague,
which resonate through it from Faustus's initial brag that through
his skill "whole cities have escap'd the plague" (I.i.21) to his final
agonized recognition that his soul "must live still to be plagu'd in
hell" (V.ii.104). For Simon Shepherd, the play's context is more distinctly conditioned by the political terror resulting from "re-in-
vigorated state repression in the late 1580s, the show trials of puritan
activists, the breaking up of presses." As he remarks, Faustus's offer
"to burn his own books, his *last line*, foregrounds the precise feeling
of error in a state that banned and burned books," and the death
by dismemberment which the 1616 text makes explicit is reminiscent
of the torture of the rack (Shepherd 139).

A more distinctly ideological component of this context is suggested by Jonathan Dollimore's argument that in *Doctor Faustus* "a
discovery of limits which ostensibly forecloses subversive questioning
in fact provokes it." By this he does not mean that the play validates
a revolt of "Renaissance man" against religious authority—for
"Faustus is constituted by the very limiting structure which he transgresses and his transgression is both despite and because of that
fact" (Dollimore 110). The play vindicates neither Faustus nor the
structure which encloses him; rather, it is interrogative—and what
it interrogates, through the representation of an identifiably Protestant mode of transgression—"despairing yet defiant, masochistic yet
wilful" (Dollimore 115)—is the Calvinistic theological orthodoxy of
Elizabethan England. A legend in which transgression had served
to legitimize orthodoxy was, in this view, reshaped by Marlowe into

"an exploration of subversion through transgression" (Dollimore 109).

The theological dimensions of the play's context, obscurely hinted at in the Prologue's suggestion of a heavenly conspiracy (lines 21-2), first become evident in the syllogism with which Faustus dismisses theology:

> *Stipendium peccati mors est.* Ha! *Stipendium, etc.*
> The reward of sin is death? That's hard.
> *Si peccasse negamus, fallimur,*
> *et nulla est in nobis veritas:*
> If we say that we have no sin
> We deceive ourselves, and there's no truth in us.
> Why then belike we must sin,
> And so consequently die.
> Ay, we must die, an everlasting death.
> (I.i.39-47)

In more than one sense this passage offers a lesson in the importance of contextualizing. Faustus misreads the words of St. Paul (Romans 6: 23) and St. John (1 John 1: 8) because he has lifted them out of their contexts, failing in each case to notice that the words he quotes form only the first half of an antithetical construction. The second clause of Romans 6: 23 ("but the gifte of God is eternal life through Jesus Christ our Lord") and the next verse in the epistle of John ("If we acknowledge our sinnes, he is faithful and just, to forgive us our sinnes, & to clense us from all unrighteousnes") conditionally withdraw the condemnations which are all that Faustus sees.

Readers who wish to see *Doctor Faustus* as a morality play, and its protagonist as no more than a witless incompetent, need go no further in restoring the context of this passage. However, a further consideration of context may suggest that to dismiss Faustus in this manner is not an adequate response to this passage. It is indeed ironically appropriate that a scholar who has arrogantly dismissed logic and law should restrict himself (in Pauline terms) to the condemnation of the Law—and with a syllogism, too. But a more suitable reaction than contempt might be the proverbial "There, but for the grace of God, go I."

Marlowe scholars have long been aware that Faustus succumbs to the same diabolical logic that was used by Despair in Spenser's *Faerie Queene* to lead Redcrosse Knight towards suicide, and, some decades previously in a dialogue written by Thomas Becon, by Satan in an attempt to undermine the faith of another Christian Knight. Both knights, unlike Faustus, escape this logic in what for sixteenth-century Protestants was the only possible way, by transcending it through an appeal to divine grace. Becon's knight, admitting his condemnation under the Law, turns to the Gospel, "that is to say, grace, favour, and remission of sins, promised in Christ" (Becon 629); Spenser's is saved by the intervention of Una:

> In heavenly mercies hast thou not a part?
> Why shouldst thou then despeire, that chosen art?
> Where justice growes, there grows eke greater grace....
> (I.ix.53)

But while Becon's knight is able "through the grace that [he has] received" (636) to appeal to God's mercy, and while Una is there to remind Redcrosse of this same grace and mercy, the notion of divine mercy is no more than hinted at in *Doctor Faustus* until after Faustus has committed apostasy and signed his pact with the devil, and it is strikingly absent from this first scene. Faustus is reminded by his Good Angel of a quite different aspect of the divine nature:

> O Faustus, lay that damned book aside,
> And gaze not on it, lest it tempt thy soul
> And heap God's heavy wrath upon thy head!
> Read, read the Scriptures; that is blasphemy.
> (I.i.71-4)

Although this may seem very much the sort of thing that a Good Angel ought to say, it offers no escape from the syllogism which Faustus has just propounded. Indeed, these words, addressed to a man whose soul has evidently already been tempted by the necromantic book he is holding, seem less akin to the intervention of Spenser's Una than to the persuasions of Despaire from which she saved Redcrosse Knight:

> Is not the measure of thy sinfull hire
> High heaped up with huge iniquitie,

Against the day of wrath, to burden thee?
(I.ix.46)

One may well wonder why the Good Angel neither suggests to Faustus the sort of question that George Herbert asks — "Art thou all justice, Lord? / Shows not thy word / More attributes?" — nor tries to prompt him to the request which follows from it: "Let not thy wrathfull power / Afflict my houre, / My inch of life..." ("Complaining", lines 11-13, 16-18). The answer would seem to be that Faustus is not among those chosen by God's inscrutable will for salvation. If this is so, the function of the Good Angel's exhortation is not to convert Faustus, but rather (in terms which readers of Calvin will find familiar) to render him inexcusable.

In the passage from which Faustus lifted the major premise of his syllogism, St. Paul contrasts a state of bondage to sin with one of bondage to God in a manner which seems to exclude any overtone either of autonomy or of free-will:

> For when ye were the servants [*douloi*, i.e. slaves] of sinne, ye were freed from righteousness. What frute had ye then in those things, whereof ye are now ashamed? For the end of those things is death. But now being freed from sinne, and made servants unto God, ye have your frute in holines and the end, everlasting life. For the wages of sinne is death: but the gifte of God is eternal life.... (Romans 6: 20-3)

Responding perversely to the passages from which he quotes, Faustus concludes (to borrow the wording of Romans 6: 21) that "the end of things is death." And in reducing Christian theology to a doctrine of necessity, he goes one step further:

> What doctrine call you this? *Che sarà, sarà*,
> What will be, shall be? Divinity, adieu!
> (I.i.48-49)

This sounds very much like a parodic reduction of the Calvinistic teachings on predestination which were the official doctrine of the Anglican church throughout the reign of Elizabeth I.

The Calvinist theology to which Marlowe is alluding is thoroughly equivocal. God summons the reprobate to repent, and therefore 'wants' them to — but they do not receive the grace to repent, and the fact that he has willed their damnation is eventually manifested in their lack of faith. The wilful self-estrangement of the reprobate from God is said to make their condemnation just — but what is this will? The Calvinist apologist Du Plessis-Mornay wrote that "God therefore to shew his power in our freedome and libertie, hath left our willes to us; and to restreyne them from loosenesse, he hath so ordered them by his wisedome, that he worketh his owne will no lesse by them, than if we had no will at all" (Du Plessis-Mornay 221).

When Faustus, having signed his pact, wonders whether it is not too late to repent, the Good Angel equivocates in a similar manner: "Never too late, if Faustus can repent" (II.iii.81). Enfolded in that conditional clause is the brute question of fact on which the doctrine of double predestination hinges. If Faustus is going to be able to repent, then he is eternally out of trouble and it is never too late; but if he cannot, it will always have been too late. Someone with an eye for theological nuances altered the B text to read "if Faustus *will* repent" (my emphasis) — thus deflecting our attention to the question of Faustus's willingness to will his own salvation. But what immediately follows confirms in a spectacular manner the A text's insinuation that the issue is not his to decide: when Faustus calls on Christ, he is answered by the appearance of a demonic trinity.

There is a sense in which Faustus's handling of scriptural texts, in addition to being a gross misreading, is also the appropriate, indeed inevitable, response for someone in a state of bondage to sin. The Bible came to sixteenth-century Protestants equipped with a theory of reading (and of misreading). Thus Elizabethan Anglicans prayed to God for "grace to love thy holie word fervently, to search the Scriptures diligently, to reade them humblie, to understand them truly, to live after them effectually" (*Prayer Book* 150). The operative word is "grace" — lacking which, scriptural study could only result in misinterpretation and mortal sin. For (to quote from another of the "Godly Prayers" printed with many editions of the Prayer Book), "the infirmitie and weaknesse of man" are such that we "can nothing doe without thy godly helpe. If man trust to himselfe, it cannot bee avoyded, but that hee must headlong runne and fall into a thousand undoings and mischiefs" (*Prayer Book* 148-49).

But this insistence upon divine grace and upon human weakness and perversity would seem to have produced a tendency to separate, if only for purposes of emphasis, the two halves of the very texts from which Faustus quotes. Roma Gill has observed that Faustus's English rendering of 1 John 1: 8 repeats the wording of the 1559 *Book of Common Prayer*, where in the order for Morning Prayer this verse is quoted without the following one—the sense of which is fully conveyed, however, by the ensuing exhortation to general confession (Gill 1990: xxv; *Prayer Book* 42). A more radical truncation of this text occurs in Article XV of the Church of England, which ends with these words: "If we say we have no sin, we deceive ourselves, and the truth is not in us." Full stop. Nothing remotely like 1 John 1: 9 appears in the following articles, or indeed anywhere among the Thirty-Nine Articles. In Calvin's *Institutes of the Christian Religion* there occurs a similar truncation, this time of the words of St. Paul. Calvin is here fulminating against the Roman Catholic distinction between mortal and venial sins:

> ...if God hath declared his will in the lawe, whatsoever is contrarie to the law, displeaseth him. Will they imagin the wrath of God to be so disarmed, that punishment of death shall not foorthwith follow upon them? And he himselfe hath pronounced it plainly.... The soule (saith he) that sinneth, the same shall die [Ezek. 18: 4, 20]. Againe, which I even now alleaged, the reward of sinne is death [Rom. 6: 23]. But albeit they grant it to be a sinne, because they cannot denie it: yet they stand stiffe in this, that it is no deadly sinne. [...] But if they continue in dotage, wee will bid them farewell: and let the children of God learne this, that all sinne is deadly, because it is a rebellion against the will of God, which of necessitie provoketh his wrath, because it is a breach of the lawe, upon which the judgement of God is pronounced without exception: and that the sinnes of the holy ones are veniall or pardonable, not of their owne nature, but because they obtaine pardon by the mercie of God. (Calvin II.viii.59, fol. 132v-133)

And so Calvin ends his chapter. The strong family resemblance between this argument and Faustus's syllogism can hardly escape notice. Calvin does supply, in the last clauses of this passage (which reads oddly like an afterthought), a loose approximation of the meaning of the latter half of Romans 6: 23. These concluding words, moreover, have scriptural authority: they echo Romans 9: 15-16, which in turn quotes Exodus 33: 19. But Calvin has chosen to emphasize the tautological nature of the Pauline doctrine: all sins without exception are mortal, he says, except those of the saints, which are forgiven not because they are saints but because they are forgiven. One can imagine a graceless reader asking, "What doctrine call you this? *Che sarà, sarà?*"

Dollimore's suggestion that Faustus "is constituted by the very limiting structure which he transgresses" is borne out by Faustus's language. For what I have spoken of as contextual is in fact embedded in this play at the most intimate level of its rhetoric. Faustus may experiment with the third-person self-objectification practised by Marlowe's Tamburlaine. But his habitual, his characteristic mode of speech is second-person self-address: "Settle thy studies Faustus" (I.i.1); "Here tire, my brains, to get a deity!" (I.i.64); "Now, Faustus, must thou needs be damn'd" (II.i.1); "What art thou, Faustus, but a man condemn'd to die?" (IV.ii.33); "Accursed Faustus, where is mercy now?" (V.i.62); "Ah Faustus, / Now hast thou but one bare hour to live, / And then thou must be damn'd perpetually" (V.ii.58-60). This mode of self-address is, very largely, what constitutes his dramatic identity—and it does so in terms of an increasingly powerful recognition of what is in store for him. At the same time as they enact a split between a perverse wilfulness and a strangely passive selfhood, his self-reflections also construct a trap of self-authenticating predication. The despairing self-definitions of Faustus would cease to be true if he could only cease from making them; but conversely, he could only cease from making them if they were not true—or rather, if he were not constituted as a subject by this very pattern of apostrophic self-address.

This rhetorical pattern is the precise equivalent of what Fulke Greville, in *Caelica*, XCIX, called a "fatal mirror of transgression": the tormented self-image which it offers "bears the faithless down to desperation." What Faustus simultaneously recognizes as his destiny and struggles to escape is also gradually revealed as the true shape of what he has desired. An eschatological awareness burns up through even his most splendid effort at forgetfulness. Helen's "sweet embracings" are to "extinguish clean" (V.i.86) the motions of penitence and despair that have wracked him, but the very language of the escapist fantasy which he constructs around her expresses through a strange inversion his actual relation to this spirit:

> Brighter art thou than flaming Jupiter
> When he appear'd to hapless Semele....
>   (V.i.106-7)

Faustus began by "level[ing] at the end of every art" (I.i.4) — that is, by challenging both the purposes and the limits of the disciplines which he had studied. Discovering in the first scene that the end of Divinity, for those who lack the grace to apply to themselves the scriptural offers of forgiveness, is "everlasting death," he opposed to this depressing conclusion the fantasies of unconditioned autonomy and limitless power inspired by the "metaphysics of magicians" (I.i.47, 50). But what C.L. Barber termed an "unstable appropriation of the divine for the human" (Barber 17) quickly collapses in this play. When in his final soliloquy Faustus begs God to "Impose some end to my incessant pain," there is a horrible irony to the ensuing recognition: "O, no end is limited to damned souls" (V.ii.93, 96). This concern with *ends*, in all of the related senses so skilfully analyzed by Edward Snow — of intention, reason for being, *telos*, finality, limit, and eschatological termination — resonates through the play, and is perhaps one reason for the place it occupies in our literary canon.

However, the self-interrogation by which Faustus constitutes himself as a subject is also an interrogation of that to which and by which he is subjected. Marlowe's play reverses the crushingly homiletic orientation of its principal source, not indeed by glorifying Faustus, whose pretensions are undermined through a sequence of mordant ironies, but rather by insistently implying that his wilfulness has itself been willed by higher powers. The intimate manner in which the protagonist's damnation is unfolded makes a detached judgment of him difficult, and the absence of that moralistic authorial condemnation which in EFB and its German original had masked the issue of predestination throws into question the nature of the divine power by whose will the action is implicitly shaped. R.G. Hunter, distinguishing in his analysis of theological contexts between the Calvinist overtones of the A text and the Pelagianism of the B-text revisions, has shown how inadequate is the widespread assumption of earlier critics "that this tragedy's didactic purpose was to terrify its audience into faith and godliness": *Doctor Faustus*, he proposed, would be rather more likely "to terrify the more intelligent and informed of its beholders out of their beliefs or at least into a serious examination of them" (R.G. Hunter 64-65).

6. The Dates of Marlowe's Doctor Faustus

The year in which this play was first written and performed cannot be established with any precision. Although the *Historia* was first printed in 1587 at Frankfurt, the first edition of EFB seems to have appeared only in May 1592 (Greg 2-5), and the earliest edition of which any copy survives was printed later the same year. However, Marlowe may perhaps have had access to this text in manuscript. In chapter 22 of EFB Pope Sixtus, who died in August 1590, is referred to in the present tense; this could mean that the translation was made before the autumn of that year. Thus, although a late date (1592-93) is more probable, the possibility that Marlowe's *Doctor Faustus* was first composed as early as 1588 cannot be wholly discounted.

Proponents of an early date point to a reference in *The Black Book* (1604) by T.M. ("like one of my Divells in Dr. Faustus when the old Theater crackt and frighted the audience"), which seems to indicate that the play was acted at the Theater in Shoreditch, presumably by the Lord Admiral's/Lord Strange's Men before their move to the Rose in 1591; it has been suggested, however, that this performance could have taken place during a brief intermission of the plague at any time up to the summer of 1594 (Greg 8-9). Further evidence for an early date is provided by Thomas Lodge's and Robert Greene's play *A Looking-Glass for London and England*, which was performed at the Rose in 1591-92, though not printed until 1594. A speech in this play appears to echo lines in Faustus's last soliloquy, and *A Looking-Glass* also contains parallels to two passages in the A text's comic scenes (Kuriyama 1975: 181-84).

However, as Roma Gill has brilliantly conjectured, the comic parallels may have been contributed by an actor who helped to shape the slapstick roles in both plays—a clown of the kind described by Hamlet, who "keepes one sute of jeasts, as a man is knowne by one

sute of Apparell" (Q1, III.ii.33-35). John Adams, who played with
Sussex's Men in 1576 and The Queen's Men in 1583 and 1588, was
well enough remembered to be linked with the famous clown
Richard Tarlton in the Induction to Jonson's *Bartholomew Fair*
(1614): "Adams, the rogue, ha' leaped and capered upon him
[Tarlton], and ha'dealt his vermin about as though they had cost him
nothing." Gill's suggestion that during the 1590s Adams was one of
the Admiral's Men and dealt his vermin about in *Doctor Faustus*
I.iv.21-29 is very appealing—as is her supposition that, having acted
the role of the Clown/Adam in *A Looking-Glass* who beats and mor-
tally wounds a devil, he subsequently contributed the "kill-devil" jest
to *Doctor Faustus* I.iv.45-49 (Gill 1990: xix-xxi). (Her further
speculation that Thomas Nashe wrote the comic scenes in Act One,
and that he and Adams supervised the assemblage of the other A-
version comic scenes, seems unwarranted.)

The evidence provided by *A Looking-Glass* is thus ambiguous.
Faustus's last speech may have influenced this play (although the
"strong correspondences" noted by Kuriyama do not include any
actual quotations), but the kill-devil jest, which is anchored in the
action of *A Looking-Glass*, seems to indicate that the borrowing was
in the other direction.

It is possible to be more precise about other dates in the early
history of this play. Between September 30, 1594 and January 5,
1597, *Doctor Faustus* was performed two dozen times by the
Admiral's Men at the Rose, with Edward Alleyn in the part of Faustus; and there was a further performance the following October
(Greg 11). The apparent withdrawal of the play from the repertory
of the Admiral's Men coincided with Alleyn's retirement from the
company in late 1597; and there is no doubt also a connection between his return in late 1602 at the time of the opening of their new
house, the Fortune, and Philip Henslowe's payment in November
1602, on behalf of the Admiral's Men, of four pounds to William
Birde and Samuel Rowley "for ther adicyones in doctor fostes"
(Greg 11-12). This revision was probably also motivated by the comparative scarcity of tragedies in the company's repertory, and by the
fact that this particular one shared certain features of the popular
genre of comedies about magicians—a genre which the revised ver-

sion of Acts Three and Four resembles still more closely (Knutson 260-74).

In the meantime, in January 1601, the play had been entered in the Stationers' Register by Thomas Bushell, who published the A text in 1604, and may have printed an earlier edition, of which no copy now survives. The text published by Bushell is presumably quite closely related to that version of the play which was performed in repertory from 1594 to 1597. By the end of that period receipts for performances of *Doctor Faustus* had fallen off; the Admiral's Men no longer had any strong reason for preventing the play from being printed.

It now seems clear that the quite different text published by John Wright in 1616 incorporates the revisions paid for by Henslowe in 1602 and belatedly announced as "new Additions" on the title page of the reprint of 1619. Until recently there was thought to be strong evidence to the contrary. However, the case of *A Looking-Glass* shows how difficult correspondences between play-texts can be to interpret; and parallels with other plays of the period which were used by Leo Kirschbaum and W.W. Greg to date the B text of *Doctor Faustus* and to argue for its priority have proved equally slippery.

The Taming of a Shrew, an anonymous and plagiaristic comedy printed in 1594, contains five distinct parallels to *Doctor Faustus* (see Boas 198-9; Kirschbaum 1946: 275-6) — one of them to a passage that occurs only in B. In IV.ii of the 1616 text, having been beheaded by the knight whom he horned at the Emperor's court, Faustus comes back to life, claiming:

> And had you cut my body with your swords,
> And hew'd this flesh and bones as small as sand,
> Yet in a minute had my spirit return'd....
> (B: 1449-51; B: IV.ii.73-75)

A Shrew contains a similar passage:

> This angrie sword should rip thy hatefull chest,
> And hewd thee smaller then the *Libian* sandes....
> (Sig. F2, scene xvi; qtd. from Greg 28)

Believing that "it is unquestionably *A Shrew* that is the debtor," Greg used this parallel in support of his argument that "none of the passages peculiar to B represent the additions paid for by Henslowe in 1602, and that structurally at any rate the B-text preserves the more original, and the A-text a maimed and debased, version of the play" (Greg 28-29). Unfortunately, though, there is strong evidence that Samuel Rowley, one of the authors of the 1602 additions, was also part-author of *A Shrew* (Kuriyama 1975: 191-6). The parallel can therefore be explained by the hypothesis that, having plagiarized from Marlowe in *A Shrew*, Rowley subsequently re-used some of his own lines from that play in the 1602 additions. This view is strengthened by Roma Gill's observation that the specifically *Libyan* sands of *A Shrew* hark back to Catullus: "quam magnus numerus Libyssae harena" (poem 7). Since it is unlikely that a writer borrowing from *Dr Faustus* "would add this magic ingredient of his own accord" (Gill 1990: 142), the B text must at this point be indebted to *A Shrew*. Elsewhere, *A Shrew* borrows the first four lines of the third scene of *Doctor Faustus*, but agrees with B in printing "shadow of the night" rather than A's "shadow of the earth" (which is demonstrably correct; see my notes to I.iii.1, 3). What Kirschbaum and Greg took to be a confirmation of B's reading is no such thing: the agreement of B with *A Shrew* suggests rather that when Rowley helped himself to parts of *Doctor Faustus* in 1594 he misunderstood I.iii.1 and changed it — and when in 1602 he was hired to tinker with the whole play he did so once again.

Greg placed greater weight upon a Shakespearean parallel. In the B text of *Doctor Faustus*, the punishment of three knights who attack Faustus includes being "Halfe smother'd in a Lake of mud and durt" (B: 1497; B: IV.iii.4); in *The Merry Wives of Windsor* (1600-01), Bardolf appears to allude to this episode when he says: "so soone as I came beyond *Eaton*, they threw me off, from behind one of them, in a slough of myre; and set spurres, and away; like three *Germane*-divels; three *Doctor Faustasses*" (First Folio, IV.v.64-8). But this can hardly be used to show that the B-text passage was written before 1602, for the allusion does not appear in the 1602 "bad quarto" of *The Merry Wives*, and the Folio text is known to have been revised (Bowers ii. 137; Gill 1990: 142-3). As Bowers remarked, a better indication of date is provided by the overwhelming probability that B: 1200, "He took his rouse with stopes of Rhennish wine," is derived from *Hamlet*: "The King doth wake to night and takes his rowse [....] / And as he draines his drafts of Rennish downe, / The kettle drumme, and trumpet, thus bray out" (Q2, I.iv.9, 11-12).

The B text printed for John Wright in 1616 appears to have been subjected to editorial alterations, presumably at the time of its publication. Philip II had died in 1598; Valdes's reference to the plate fleet "That yearely stuffes olde *Philips* treasury" (A: 165; I.i.133) was therefore put into the past tense ("stuff'd"). The same editorial hand was probably responsible for smoothing out compacted or ambiguous syntax: in the Prologue, for instance, "whose sweete delight disputes / In heavenly matters of *Theologie*" (18-19) is replaced by "and sweetly can dispute / In th'heavenly matters of Theologie."

The B text was also censored to avoid the fine of ten pounds specified in the "Acte to restraine Abuses of Players" (1606) for each occasion on which actors "in any Stage play [...] jestingly or prophanely speake or use the holy Name of God or of Christ Jesus, or of the Holy Ghoste or of the Trinitie, which are not to be spoken but with feare and reverence" (Gill 1990: xvii). Thus Faustus's dismissal of Divinity in the A text as "Unpleasant, harsh, contemptible and vile" (I.i.110) is eliminated; he is counselled by Mephastophilis to abjure not "the Trinity" (I.iii.53) but "all godliness"; and in his last soliloquy he tries to leap up, not "to [his] God" (V.ii.70), but "to heaven". More significantly, Faustus's vision of Christ's blood streaming in the firmament disappears from the text, and the vision which succeeds it — "see where God stretcheth out his arm / And bends his ireful brows!" (V.ii.76-77) — is almost effaced: as Roma Gill remarks, the "threatening arm" and "angry brow" of the B text "do not belong to anyone" (Gill 1990: xvii).

While mutilating some of the finest lines in the play, this censorship also alters its theological resonance. In the words of R.G. Hunter, "What Marlowe is doing in the A version is characterizing the God who sends his creatures to hell and this the B version will not allow." The entrance of God into the theater of God's judgments, though visible only to Faustus, is terrifying; but this terror "is mitigated in the B version, its vividness generalized out of existence" (R.G. Hunter 62).

As a comparison of the two versions of the play will reveal, other alterations in the B text display a similar tendency. Whether they be ascribed to the revision of 1602, the overt censorship of 1606, or the editorial work of 1616, these changes are systematic in nature: taken together, they amount to a deformation of the originally interrogative thrust of the play.

7. *A and B: Memorial transmission and censorship*

The most detailed comparative analysis of the A and B texts remains that of W.W. Greg, in his parallel-text edition of *Doctor Faustus*. Greg believed that B represented something very close to the original form of the play, and that A was a reduced version which had been cut for performance in the provinces during the plague years of the early 1590s, and further corrupted by memorial transmission. In other words, as Leo Kirschbaum had already asserted, A was a "bad quarto" derived not from an authorial manuscript, but from one based on actors' recollections of their parts (Greg 60). Greg thought that B, in contrast, could be traced back to an authorial manuscript — one which was not solely Marlowe's work, but could be taken to express his intentions. He explained the presence of Samuel Rowley's stylistic traits in scenes unique to B by supposing that Rowley had collaborated with Marlowe in writing the play, and he found it convenient to assume that the 1602 additions written by Rowley and Birde must have been lost.

This view of the play's textual history was conclusively refuted in 1973 by Fredson Bowers, who showed that a large part of B consists precisely of the 1602 additions. The work of Constance Brown Kuriyama (1975) and of Michael Warren has since made it evident that Greg's analyses of specific instances of supposed memorial corruption in A are likewise far from trustworthy. What then remains of the authority claimed for B by Greg and Kirschbaum? By Greg's own account, some 500 lines in the B text (out of a total of just over 800 which he thought to have been written by Marlowe) were printed from the 1611 reprint of A, known as A3 — though Greg believed that sporadic use was also made of a manuscript of the play (Greg 64-74, 138-9). The 1616 quarto is thus a heterogeneous text; and to the extent that its tragic action is largely derived from A3, and that most of what remains is the work of Birde and Rowley, one may be tempted to conclude that the several different moments of textual reproduction conflated in B are all subsequent to A. However, it is obvious that the person who supervised the printing of B must have had access to a manuscript which, in addition to containing the 1602 additions and embodying the alterations of a censor, also offered many readings in parallel passages which differ from those of A. But what kind of manuscript was this?

Greg explained the 1616 editor's reliance on A3 by hypothesizing that the manuscript available to him was "in all probability incomplete, mutilated, and illegible" — and he took the very large further step of assuming that it must have been a bundle of authorial "foul papers" (Greg 85). Recognizing that there are no grounds for such an assumption, and that this hypothetically dilapidated manuscript might just as easily have been a reported text as an authorial one (Warren 128-9), recent editors have tended to resist the view that B has any substantive value. David Ormerod and Christopher Wortham, while regarding A as a "memorially reconstructed" text, refuse to concede any form of priority to B. "In closely parallel passages B has some superior readings," they write, "but these can be put down to intelligent editorial emendation rather than access to a supposed manuscript by Marlowe" (Ormerod and Wortham xxvii-xxviii). In a similar vein Roma Gill has remarked that "For the most part the edited and censored B text is of historical interest rather than practical use in preparing a modern edition of *Dr Faustus*" (Gill 1990: xvii).

In my opinion, the evidence points to a more nuanced conclusion. Thanks to the work of Annabel Patterson and to William Empson's sometimes extravagant study of *Faustus and the Censor*, the issue of censorship has attracted renewed attention. All textual critics agree that B is a censored text, and it can be shown that some of the textual variants which Greg took to exemplify memorial corruption in A are more probably the result of censorship in B. However, it is also possible to demonstrate that in other cases the readings of A are, as Greg asserted, secondary to those of B. This does not mean that the manuscript used in the printing of B was necessarily an authorial one, for traces of memorial transmission are detectable in B as well as in A. But it does mean that B is of value to editors for what it can reveal at certain points of something close to the originary moment of textual production.

Let me review these claims in sequence. The activity of the censor is most obvious in the last scene of the play, where Faustus's magnificent outcry in the A-text—

> O Ile leape up to my God: who pulles me downe?
> See see where Christs blood streames in the firmament,
> One drop would save my soule, halfe a drop, ah my Christ
> (A: 1462-4; V.ii.70-72)

—is reduced in B to the barely intelligible

> O I'le leape up to heaven: who puls me downe?
> One drop of bloud will save me; oh my Christ....
> (B: 2048-49)

Another desperate plea in the same speech—

> Oh God, if thou wilt not have mercy on my soule,
> Yet for Christs sake, whose bloud hath ransomd me,
> Impose some end to my incessant paine
> (A: 1483-5; V.ii.91-93)

—is transformed into something at once less vivid and more moralistic:

> O, if my soule must suffer for my sinne,
> Impose some end to my incessant paine....
> (B: 2067-68)

More has been excised here than the names of God and Christ: the alarming implication of a refusal of divine mercy has disappeared from the B text, to be replaced by an acknowledgment of the due connection between sinfulness and suffering.

In the immediately preceding scene a similar effect can be noted. The Old Man tells Faustus in the A text that the "stench" of his "most vilde and loathsome filthinesse"

> corrupts the inward soule
> With such flagitious crimes of hainous sinnes,
> As no commiseration may expel,
> But mercie Faustus of thy Saviour sweete,
> Whose bloud alone must wash away thy guilt.
> (A: 1308-13; V.i.41-46)

Like the Good Angel's first speech, this is not a comforting intervention; for although the Old Man wishes to guide Faustus "unto the way of life" (A: 1303), what his words convey most distinctly is a violent revulsion from him. Faustus already believes that God "loves [him] not" (A: 447; II.i.10); the same is apparently true of God's spokesman in this scene. The B text gives the Old Man an altogether different speech, which provides a deliberate contrast to the loveless rhetoric of his A-text counterpart:

> It may be this my exhortation
> Seemes harsh, and all unpleasant; let it not,
> For gentle sonne, I speake it not in wrath,
> Or envy of thee, but in tender love,
> And pitty of thy future miserie.
> (B: 1823-7; B: V.i.43-47)

The theology of the B-text speech is also different. Christ's blood has again been effaced, and the A-text's suggestion that an unmerited divine mercy is Faustus's only hope of salvation gives way to the implication that it is within his own power to repent:

> Though thou hast now offended like a man,
> Doe not persever in it like a Divell;
> Yet, yet, thou hast an amiable soule,
> If sin by custome grow not into nature....
> (B: 1816-19; B: V.i.36-39)

Faustus responds to the Old Man's intervention with an outburst of despair — "Where art thou Faustus? wretch what hast thou done? / Damnd art thou Faustus, damnd, dispaire and die" (A: 1314-15; V.i.47-48) — the second line of which is missing in B. To the suicidal gesture which follows, the Old Man reacts in both texts with the vision of an angel that hovers over Faustus, "And with a violl full of precious grace, / Offers to powre the same into thy soule" (A: 1321-2; V.i.54-55). But in neither text does Faustus seem to receive this grace: the Old Man leaves him, in A, "with heavy cheare, / fearing the ruine of thy hopelesse soule" (A: 1327-8; V.i.60-61) — and in B, "with griefe of heart, / Fearing the enemy of thy haplesse soule" (B: 1841-2). Faustus then asks himself, in A, "Accursed Faustus, where is mercie now?" (A: 1329; V.i.62) — a question for which B, re-using an earlier line, substitutes "Accursed *Faustus*, wretch what hast thou done?" (B: 1843). These variants result in a distinct shift in the meaning of this passage: where A implies that there is a link between Faustus's despair and the divine mercy which hovers just beyond his reach, B emphasizes instead his own perverse agency and that of the "enemy" whose victim he has made himself.

Whether the above alterations be ascribed to the 1602 additions or to the subsequent censorship of the play, they are consistent in substituting for A's foregrounding of the harshness of Calvinist theology an orientation that might be described as semi-Pelagian. In these passages in B the view that Faustus has the capacity to repent, and is therefore wholly responsible for his sinful failure to do so, supplants the A text's insistent suggestion that his despairing inability to will his own salvation is due to the withholding of divine grace.

Although the disturbing notion of a refusal of divine mercy was thus removed from the last act of the B text, it remains in evidence elsewhere, most notably in Act Two, where, encouraged by his Good Angel to repent, Faustus calls on Christ — only to be answered by the terrifying entrance of a demonic trinity: Lucifer, Belzebub, and Mephastophilis. Not surprisingly, in this passage also there are signs, though less obtrusive, of revision in the B text.

Faustus cries in his brief prayer: "Ah Christ my Saviour, / seeke [B: Helpe] to save distressed Faustus soule" (A: 711-12; II.iii.84-85). Greg cited this variant as one of several in which — sure evidence of memorial corruption — the reading of A implies a definite misunderstanding of the theological situation. "To seek to do something," he wrote, "implies a doubtful issue: but whereas it is heretical to question Christ's power to save, it is true belief that that power is only exercised in aid of the sinner's own endeavour" (Greg 46). In at least two respects this statement is curiously revealing. It implies, first, that theological orthodoxy can be used — in this of all plays — as a textual criterion. This naivety is compounded by a strange disregard of historical context in Greg's definition of "true belief." Given that the theology of the Anglican church in the latter decades of the sixteenth century was overwhelmingly Calvinistic in orientation, most educated Anglicans of Marlowe's time would have rejected this definition as arrant Pelagianism: to them it was axiomatic that a sinner was powerless to help himself until Christ's saving power was exercised on his behalf.

Greg's words amount to saying that the reading of the 1616 text in this line is authentic because he agrees with its theological implications. But since there may be better reasons for preferring the reading of the 1604 text, it is worth lingering a moment longer over Faustus's prayer. Greg's perception of an undertone of doubt in the A text's "seeke to save" is acute, but should if anything serve to confirm the appropriateness of this expression in the mouth of one whose problem is precisely that he lacks faith. More obviously, though, "seeke" carries two other implications: first, that it is primarily up to Christ to save Faustus's soul; and second, that he has not previously been trying to. A simple cry for help—the B text's "Helpe to save"—does not imply anything about the previous stance of the person to whom it is addressed, but the A text's imploring "seeke" contains an element of persuasion which can only suggest that at some level Faustus thinks persuasion to be necessary. It takes no leap of the imagination to see how the censoring editor who in the final scene substituted Faustus's bland acknowledgment of sin for the A text's refusal of divine mercy might have recognized these implications. On the other hand, there is no reason for believing that an actor's faulty memory might have effected the reverse substitution.

The words which I have quoted from Greg's commentary represent not a momentary aberration, but rather the basic orientation of his approach to the play. I have remarked that Faustus's prayer in II.iii was preceded by the Good Angel's encouragement to repent: but the precise nature of this encouragement needs closer examination. When, having broken angrily with Mephastophilis, Faustus wonders aloud whether it is not too late, his Good Angel reassures him with the words: "Never too late, if Faustus can [B: will] repent" (A: 708; II.iii.81). Here again, Greg argues that the reading of A is corrupt: "A is wrong in making the Angel doubt Faustus' ability to repent if he has the will to do so" (Greg 338). But this is not what the line means. The Angel does not oppose ability and will in this manner; rather, he is suggesting that Faustus is perhaps unable to will to repent. Greg writes: "It is not a question of the possibility of repentance—that is assumed—but of the will to repent" (Greg 45). One must ask: assumed by whom?

Far from being a theological absurdity, as Greg's words seem to imply, the A-reading would have been immediately comprehensible to Marlowe's audiences: for the predicament of the reprobate, of those who have not been chosen by God for salvation, is quite simply that they cannot repent—or, more precisely, that they are unable to will to repent. To twentieth-century minds this may seem paradoxical: the very notion of will is commonly taken to imply freedom and autonomy. But, as Calvin wrote, "[if] this, that it is of necessitie that God doe well, doe not hinder the free will of God in doing well, if the divell which cannot do but evil yet willingly sinneth, who shall then say that a man doeth therefore lesse willingly sinne for this that hee is subject to necessitie of sinning?" Greg's belief that the possibility of repentance and the will to repent are separate matters could only indicate to Elizabethan Anglicans that he had fallen into the error of Peter Lombard, who, in Calvin's words, "could not distinguish necessitie from compulsion," and thus "gave matter to a pernicious errour" (Calvin II.iii.5, fol. 88v).

The Good Angel's words in the 1604 text suggest a question that may already have occurred to members of the audience. Can Faustus repent? It would seem that Anglican theologians of the period, if consulted on the matter at this point in the play, would have responded with a unanimous negative. Even if, disregarding the stern Calvinists for whom a failure to persevere in grace would provide sure evidence of reprobation (see Calvin III.xxii.7; III.xxiv.6), one seeks instead the opinion of their opponent Richard Hooker, the answer is the same. Faustus, one remembers, abjured the Trinity in his invocation of Mephastophilis in the third scene of the play (see Keefer 1987: 520-1, n. 51), thus denying the very foundation of the Christian faith. In Hooker's opinion, "if the justified err, as he may, and never come to understand his error, God doth save him through general repentance: but if he fall into heresy, he calleth him either at one time or other by actual repentance; but from infidelity, which is an inward direct denial of the foundation, preserveth him by special providence for ever" (Hooker i. 49-50). Faustus has not been so preserved—and if he is therefore not one of the justified, he cannot repent. What then of the agonies which Faustus undergoes? For Calvin and his followers, at least, the answer is brutally simple: "...that blinde torment wherewith the reprobate are diversly drawen, when they see that they must needes seeke God, that they may find remedy for their evils, and yet doe flee from his presence, is unproperly called Conversion and prayer" (Calvin III.iii.24; fol. 201v).

These observations cannot be held to demonstrate that the A-reading of the Good Angel's speech is Marlovian and the B-reading inauthentic: as I have already observed, it is naive to think that theological orthodoxy can be used as a textual criterion. However, taken in conjunction with what has already been said about context in section 5 above, they do establish the likelihood that B's variant readings in such passages as the ones I have discussed result from an ideologically-motivated revision.

A similar ideological motivation is evident throughout Greg's comparison of the A and B texts. Nonetheless, some at least of his repeated claims for the priority of B's readings over A's are justified. Two examples—which are of particular interest because in both cases the editions of Ormerod and Wortham and of Gill (1989, 1990) follow the readings of A—will suffice to demonstrate the point.

In the 1604 quarto the Chorus to Act Three consists of only eleven lines: we read in this text that

> Learned Faustus,
> To know the secrets of *Astronomy*,
> Graven in the booke of *Joves* hie firmament,
> Did mount himselfe to scale *Olympus* top,
> Being seated in a chariot burning bright,
> Drawne by the strength of yoky dragons neckes,
> He now is gone to proove *Cosmography*,
> And as I guesse, wil first arive at *Rome*....
> (A: 813-17)

The seventh line comes as a surprise: its sudden shift of subject produces such a naively bathetic effect that even if no alternative text were available, one would suspect that something had dropped out of this passage. I do not think that any reader who compares these lines with this chorus as printed in the present edition will be tempted to believe that the fourteen additional B-version lines represent an interpolation.

The priority of B is still more evident in a sequence of near-synonymous variants that occurs in the third scene of Act Two. In this passage the B-text (with its variants from A italicized) reads as follows:

> *Speake*, are there many *Spheares* above the Moone?
> Are all Celestiall bodies but one Globe,
> As is the substance of this centricke earth?
> **Meph.** As are the elements, such are the *heavens*,
> *Even from the Moone unto the Emperiall Orbe*,
> Mutually folded in each others *Spheares*....
>   (B: 604-9; II.iii.35-40)

There is no obvious reason to prefer most of these readings to the A text's variants ("Tel me" for "Speake" and "heavens" for "Spheares" in the first line, "spheares" for "heavens" in the fourth, and "orbe" for "Spheares" in the sixth). However, the fact that the fifth line is missing in A shows that text to be defective. The assumption that A is original would require an interpolator who supplied the fifth line as in B, noticed that he then had two consecutive lines ending with "orb," and to remove that embarrassment substituted "spheres" for "orb" in the sixth line. Faced with the clumsiness of "spheres...folded in each others' spheres," he would then have had to work backwards through the passage, substituting "heavens" for "spheres" in the fourth line, and "spheres" for "heavens" in the first. It will, I think, be admitted that this is unlikely.

If we assume instead the relative priority of B, it is easy to see how an apparently insignificant error, the substitution of "heavens" for "spheres" in the first line, could have produced a sequence of displacements. The reverse substitution of "spheres" for "heavens" in the fourth line, while compensating for the initial displacement, creates the absurdity of "spheres...folded in each others' spheres." A displacement of the second "spheres" by "orb" (for "heaven" would not make sense in the sixth line) removes this clumsiness, but results in the further problem of two consecutive lines ending with "orb" — the easiest solution for which is simply to drop the first of these lines.

Although the rotation of variants points to the conclusion that in these lines B is preferable to A, it does not follow that this passage in A was printed from a reported text. An actor's defective memory may very well have been responsible for the sequence of displacements in A, but the same effects could also have been produced by a compositor who, having set the first four lines of this passage, might have found it easier to omit the fifth line and use "orb" in the sixth than to correct "spheres" and "heavens" in the first and fourth lines. However, the next line in A—"And [*Faustus* all] jointly move upon one axletree" (A: 669; the bracketed words are not in B)—does bear the marks of memorial transmission in its hypermetrical vocative and redundant "all."

Elsewhere in A the signs of memorial transmission are equally prominent. In the first scene of Act Two, Faustus exclaims, in the B text:

> Nay, and this be hell, I'le willingly be damn'd.
> What sleeping, eating, walking and disputing?
> (B: 530-1; II.i.139-40)

A reads instead: "How? now in hell? nay and this be hell, Ile willingly be damnd here: what walking, disputing, &c." (A: 585-6). The repetition of the last words of the preceding speech ("now in hell"), the redundant "here," the vagueness of "&c.," and the slack prose rhythm of A are all suggestive of the imperfections of memory. By the same tokens, however, a part of this same scene in B can be identified as having been memorially transmitted. Faustus says, in A:

> Loe *Mephastophilus*, for love of thee,
> I cut mine arme, and with my proper blood
> Assure my soule to be great *Lucifers*....
> (A: 493-5; II.i.53-55)

In B he says:

> Loe *Mephosto*: for love of thee Faustus hath cut his arme,
> And with his proper bloud assures his soule to be great
> *Lucifers*....
> (B: 441-2)

This makes equally good sense, but if a disruption of lineation and of blank verse rhythms is a sign of memorial 'corruption,' then these lines are corrupt.

8. *The Present Edition*

(a) Copy-text

In this edition I have taken the 1604 or A text of *Doctor Faustus* as copy-text, while at the same time recognizing the substantive value of parallel passages in the 1616 or B text. I have thus striven to resist that "tyranny of the copy-text" (Greg "Copy-text" 49) which arises out of the common habit of assuming that the local readings of a text identified as historically more authentic should without question be preferred over those of other demonstrably substantive texts. For, as I have already indicated, the claim that A represents a relatively more authentic *version* of the play is in no way contradicted by the assertion that in parallel passages the readings of the B *text* are sometimes superior. B is a heavily revised and censored text, which in some parallel passages is derived from the 1611 reprint of A. But in other parallel passages where A is defective B can be shown to have manuscript authority.

Needless to say, I have not extended the process of editorial conflation to the level of the play's structure. Those scenes in the B text which diverge from the A version of the play have been relegated to Appendix 1 (where, for purposes of comparison, I have given them act and scene numbers corresponding to those of the scenes in A which they were intended to displace).

The text printed here contains one novel conjecture, at I.i.52. This line does not appear in B; A gives it as "Lines, circles, sceanes, letters and characters" (A: 81). "Seals" (my conjecture for the unintelligible "sceanes") carries a meaning in Renaissance magic close to that of "letters" and "characters;" it translates the Latin words *sigilla* and *signacula*. Petrus de Abanus, who may be the "Albanus" of I.i.155, lists the *sigilla* of the planetary angels in his *Heptameron seu elementa magica* (see Agrippa 1970: i. 574-87). Similarly, Cornelius Agrippa gives the "letters or characters" (*literae seu characteres*) of the planets in his *De occulta philosophia* I. xxxiii, and at II. xxii of the same work lists the "seals or characters" (*signacula sive characteres*) of the planetary intelligences (Agrippa 1970: i. 61, 221-25). "Seals," it can be added, overlaps in meaning with "figures," a word which appears in the first chapter of EFB: "Figures, Characters, Conjurations, Incantations...."

(b) Act and scene divisions

One characteristic of authorial and scribal manuscripts of play-texts in this period, and of the printed texts immediately derived from them, appears to have been the presence of act and scene divisions; these are commonly lacking in texts printed from playhouse manuscripts. The 1604 and 1616 quartos of *Doctor Faustus* contain no act or scene divisions: all such divisions in modern editions of this play are therefore editorial. During the present century an interesting divergence in editorial practice has become evident. B-version editors have tended to think of the play as having a five-act structure (the only deviants being Jump, who numbered the play's scenes consecutively from the start, and Bowers, who allowed his readers to choose between act and scene numbers and consecutively numbered scenes). In contrast, A-version editors have either eschewed act and scene divisions altogether (Tucker Brooke, Ormerod and Wortham) or else have divided the play only into scenes (Kocher, Wright and LaMar, and Gill [1989, 1990]).

This divergence may seem paradoxical, for since the B text lacks the chorus to Act IV, its five-act structure is actually less clearly marked than is that of the A text. But that both versions of the play have such a structure is, I think, evident. (G.K. Hunter's analysis of the matter, though vitiated by his belief in the authenticity of B and his blindness to the stylistic oddities of the B-text additions, seems to me to be correct, in its broad outlines at least.)

In the A version, what I would call Acts I, III, and IV all begin with a choral prologue or introduction. If the stage direction at B: 557, where Wagner enters to speak lines belonging to the Chorus, can be taken to indicate that he took the part of the Chorus throughout, then Act V also has a quasi-choral introduction in Wagner's speech at V.i.1-8. Moreover, the opening lines of what I would call Act II announce a shift in mood, from a note of defiant transgression to a wavering between despairing recklessness and a nostalgic desire for communion with the sacred. This, I think, is sufficient reason to accept a division of the play into acts. (There is no more need to suspect that a choral speech designed to preface

Act II has been lost than there is to believe that the last three acts of Shakespeare's *Romeo and Juliet* were once supplied with choral introductions.)

I have assumed that a new scene begins either when the stage is voided or when there is a major change in locale. The act divisions in this edition are not meant to imply any claim with respect to a recovery of authorial presence in this text.

(c) Restoration of misplaced scenes

In other respects as well, to the extent that the textual evidence permits, I have sought to repair the defects of the A text. In the 1604 quarto two comic scenes intrude between the chorus to Act IV and the action in the Imperial court which that chorus introduces. Most textual scholars have long since recognized that these scenes are misplaced, although few have made any serious attempt to determine where they properly belong. Some editions based on the A text (those of Dyce, Ward, Tucker Brooke, and Ormerod and Wortham) simply print these scenes in the order in which they occur in the 1604 quarto, while others (Kocher, and Wright and LaMar) make the two comic scenes precede the chorus to Act IV. Roma Gill, in her most recent editions, has taken the further step of removing the first of these two scenes to the place occupied by the corresponding scene in the B text. This is an improvement, though not an adequate solution to the problem. It has been argued that the comic scene in B which Gill used as a guide is itself misplaced (Eriksen 1981: 249-53); my own view is that this B-text scene occupies the position for which it was written, but that its placement there was part of the process by which the B version of the play was created. I believe that the loosely parallel scene in A originally followed the fifth scene of the play—and that to restore it to that position is also, in large part, to restore the structural integrity of the A text.

The following tabulation of the scenes of the play, and of the order in which they appear in the quartos of 1604 and 1616 and in the present edition, will make clear the manner in which this edition differs from all previous ones. (A few words of clarification. The fifth scene in the 1604 quarto, though continuous in that text, is actually composed of two scenes run together: hence the scene numbers A: v (a) and v (b). And although I regard scene xi of the 1616 quarto as a single scene, and have printed it in Appendix 1 as Act IV, scene i, the scene numbers B: xi (a) and xi (b) are a concession to the fact that many editors of the 1616 version of *Doctor Faustus* have started a new scene with the entrance of the Emperor.)

A text (1604)	B text (1616)	This edition
A: chorus 1.	B: chorus 1 (parallel).	Prologue
i.	i (parallel).	I.i. (Faustus, Angels, Valdes and Cornelius)
ii.	ii (parallel).	I.ii. (Wagner and Scholars)
iii.	iii. (parallel).	I.iii. (Faustus' conjuration of Mephastophilis)
iv.	iv. (parallel action).	I.iv. (Wagner hiring clown = A: iv.)
v (a).	v. (parallel, but with excision of concluding lines).	II. i. (pact scene = A: v (a))
—	B: chorus 2a. (lines 1-6, 20, 22-25 of B: chorus 2b.)	—
		II.ii. (Robin and Rafe with stolen book = A: vii.)
v (b).	vi. (parallel)	II.iii. (disputation, seven deadly sins = A: v. (b))
	vii. (Robin and Dick: loosely parallel to A: vii.)	
A: chorus 2. (= 1-6, 20, 22-5 of B: chorus 2b.)	B: chorus 2b.	Act III, Chorus. (= B: chorus 2b.)
vi.	viii. (initially parallel to A: vi.)	III.i. (Papal scene = A: vi.)
	ix. (Papal banquet: conclusion parallel to A: vi.)	
		III.ii. (Robin and Rafe with stolen cup = A: viii.)
A: chorus 3.	—	Act IV, Chorus. (= A: chorus 3.)

A	B	
vii. (Robin and Rafe with stolen book).		
viii. (Robin and Rafe with stolen cup.)	x. (action parallel to A: viii.)	
—	xi (a) (Imperial courtiers anticipate Faustus' arrival.)	—
ix.	xi (b) (action parallel to A: ix.)	IV.i. (Imperial court = A: ix.)
—	xii. (Benvolio's revenge.)	—
—	xiii. (Benvolio and his friends horned.)	—
x.	xiv. (parallel action.)	IV.ii. (Faustus and horse-courser = A: x.)
—	xv. (Clowns at an inn.)	—
xi.	xvi. (parallel action followed by intrusion of clowns.)	IV.iii. (Court of Vanholt = A: xi.)
xii.	xvii. (parallel action.)	V.i. (Faustus, Old Man, Helen = A: xii.)
xiii.	xviii. (parallel, but with extensive additions).	V.ii. (Faustus's confession to the scholars and last solilquy = A: xiii.)
A: chorus 4.	B: chorus 3. (= A: chorus 4.)	Epilogue.

It is immediately apparent that both the A and B texts are defective at the join between A: v (a) and v (b), or B: v and vi. The fifth scene begins in both texts with Faustus wavering between penitence and despair, and then, at the prompting of his Evil Angel, summoning Mephastophilis and writing with his own blood a "deede of gift of body and of soule" (A: 534). Having consigned himself to Lucifer in exchange for twenty-four years of demonic service, Faustus begins to discover the nature of that service when he asks for "a wife, the fairest maid in *Germany*" (A: 587-8), and gets instead a "hote whore," *"a divell drest like a woman, with fier workes"* (A: 598, 595-6). As though to make up for this trick, Mephastophilis gives him a book of magic spells. Scene B: v ends at this point:

Faust. Thankes *Mephostophilis* for this sweete booke.
This will I keepe, as chary as my life.   *Exeunt.*
(B: 555-6)

Yet while in B this and the following scene are distinct, they are separated by the same eleven lines from the chorus to Act III (B: chorus 2b) which appear in the A text as A: chorus 2. The fact that these lines are assigned to Wagner (B: 557) is of interest as suggesting that Wagner speaks the part of the chorus (it can be noted that the speech of Wagner's which begins Act V is clearly choral in nature). Moreover, this piece of patchwork, while casting doubt on Fredson Bowers's claim that the B version of the play is "textually coherent and historically a unit" (Bowers ii. 143), also signals the 1616 editor's awareness that his text was defective.

In A, though, the scene continues. Faustus requests additional books, but is told that what he wants is already contained in the book he has (A: 614-27; II.i.166-79 in the present edition). From the fact that these lines parody a passage from the apocryphal Wisdom of Solomon (7: 17-22) which precedes by only a few verses the words of Solomon (7: 26, 29, 8: 2) parodied by Faustus in his address to Helen, it can be argued that they formed part of the original design of the play, and that their absence in B is an indication of revision. A further indication is provided by the fact that the last line in B's fifth scene (a line absent in A) occurs again in both texts immediately following the pageant of the seven deadly sins, when Lucifer gives Faustus a second magic book (A: 805, B: 739; III.iii.171). It seems probable that whoever cut short the first book-giving scene in B simply inserted this same line at B: 556.

In A, immediately after his exchanges with Mephastophilis over the first magic book (A: 614-27; II.i.166-79), Faustus declares:

When I behold the heavens, then I repent,
And curse thee wicked *Mephastophilus*,
Because thou hast depriv'd me of those joyes.
(A: 628-30)

However, it soon becomes evident that a considerable expanse of time has elapsed since the signing of the blood pact: Faustus says he would have killed himself "long ere this" (A: 653), had not his despair been conquered by the pleasure of hearing Homer sing and

Amphion play duets with Mephastophilis. Clearly, then, A: v (a) and v (b) are distinct scenes, and the scene which separated them is either missing or displaced.

The two displaced comic scenes in A have to do with Robin the ostler (whom one may choose to identify with the Clown recruited by Wagner in I.iv) and his companion Rafe. In the first of these Robin explains to Rafe the use he intends to make of a conjuring book that he has stolen from Doctor Faustus; in the second, when the two of them are challenged by a Vintner over a cup they have stolen from him, Robin uses the stolen book to summon up Mephastophilis. The proper location of the latter scene is easy enough to determine: a loosely parallel scene in B follows Faustus's escapades at the Pope's banquet (which include snatching the Pope's cup out of his hand). This scene provides a low-life commentary on Faustus's actions in much the same way as the comic scenes of Act I parody and deflate his early aspirations. I have therefore followed the lead of Kocher, of Wright and LaMar, and of Roma Gill's A-version editions in making A's cup-stealing scene follow the papal scene.

The other displaced A-text scene is less easy to reposition. The loosely parallel scene in B follows Lucifer's gift to Faustus of a second magical book after the pageant of the seven deadly sins; on this basis Roma Gill places the A-text scene in the same position. However, there is reason to believe that the placing of the stolen book scene in B does not reflect the original order of the play.

It seems evident that the A-text scene should follow one of the two gifts of magical books to Faustus. In A the first of these episodes is much more prominent than the second, and not just because Mephastophilis (as in B) devotes seven lines to an account of the contents of the book. It will be remembered that, having frustrated Faustus's request for "a wife, the fairest maid in *Germany*" (A: 587-8), Mephastophilis gives him this conjuring book as though it were a kind of consolation. Faustus then asks, three times in succession, for another book which will provide him with one or another kind of lore (the things he lists are reminiscent of what Solomon says Wisdom has taught him) — but each time he is shown, to what seems his mounting irritation, that what he wants is already contained in the book he has in his hands. This sequence may remind one of Faustus's inability, when in the first scene he held a bible in his hands, to make sense of its conditional promises of salvation. It is also echoed in the displaced comic scene which in the present edition follows Mephastophilis's gift.

After asking for a wife and receiving instead "a hote whore" (A: 598), Faustus was given the book, along with instructions as to how to use it:

> The iterating of these lines brings golde,
> The framing of this circle on the ground,
> Brings whirlewindes....
>
> (A: 608-10)

Robin, having stolen what is presumably the same book, appears to revert to the desire from which the book had distracted Faustus: "ifaith I meane to search some circles for my owne use: now wil I make al the maidens in our parish dance at my pleasure starke naked before me..." (A: 950-2). The two scenes appear, then, to be deliberately linked.

The linkages in B's distantly parallel version of this scene are of a different order. Robin's bawdy quibble on circles is gone, and at the end of the scene Robin and his companion (here named Dick) set off to conjure themselves some free wine at the tavern — presumably the same one from which they have just emerged, pursued by the Vintner, in the comic scene which follows Faustus's escapades in Rome. A deliberate (if sometimes unskilful) interconnection of comic scenes is noticeable elsewhere in B; this particular connection provides one reason for thinking that the B-text scenes involving the stolen book and the stolen cup were not designed to be separated by more than the papal scenes — and hence that Eriksen (1981) was mistaken in arguing that B's stolen book scene properly belongs in the gap between the fifth and sixth scenes. In the B text that gap remains obstinately empty.

In A, the stolen book and stolen cup scenes are linked, not to one another, but rather to the scenes in the principal action which they parody. Restored to their proper place, they permit the play's patterns of meaning to be more fully appreciated than has been possible in the past.

9. *Abbreviations: Editions of* Doctor Faustus

(a) Early Editions

A1

THE / TRAGICALL / History of D. Faustus. / *As it hath bene Acted by the Right / Honorable the Earle of Nottingham his seruants.* Written by Ch. Marl. / [Device] / LONDON / Printed by V. S. [Valentine Simmes] for Thomas Bushell. 1604. (Bodleian Library, shelf-mark Malone 233 [3]; STC 17429; facsimile rpt. in *Christopher Marlowe: Doctor Faustus 1604 and 1616* [Menston, England: Scolar Press, 1970].)

A2, A3.

Reprints of the A text, printed by George Eld for John Wright in 1609 and 1611 respectively.

B1

The Tragicall History / of the Life and Death / of *Doctor Faustus.* / Written by *Ch. Mar.* / [Woodcut of Faustus conjuring a devil] / LONDON, / Printed for *Iohn Wright*, and are to be sold at his shop / without Newgate, at the si[gne] of the / Bibl[e.] 1616. (British Library, shelf-mark C. 34. d. 26; STC 17432; facsimile rpt. in *Christopher Marlowe: Doctor Faustus 1604 and 1616* [Menston, England: Scolar Press, 1970].)

B2, B3, B4.

Reprints of the B text, for John Wright, in 1619, 1620, and 1624 respectively. The title pages of these editions contain the words "With new Additions" (Wright published two further reprints, B5 and B6, in 1628 and 1631.).

(b) Editions containing both versions

Cunningham

Cunningham, Francis, ed. *The Works of Christopher Marlowe.* 1870; rpt. London, 1889.

Dyce

Dyce, Alexander, ed. *The Works of Christopher Marlowe.* 2nd ed.; London, 1858.

Greg

Greg, W.W., ed. *Marlowe's "Doctor Faustus" 1604-1616: Parallel Texts.* 1950; rpt. Oxford: Clarendon P, 1968.

(c) A-version editions

Bullen

Bullen, A. H., ed. *The Works of Christopher Marlowe*. 3 vols.; London, 1885.

Ellis

Ellis, Havelock, ed. *Christopher Marlowe*. Mermaid Series; London, 1887.

Gill 1989

Gill, Roma, ed. *Dr Faustus / Christopher Marlowe*. 2nd edition based on the A text. The New Mermaids; London: Black; New York: Norton, 1989.

Gill 1990

Gill, Roma, ed. *The Complete Works of Christopher Marlowe, vol. 2: Doctor Faustus*. Oxford: Clarendon P, 1990.

Kocher

Kocher, Paul H., ed. *Christopher Marlowe: The Tragical History of Doctor Faustus*. New York: Appleton-Century-Crofts, 1950.

Ormerod and Wortham

Ormerod, David, and Christopher Wortham, ed. *Christopher Marlowe: Dr Faustus: The A-Text*. Nedlands: U of Western Australia P, 1985.

Tucker Brooke

Tucker Brooke, C.F., ed. *The Works of Christopher Marlowe*. 1910; rpt. Oxford: Clarendon P, 1941.

Wagner

Wagner, W., ed. *Christopher Marlowe's Tragedy of Doctor Faustus*. London, 1877.

Ward

Ward, A.W., ed. *Marlowe: Tragical History of Dr. Faustus; Greene: Honourable History of Friar Bacon and Friar Bungay*. 4th ed.; Oxford: Clarendon P, 1901.

Wright and LaMar

Wright, Louis B., and Virginia A. LaMar, ed. *The Tragedy of Doctor Faustus / Christopher Marlowe*. 1959; rpt. New York: Washington Square P, 1968.

(d) B-version editions

Barnet
> Barnet, Sylvan, ed. *Christopher Marlowe: Doctor Faustus*. 1969; 2nd ed.; New York: Signet, 1980.

Boas
> Boas, F.S., ed. *The Tragical History of Doctor Faustus*. 1932; rpt. London: Methuen, 1949.

Bowers
> Bowers, Fredson, ed. *The Complete Works of Christopher Marlowe*. 2 vols.; Cambridge: Cambridge UP, 1973.

Dilke
> [Dilke, C.W., ed.] *Old English Plays*. 6 vols.; London, 1814-15.

Gill 1965
> Gill, Roma, ed. *Doctor Faustus / Christopher Marlowe*. The New Mermaids; London: Benn, 1965.

Gill 1971
> Gill, Roma, ed. *The Plays of Christopher Marlowe*. London, New York: Oxford UP, 1971.

Greg "Conj."
> Greg, W.W., ed. *The Tragical History of the Life and Death of Doctor Faustus by Christopher Marlowe: A Conjectural Reconstruction*. Oxford: Clarendon P, 1950.

Jump
> Jump, John D., ed. *Doctor Faustus / Christopher Marlowe*. The Revels Plays. 1962; rpt. London: Methuen, 1974.

Kirschbaum
> Kirschbaum, Leo, ed. *The Plays of Christopher Marlowe*. 1962; rpt. Cleveland: Meridian Books, 1968.

Oxberry
> [Oxberry, W., ed.] *The Tragicall Historie of the Life and Death of Doctor Faustus, with New Additions. Written by Ch. Mar.* London, 1818.

Pendry and Maxwell
> Pendry, E.D., and J.C. Maxwell, ed. *Christopher Marlowe: Complete Plays and Poems*. 1976; rpt. London: Dent, 1983.

Ribner
    Ribner, Irving, ed. *The Complete Plays of Christopher Marlowe.* New York: Odyssey, 1963.

Robinson
    [Robinson, G., ed.] *The Works of Christopher Marlowe.* 3 vols.; London, 1826.

Steane
    Steane, J.B., ed. *Christopher Marlowe: The Complete Plays.* Harmondsworth: Penguin, 1969.

10. Works Cited: Abbreviations

Citations from classical and patristic writers are in most cases keyed to the editions in the Loeb Classical Library and the Ante-Nicene Christian Library respectively. Unless otherwise indicated, Shakespeare is quoted from the Riverside text; other major English Renaissance writers are cited from standard editions. With the exception of certain patristic writings of particular importance in the development of the Faustus legend, these texts are not listed here.

Acts of Peter
    In Hennecke, E., ed. *New Testament Apocrypha.* Rev. ed. W. Schneemelcher, trans. R. McL. Wilson *et al.* 2 vols. 1963-65; rpt. London: SCM, 1973-74.

Acts of Peter and Paul
    In Walker, A., trans. *Apocryphal Gospels, Acts, and Revelations.* Ante-Nicene Christian Library, vol. 16. Edinburgh: T. and T. Clark, 1870.

Agrippa 1530
    Agrippa, Henricus Cornelius. *Splendidae nobilitatis viri et armatae militiae equitis aurati ac utriusque Iuris doctoris sacrae caesareae maiestatis a consilijs et archiuis inditiarij Henrici Cornelij Agrippae ab Nettesheym De Incertitudine et Vanitate Scientiarum et Artium atque excellentia Verbi Dei declamatio.* Antwerp, 1530.

Agrippa 1533
    Henrici Cornelii Agrippae ab Nettesheym a consiliis & archiuis inditiarii sacrae caesarae maiestatis: De occulta philosophia libri tres. [Cologne], 1533.

Introduction

Agrippa 1575

Henrie Cornelius Agrippa, of the Vanitie and vncertaintie of Artes and Sciences: Englished by Ia[mes]. San[ford]. Gent.. 1569; rpt. London: Henrie Bynneman, 1575.

Agrippa 1970

Agrippa, H.C. *Opera.* Ed. R.H. Popkin. 2 vols.; c. 1600; facsimile rpt. Hildesheim and New York: Georg Olms, 1970.

Agrippa 1974

Of the Vanitie and Vncertainty of the Artes and Sciences, by Henry Cornelius Agrippa. Ed. Catherine M. Dunn. Northbridge: California State U.P., 1974

Allen

Allen, Marguerite de Huszar. *The Faust Legend: Popular Formula and Modern Novel.* New York, Berne, Frankfurt: Peter Lang, 1985.

Bakeless

Bakeless, John. *The Tragicall History of Christopher Marlowe.* 2 vols.; 1942; rpt. Hamden, Conn.: Archon Books, 1964.

Barber

Barber, C.L. *Creating Elizabethan Tragedy: The Theater of Marlowe and Kyd.* Ed. Richard P. Wheeler. Chicago: U of Chicago P, 1988.

Barnes

Barnes, Celia. "Matthew Parker's Pastoral Training and Marlowe's *Doctor Faustus. CD* 15 (1981): 258-67.

Baron 1978

Baron, Frank. *Doctor Faustus from History to Legend.* Munich: Wilhelm Fink, 1978.

Baron 1982

Faustus: Geschichte, Sage, Dichtung. Munich: Winkler, 1982.

Baron 1985

"The Faustbook's Indebtedness to Augustin Lercheimer and Wittenberg Sources." *Daphnis* 14 (1985): 517-45.

Baskervill

Baskervill, C. R. *The Elizabethan Jig and Related Song Drama.* 1929; rpt. New York: Dover, 1965.

Becon
> Becon, Thomas. *The Catechism of Thomas Becon ... with other pieces written by him in the reign of King Edward the Sixth*. Ed. John Ayre. Cambridge, 1844.

Bloom
> Bloom, Harold, ed. *Christopher Marlowe*. New York: Chelsea House, 1986.

Boas 1940
> Boas, F.S. *Christopher Marlowe: A Biographical and Critical Study*. Oxford: Clarendon P, 1940.

Bodin
> Bodin, Jean. *De la démonomanie des sorciers ... par I. Bodin Angevin*. Paris, 1581.

Bowers, "Editing"
> Bowers, Fredson. *On Editing Shakespeare*. Charlottesville: UP of Virginia, 1966.

Bowers, "Additions"
> "Marlowe's *Doctor Faustus*: The 1602 Additions." *SB* 26 (1973): 1-18.

Brockbank
> Brockbank, J. P. *Marlowe: Dr. Faustus*. London: Arnold, 1962.

Calvin
> Calvin, Jean. *The Institution of Christian Religion, written in Latine by M. John Caluine, and translated into English according to the Authors last edition [...] by Thomas Norton*. London: H. Midleton, for W. Norton, 1587.

Dido
> Marlowe, Christopher. *Dido Queen of Carthage* and *The Massacre at Paris*. Ed. H.J. Oliver. The Revels Plays. London: Methuen, 1968.

Dollimore
> Dollimore, Jonathan. *Radical Tragedy: Religion, Ideology and Power in the Drama of Shakespeare and his Contemporaries*. Chicago: U of Chicago P, and Brighton: Harvester P, 1984.

Du Plessis-Mornay

Du Plessis-Mornay, Philippe. *A Woorke concerning the trewnesse of the Christian Religion*. Trans. Sir Philip Sidney and Arthur Golding. London, 1587.

Edwards

Edwards, Mark U., Jr. *Luther and the False Brethren*. Stanford: Stanford UP, 1975.

EFB

The Historie of the damnable life, and deserued death of Doctor Iohn Faustus, Newly imprinted, and in conuenient places imperfect matter amended: according to the true Copie printed at Franckfort, and translated into English by P.F. Gent. [....] London: Thomas Orwin, for Edward White, 1592. (British Library, shelf mark C. 27 b. 43; this unique copy of the earliest surviving edition of the English Faustbook is reprinted in Palmer and More, pp. 134-236.)

Ellis-Fermor

Ellis-Fermor, Una. *Christopher Marlowe*. London: Methuen, 1927.

Empson

Empson, William. *Faustus and the Censor: The English Faustbook and Marlowe's "Doctor Faustus"*. Ed. John Henry Jones. Oxford: Blackwell, 1987.

Eriksen 1981

Eriksen, Roy T. "The Misplaced Clownage-scene in *The Tragedie of Doctor Faustus* (1616) and its Implications for the Play's Total Structure." *ES* 62 (1981): 249-58.

Eriksen 1987

"The Forme of Faustus Fortunes": A Study of The Tragedie of Doctor Faustus (1616). Oslo: Solum Forlag; Atlantic Highlands, N.J.: Humanities P, 1987.

First Folio

Mr. William Shakespeares Comedies, Histories, & Tragedies. Ed. Helge Kükeritz, intro. C.T. Prouty. Facsimile rpt. New Haven and London: Yale UP, 1954.

Gill 1987

Gill, Roma, ed. *The Complete Works of Christopher Marlowe, vol. 1: All Ovids Elegies, Lucans First Booke, Dido Queene of Carthage, Hero and Leander*. Oxford: Clarendon P, 1987.

Gill 1988
Gill, Roma. *"Doctor Faustus*: The Textual Problem." *UHSL* 20 (1988): 52-60.

Greg, "Copy-Text"
Greg, W.W. "The Rationale of Copy-Text." *Studies in Bibliography* 3 (1950): 19-36; rpt. in O. M. Brack, Jr., and Warner Barnes, ed., *Bibliography and Textual Criticism*. Chicago: U of Chicago P, 1969: 41-58.

Greville
Greville, Fulke. *Selected Writings of Fulke Greville*. Ed. Joan Rees. London: Athlone P, 1973.

Hamlet Q2
Shakespeare, William. *Hamlet: Second Quarto: 1605*. Facsimile rpt. London: Scolar P, 1969.

Headley
Headley, John M. *Luther's View of Church History*. New Haven and London: Yale UP, 1963.

Herbert
Herbert, George. *The English Poems of George Herbert*. Ed. C.A. Patrides. 1974; rpt. London: Dent, 1977.

Herminjard
Herminjard, A.L., ed. *Correspondance des réformateurs dans les pays de langue française*. 9 vols. 1866-97; rpt. Nieuwkoop: B. de Graaf, 1965-66.

Historia
Historia von D. Johann Fausten. Text des Druckes von 1587. Kritische Ausgabe. Ed. Stephan Füssel and Hans Joachim Kreutzer. Stuttgart: Philipp Reclam Jun., 1988.

Hjort
Hjort, Anna Mette. "The Interests of Critical Editorial Practice." *Poetics* 15 (1986): 259-77.

Hooker
Hooker, Richard. *Of the Laws of Ecclesiastical Polity*. Ed. Christopher Morris. 2 vols. London: Dent, 1954.

G.K. Hunter
Hunter, G.K. "Five-act structure in *Doctor Faustus*." In Hunter, *Dramatic Identities and Cultural Tradition: Studies in Shakespeare and his Contemporaries*. Liverpool: Liverpool UP, 1978: 335-49.

R.G. Hunter
> Hunter, R. G. *Shakespeare and the Mystery of God's Judgments.* Athens, Georgia: U of Georgia P, 1976.

Irenaeus
> Irenaeus, Bishop of Lyons. *Against Heresies.* In *The Writings of Irenaeus*, vol. 1. Trans. A. Roberts and W.H. Rambaut. Ante-Nicene Christian Library, vol. 5. Edinburgh: T. and T. Clark, 1868.

Jew of Malta
> Marlowe, Christopher. *The Jew of Malta.* Ed. N.W. Bawcutt. The Revels Plays. Manchester and Baltimore: Manchester UP and Johns Hopkins UP, 1978.

Johnson 1945
> Johnson, F. R. "Marlowe's 'Imperiall Heaven'." *ELH* 12 (1945): 35-44.

Johnson 1946
> "Marlowe's Astronomy and Renaissance Skepticism." *ELH* 13 (1946): 241-54.

Keefer 1983
> Keefer, Michael H. "Verbal Magic and the Problem of the A and B Texts of *Doctor Faustus.*" *JEGP* 82.3 (1983): 324-46.

Keefer 1985-86
> "Misreading Faustus Misreading: The Question of Context." *DalR* 65.4 (Winter 1985-86): 511-33.

Keefer 1987
> "History and the Canon: The Case of *Doctor Faustus.*" *UTQ* 56.4 (1987): 498-522.

Keefer 1988
> "Agrippa's Dilemma: Hermetic 'Rebirth' and the Ambivalences of *De vanitate* and *De occulta philosophia.*" *RQ* 41.4 (1988): 614-53.

Keefer 1989
> "Right Eye and Left Heel: Ideological Origins of the Legend of Faustus." *Mosaic* 22.2 (1989): 79-94.

Kirschbaum 1943
> Kirschbaum, Leo. "Marlowe's Faustus: A Reconsideration." *RES* 19 (1943): 225-41.

Kirschbaum 1946
"The Good and Bad Quartos of *Doctor Faustus*." *The Library* 2nd series, 26 (1946): 272-94.

Knutson
Knutson, Roslyn L. "Influence of the Repertory System on the Revival and Revision of *The Spanish Tragedy* and *Dr. Faustus*." *ELR* 18 (1988): 257-74.

Kuriyama 1975
Kuriyama, Constance Brown. "Dr. Greg and *Doctor Faustus*." *ELR* 5 (1975): 171-97.

Kuriyama 1988a
"Marlowe's Nemesis: The Identity of Richard Baines." In Kenneth Friedrich, Roma Gill, and Constance B. Kuriyama, ed., *"A Poet and a filthy Play-maker": New Essays on Christopher Marlowe.* New York: AMS P, 1988. 343-60.

Kuriyama 1988b
"Marlowe, Shakespeare, and the Nature of Biographical Evidence." *UHSL* 20 (1988): 1-12.

Kuriyama 1989
Rev. of *Christopher Marlowe: Dr Faustus: The A-Text*, ed. David Ormerod and Christopher Wortham. *MSABR* 8.1 (Summer 1989): 1-6.

Lake
Lake, David J. "Three Seventeenth-Century Revisions: *Thomas of Woodstock, The Jew of Malta,* and *Faustus B*." *NQ* 30 (April 1983): 133-43.

Leech
Leech, Clifford. *Christopher Marlowe: Poet for the Stage.* Ed. Anne Lancashire. New York: AMS P, 1986.

Maclure
Maclure, Millar, ed. *Marlowe: The Critical Heritage 1588-1896.* London: Routledge & Kegan Paul, 1979.

Massacre at Paris
See entry for *Dido*.

McDaniel
McDaniel, W.B. "An Hermetic Plague-Tract by Johannes Mercurius Corrigiensis." *Transactions and Studies of the College of Physicians of Philadelphia* 4th ser. 9 (1941-42): 96-111, 217-25.

McGann 1983
> McGann, Jerome J. *A Critique of Modern Textual Criticism*. Chicago:
> U of Chicago P, 1983.

McGann 1985
> "The Monks and the Giants: Textual and Bibliographical Studies and
> the Interpretation of Literary Works." In McGann, ed., *Textual
> Criticism and Literary Interpretation*. Chicago: U of Chicago P, 1985:
> 180-199.

Mebane
> Mebane, John S. *Renaissance Magic and the Return of the Golden
> Age*. Lincoln and London: U of Nebraska P, 1989.

Nauert
> Nauert, Charles G., Jr. *Agrippa and the Crisis of Renaissance Thought*.
> Urbana: U of Illinois P, 1965.

Norton-Smith
> Norton-Smith, John. "Marlowe's *Faustus* (I.iii, 1-4)." *NQ* 25 (1978):
> 436-37.

Nuttall
> Nuttall, A. D. *Overheard by God: Fiction and Prayer in Herbert, Mil-
> ton, Dante and St John*. London: Methuen, 1980.

Oberman
> Oberman, Heiko. *Masters of the Reformation: The Emergence of a
> New Intellectual Climate in Europe*. Trans. Dennis Martin.
> Cambridge: Cambridge UP, 1981.

Oliver
> Oliver. L.M. "Rowley, Foxe, and the *Faustus* Additions." *MLN* 60
> (1945): 391-94.

Ong
> Ong, Walter J. *Ramus, Method, and the Decay of Dialogue*. 1958; rpt.
> Cambridge, Mass.: Harvard UP, 1983.

Orgel
> Orgel, Stephen. "What is a Text?" *RORD* 24 (1981): 3-6.

Ozment
> Ozment, Steven. *Mysticism and Dissent: Religious Ideology and Social
> Protest in the Sixteenth Century*. New Haven: Yale UP, 1973.

Patterson
> Patterson, Annabel. *Censorship and Interpretation: The Conditions of Writing and Reading in Early Modern England*. Madison: U of Wisconsin P, 1984.

Penry
> Penry, John. *The Notebook of John Penry 1593*. Ed. Albert Peel. Camden third series, vol. 67. London: Royal Historical Society, 1944.

Pettitt 1988a
> Pettitt, Thomas. "Formulaic Dramaturgy in *Doctor Faustus*." In Kenneth Friedenreich, Roma Gill, and Constance B. Kuriyama, ed., *"A Poet and a filthy Play-maker": New Essays on Christopher Marlowe*. New York: AMS P, 1988: 167-91.

Pettitt 1988b
> "Oral Transmission, Incremental Repetition, and the 'Bad' Quarto: Folkloristic Perspectives on the Text of *Doctor Faustus*." Paper presented at the MSA Second International Marlowe Conference, Oxford 1988.

Pizer
> Pizer, Donald. "Self-Censorship and Textual Editing." In Jerome J. McGann, ed., *Textual Criticism and Literary Interpretation*: 144-61.

PM
> Palmer, Philip Mason, and Robert Pattison More, ed. *The Sources of the Faust Tradition: From Simon Magus to Lessing*. London, New York: Oxford UP, 1936.

Prayer Book
> *The Prayer-Book of Queen Elizabeth, 1559*. London, 1890.

Recognitions
> Clement I (Pope, pseud.). *Recognitions of Clement*. In *The Writings of Tatian and Theophilus; and The Clementine Recognitions*. Trans. B. P. Pratten, M. Dods, and T. Smith. Ante-Nicene Christian Library, vol. 3. Edinburgh: T. and T. Clark, 1867.

Richardson
> Richardson, E.C. "Faust and the Clementine Recognitions." *Papers of the American Society of Church History* 6 (1894): 133-45.

Ricks
> Ricks, Christopher. "*Doctor Faustus* and Hell on Earth." *EC* 35 (1985): 101-20.

Robbins
Robbins, R.H. *The Encyclopedia of Witchcraft and Demonology.* 1959; rpt. London: Spring Books, 1967.

Scholem
Scholem, Gershom. *Kabbalah.* New York: Quadrangle/New York Times Books, 1974.

Shepherd
Shepherd, Simon. *Marlowe and the Politics of Elizabethan Theatre.* Brighton: Harvester P, 1986.

Sinfield
Sinfield, Alan. *Literature in Protestant England, 1550-1650.* London: Croom Helm, and Totowa, N. J.: Barnes & Noble, 1983.

Snow
Snow, Edward A. "Marlowe's *Doctor Faustus* and the Ends of Desire." In Alvin Kernan, ed., *Two Renaissance Mythmakers: Christopher Marlowe and Ben Jonson.* Baltimore and London: Johns Hopkins UP, 1977: 70-110.

Snyder
Snyder, Susan. "The Left Hand of God: Despair in Medieval and Renaissance Tradition." *SR* 12 (1965): 18-59.

Thevet
Thevet, André. *Les vrais pourtraits et vies des hommes illustres.* 2 vols. Paris, 1584.

Thomas
Thomas, Keith. *Religion and the Decline of Magic.* 1971; rpt. Harmondsworth: Penguin, 1973.

Tille
Tille, Alexander. *Die Faustsplitter in der Literatur des sechzehnten bis achtzehnten Jahrhunderts.* Berlin: Emil Felber, 1900.

Tilley
Tilley, M. P. *A Dictionary of the Proverbs in England in the Sixteenth and Seventeenth Centuries.* Ann Arbor: U of Michigan P, 1950.

Urry
Urry, William. *Christopher Marlowe and Canterbury.* Ed. Andrew Butcher. London: Faber and Faber, 1988.

WA
> D. *Martin Luthers Werke.* Ed. P. Pietsch *et al.* 93 vols.; Weimar: Hermann Bühlaus, 1883-1987. (*WA*=Weimarer Ausgabe; *WATr*=Tischreden; *WABr*=Briefwechsel.)

Warren
> Warren, Michael J. "*Doctor Faustus*: The Old Man and the Text." *ELR* 11 (1981): 111-47.

Wentersdorf
> Wentersdorf, Karl P. "Some Observations on the Historical Faust." *Folklore* 89 (1978): 201-23.

Williams
> Williams, G.H. *The Radical Reformation.* Philadelphia: Westminster P, 1962.

Yates
> Yates, Frances A. *Giordano Bruno and the Hermetic Tradition.* London: Routledge and Kegan Paul, 1964.

Zambelli
> Zambelli, Paola. "Magic and Radical Reformation in Agrippa of Nettesheim." *JWCI* 39 (1976): 104-38.

Further Reading

Altman, Joel B. *The Tudor Play of Mind: Rhetorical Inquiry and the Development of Elizabethan Drama.* Berkeley: U of California P, 1978.

Bevington, David. *From "Mankind" to Marlowe.* Cambridge, Mass.: Harvard UP, 1962.

Bluestone, Max. "*Libido Speculandi*: Doctrine and Dramaturgy in Contemporary Interpretations of Marlowe's *Doctor Faustus*." In *Reinterpretations of Elizabethan Drama.* Ed. Norman Rabkin. New York: Columbia UP, 1969: 33-88.

Cole, Douglas. *Suffering and Evil in the Plays of Christopher Marlowe.* 1962; rpt. New York: Gordian, 1972.

Gatti, Hilary. *The Renaissance Drama of Knowledge: Giordano Bruno in England.* London and New York: Routledge, 1989.

Introduction

Jacquot, Jean. "Marlowe: De quelques problèmes d'interprétation." In *Théâtre et Idéologies: Marlowe, Shakespeare*. Ed. M.T. Jones-Davies. Paris: Jean Touzot, 1982: 201-236.

Kuriyama, Constance Brown. *Hammer or Anvil: Psychological Patterns in Christopher Marlowe's Plays*. New Brunswick, NJ: Rutgers UP, 1980.

Levin, Harry. *Christopher Marlowe: The Overreacher*. London: Faber and Faber, 1961.

Sanders, Wilbur. *The Dramatist and the Received Idea: Studies in the Plays of Marlowe and Shakespeare*. Cambridge: Cambridge UP, 1968.

Traister, Barbara. *Heavenly Necromancers: The Magician in English Renaissance Drama*. Columbia: U of Missouri P, 1984.

Weil, Judith. *Christopher Marlowe: Merlin's Prophet*. Cambridge: Cambridge UP, 1977.

Also:

Birringer, Johannes H. *Marlowe's "Dr Faustus" and "Tamburlaine": Theological and Theatrical Perspectives*. Frankfurt, Bern, New York: Peter Lang, 1984

Marcus, Leah. "Textual Indeterminacy and Ideological Difference: The Case of *Doctor Faustus*." Renaissance Drama n.s. 20 (1989): 1 - 29

Stachniewski, John. *The Persecutory Imagination: English Puritanism and the literature of Religious Despair*. Oxford; Clarendon P. 1991

Steane, J.B. *Marlowe: A Critical Study*. Cambridge; Cambridge U.P., 1964.

Wilks, John S. *The Idea of Conscience in Renaissance Tragedy*. London and New York; Routledge, 1990.

Periodicals: Abbreviations:

CD	Comparative Drama
DalR	The Dalhousie Review
EC	Essays in Criticism
ELH	English Literary History
ELR	English Literary Renaissance
ES	English Studies
JEGP	Journal of English and Germanic Philology
MLN	Modern Language Notes
MSABR	MSA [Marlowe Society of America] Book Reviews
NQ	Notes and Queries
RES	Review of English Studies
RQ	Renaissance Quarterly
RORD	Research Opportunities in Renaissance Drama
SB	Studies in Bibliography
SEL	Studies in English Literature 1500-1900
SR	Studies in the Renaissance
UHSL	University of Hartford Studies in English
UTQ	University of Toronto Quarterly

THE TRAGICAL
HISTORY OF
DOCTOR FAUSTUS

DRAMATIS PERSONAE

JOHN FAUSTUS, doctor of theology.

WAGNER, a student, and Faustus's servant; also speaks the part of CHORUS.

GOOD ANGEL.

EVIL ANGEL.

VALDES and CORNELIUS, magicians.

THREE SCHOLARS, colleagues of Faustus at Wittenberg University.

MEPHASTOPHILIS, a devil.

CLOWN (ROBIN).

RAFE, another clown.

LUCIFER.

BELZEBUB.

THE SEVEN DEADLY SINS.

POPE.

CARDINAL OF LORRAINE.

FRIAR.

VINTNER.

CHARLES V, Emperor of Germany.

KNIGHT.

ALEXANDER THE GREAT and his PARAMOUR, spirits.

HORSE-COURSER.

DUKE OF VANHOLT and his DUCHESS.

HELEN OF TROY, a spirit.

OLD MAN.

Devils, Friars, Attendants.

THE TRAGICAL HISTORY OF
DOCTOR FAUSTUS

PROLOGUE.

Enter Chorus.

Chorus.
 Not marching now in fields of Thracimene
 Where Mars did mate the Carthaginians,
 Nor sporting in the dalliance of love
 In courts of kings where state is overturn'd,
 Nor in the pomp of proud audacious deeds   5
 Intends our muse to vaunt his heavenly verse.
 Only this, gentlemen: we must perform
 The form of Faustus' fortunes, good or bad.
 To patient judgments we appeal our plaud,
 And speak for Faustus in his infancy: 10
 Now is he born, his parents base of stock,
 In Germany, within a town call'd Rhodes;

2. *Mars did mate*] Mars allied himself with or rivalled. Hannibal's Carthaginian army inflicted a crushing defeat upon the Romans at the battle of Lake Trasummenus in 217 B.C. The mention of Mars is an allusion to Livy's *Historiae* XXII. i. 8-12, according to which the battle was preceded by terrifying portents in which the war-god figured prominently. Since these portents demoralized the Romans, Livy's text could suggest either that Mars had allied himself with the Carthaginians or that he had rivalled them in destroying the Roman army.
3-5.] These lines may refer to other plays by Marlowe: lines 3-4 to *Dido, Queen of Carthage* or to *Edward II*, and line 5 to *Tamburlaine*. There is no evidence that he ever wrote a play about Hannibal.
6. *our Muse*] the poet. A metonymic equation of muse with poet is evident in Shakespeare, Sonnet xxi. 1-2, and Milton, *Lycidas*, lines 19-21. Here Marlowe may also be playing with the notion that the dramatist puts words into the actors' mouths just as the muse was said to do with poets.   *vaunt*] display proudly.
8. *Faustus*] pronounced as spelled by Henslowe in his *Diary*: "Fostes".
9. *our plaud*] for our applause.
12. *Rhodes*] Roda (now Stadtroda), near Weimar.

Of riper years to Wittenberg he went,
Whereas his kinsmen chiefly brought him up.
15 So soon he profits in divinity,
The fruitful plot of scholarism grac'd,
That shortly he was grac'd with doctor's name,
Excelling all whose sweet delight disputes
In heavenly matters of theology,
20 Till swoll'n with cunning of a self-conceit,
His waxen wings did mount above his reach
And melting heavens conspir'd his overthrow:
For falling to a devilish exercise,
And glutted now with learning's golden gifts,
25 He surfeits upon cursed necromancy;
Nothing so sweet as magic is to him,
Which he prefers before his chiefest bliss:
And this the man that in his study sits.

Exit.

---

13. *Wittenberg*] The University of Wittenberg was famous under Martin Luther and Philipp Melancthon as a Protestant centre of learning.

17. *grac'd*] At Cambridge it was and still is by the "grace" or decree of the university Senate that degrees are conferred; Marlowe's name appears in the Grace Book in 1584 and in 1587 for the B.A. and M.A. degrees respectively.

18. *whose sweet delight disputes*] It is possible to construe "disputes" as a verb; more probably, the expression is elliptical and means "whose sweet delight consists in disputes...." Bowers emends to "whose sweet delight's dispute".

21. *waxen wings*] an allusion to the story of Icarus (cf. Ovid, *Metamorphoses* VIII. 183-235): escaping with his father Daedalus from Minos's island kingdom of Crete, Icarus ignored his father's warning about the wings he had made for them and flew too close to the sun. The episode was a favourite of Renaissance moralists and emblem writers. Compare *Dido, Queen of Carthage* V.i. 243-45.

22. *heavens conspir'd his overthrow*] Compare *1 Tamburlaine* IV.ii. 8-11, where the possibility of heaven conspiring refers to astrological causation as opposed to the will of "the chiefest god".

23. *falling to*] These words link the metaphors of an Icarian fall and that of gluttonous surfeit. A distant secondary overtone in line 23 ("falling to" in the sense of eating, as in the B-version III.ii. 59, 61) comes suddenly to the fore in line 24 with "glutted now".

ACT I

Act I Scene i.

Faustus in his study.

Faustus.

Settle thy studies Faustus, and begin
To sound the depth of that thou wilt profess.
Having commenc'd, be a divine in show,
Yet level at the end of every art,
And live and die in Aristotle's works.   5
Sweet *Analytics*, 'tis thou hast ravish'd me:
Bene disserere est finis logices.
Is to dispute well logic's chiefest end?
Affords this art no greater miracle?
Then read no more, thou hast attain'd that end.   10
A greater subject fitteth Faustus' wit:

1-37.] Jump suggests that these lines may be indebted to Lyly's *Euphues* (ed. Bond, i. 241): "Philosophy, Physic, Divinity, shall be my study. O the hidden secrets of Nature, the express image of moral virtues, the equal balance of Justice, the medicines to heal all diseases, how they begin to delight me. The *Axiomaes* of *Aristotle*, the *Maxims* of *Justinian*, the *Aphorismes* of *Galen*, have suddenly made such a breach into my mind that I seem only to desire them which did only erst detest them."
2. *profess*] affirm faith in or allegiance to; also, perhaps secondarily, "adopt as the subject of public teaching" (Ward).
3. *commenc'd*] taken a degree.   **4.** *level at*] take aim at.
5.] A reminiscence, Roy T. Eriksen suggests, of Giordano Bruno's dialogue *La cena de le ceneri* (1584), I.34, where the scoffer Frulla mocks those who, without understanding so much as the titles of his books, *"voglion vivere e morire per Aristoteles....."*
6. Analytics] the name of two treatises on logic by Aristotle, whose works still dominated the university curriculum.
7. bene...logices] "To argue well is the end or purpose of logic." This definition, derived not from Aristotle but from Cicero, recurs in the many works on logic and dialectic by Petrus Ramus (1515-72), who hoped to supplement and supplant Aristotelian logic with his own dichotomizing method. Ramus's method was controversial at Cambridge when Marlowe was a student there: attacked by Everard Digby, it was defended by William Temple (see Walter J. Ong, *Ramus*, pp. 160, 178). In *The Massacre at Paris*, the Duke of Guise, before ordering Ramus's murder, calls him a "flat dichotomist" (ix. 28), one who, "having a smack in all, / ...yet didst never sound anything to the depth" (ix. 24-5).
11. *wit*] understanding.

Bid *on kai me on* farewell; Galen come,
Seeing *ubi desinit philosophus, ibi incipit medicus.*
Be a physician Faustus, heap up gold,
15   And be eterniz'd for some wondrous cure!
Summum bonum medicinae sanitas:
The end of physic is our bodies' health.
Why Faustus, hast thou not attain'd that end?
Is not thy common talk sound aphorisms?
20   Are not thy bills hung up as monuments,
Whereby whole cities have escap'd the plague,
And thousand desperate maladies been eas'd?
Yet art thou still but Faustus, and a man.
Couldst thou make men to live eternally,
25   Or being dead, raise them to life again,
Then this profession were to be esteem'd.
Physic farewell; where is Justinian?
Si una eademque res legatur duobus,
alter rem, alter valorem rei, etc.
30   A petty case of paltry legacies!
Exhereditare filium non potest pater, nisi—
Such is the subject of the *Institute*
And universal body of the law.

12. on kai me on] a transliteration of Greek words meaning "being and not being". As Jump was the first to recognize, the phrase is again not Aristotelian; its source is a text of the sophist Gorgias, *On Nature or that which is not* (*peri tou me ontos*), as preserved by the sceptic Sextus Empiricus in his *Adversus mathematicos* VII. 66. Latin editions of the works of Sextus Empiricus were published in 1562 and 1569.
13. ubi...medicus] "Where the philosopher leaves off, there the physician begins." Freely translated from Aristotle, *De sensu 436a.*
16. Summum...sanitas] "The supreme good of medicine is health." Translated from Aristotle, *Nicomachean Ethics* 1094a; a similar formulation occurs in Aristotle's *Politics* 1258a.
19. *sound aphorisms*] reliable medical precepts. Hippocrates's *Aphorisms* consisted of more than four hundred short sentences containing the basis of his teachings. Originally applied to medicine alone, the term came to refer to pithy sentences containing the gist of any subject.
20. *bills*] prescriptions.
28-29. Si...rei] "If one and the same thing is bequeathed to two persons, one of them shall have the thing, the other the value of the thing." Derived in part from II.xx of the *Institutes*, a compilation of Roman law carried out at the command of the emperor Justinian in the sixth century.
31. Exhereditare...nisi—] "A father cannot disinherit his son except—." An incomplete formulation of a rule from Justinian's *Institutes* II.xii.

This study fits a mercenary drudge
Who aims at nothing but external trash—   35
Too servile and illiberal for me.
When all is done, divinity is best:
Jerome's Bible, Faustus, view it well.
Stipendium peccati mors est. Ha! *Stipendium, etc.*
The reward of sin is death? That's hard.   40
Si peccasse negamus, fallimur,
et nulla est in nobis veritas:
If we say that we have no sin
We deceive ourselves, and there's no truth in us.
Why then belike we must sin,   45
And so consequently die.
Ay, we must die, an everlasting death.
What doctrine call you this? *Che sarà, sarà,*
What will be, shall be? Divinity, adieu!
These metaphysics of magicians   50
And necromantic books are heavenly!

---

38. *Jerome's Bible*] The Vulgate, prepared mainly by St. Jerome, was the Latin edition of the Bible used by the Roman Catholic church. Faustus's quotations in lines 39 and 41-42 differ from the wording of the Vulgate: the Latin appears to be Marlowe's translation of an English text, probably that of the Geneva Bible (1560).

39. *Stipendium...est*] the first half of Romans 6:23, a verse which in the Geneva Bible is translated as follows: "For the wages of sin is death: but the gift of God is eternal life through Jesus Christ our Lord."

41-42. *Si peccasse...veritas*] 1 John 1:8. Faustus has again quoted only the first half of an antithetical statement: he notices the condemnation of sinners by the law of God, but not the conditional promise of divine mercy which immediately follows in 1 John 1:9. In the Geneva Bible, 1 John 1:8-9 is rendered as follows: "If we say that we have no sin, we deceive our selves, and truth is not in us. If we acknowledge our sins, he is faithful and just, to forgive us our sins, and to cleanse us from all unrighteousness."

43-47.] *If...death*] In Thomas Becon's *Dialogue Between the Christian Knight and Satan* (1564), Satan attempts to reduce the Knight to despair with a similar syllogism; the Knight, recognizing his guilt according to the Law, appeals to the Gospel, "that is to say, grace, favour, and remission of sins, promised in Christ" (*The Catechism of Thomas Becon...*, ed. J. Ayre, pp. 628-29). In Spenser's *Faerie Queene*, Una rescues the Red Cross Knight from the arguments of Despair with a similar reminder: "Why shouldst thou then despair, that chosen art? / Where justice grows, there grows eke greater grace" (I.ix. 53). This kind of appeal to divine grace and election provided the only escape from what Luther called "the devil's syllogism"; see Susan Snyder, "The Left Hand of God: Despair in Medieval and Renaissance Tradition," *Studies in the Renaissance* 12 (1965), 30-31.

48-49. *What...adieu*] a reprobate's version of the Calvinist doctrine of predestination. The proverb recurs in *Edward II* IV.vi. 94.

Lines, circles, seals, letters and characters:
Ay, these are those that Faustus most desires.
O, what a world of profit and delight,
55   Of power, of honor, of omnipotence,
Is promis'd to the studious artisan!
All things that move between the quiet poles
Shall be at my command. Emperors and kings
Are but obey'd in their several provinces,
60   Nor can they raise the wind, or rend the clouds;
But his dominion that exceeds in this
Stretcheth as far as doth the mind of man!
A sound magician is a mighty god:
Here tire, my brains, to get a deity!

Enter Wagner.

65   Wagner, commend me to my dearest friends,
The German Valdes and Cornelius;
Request them earnestly to visit me.

Wagner.
    I will, sir.

Exit.

Faustus.
    Their conference will be a greater help to me
70   Than all my labors, plod I ne'er so fast.

Enter the Good Angel and the Evil Angel.

Good Ang.
    O Faustus, lay that damned book aside,

---

52. *lines*] a reference, Ormerod and Wortham suggest, to the occult art of geomancy, or divination by means of astrologically determined patterns of points and lines. See Henricus Cornelius Agrippa, *In geomanticam disciplinam lectura*, in his *Opera*, ed. Popkin, i. 506-7. *circles*] See I.iii. 8-13. A primary function of magic circles was to protect the practitioner of ceremonial magic from evil spirits. *seals, letters and characters*] talismanic symbols of the planets and of the angels, spiritual intelligences and daemons that were believed to govern them.
56. *artisan*] practitioner of an art.   61. *exceeds*] excels.   64. *get*] beget.
69. *conference*] conversation.

And gaze not on it, lest it tempt thy soul
And heap God's heavy wrath upon thy head!
Read, read the Scriptures; that is blasphemy.

Evil Ang.

Go forward, Faustus, in that famous art   75
Wherein all nature's treasury is contain'd:
Be thou on earth as Jove is in the sky,
Lord and commander of these elements!

Exeunt Angels.

Faustus.

How am I glutted with conceit of this!
Shall I make spirits fetch me what I please,   80
Resolve me of all ambiguities,
Perform what desperate enterprise I will?
I'll have them fly to India for gold,
Ransack the ocean for orient pearl
And search all corners of the new found world   85
For pleasant fruits and princely delicates;
I'll have them read me strange philosophy
And tell the secrets of all foreign kings;
I'll have them wall all Germany with brass
And make swift Rhine circle fair Wittenberg;   90
I'll have them fill the public schools with silk
Wherewith the students shall be bravely clad;
I'll levy soldiers with the coin they bring,

73. *heap God's heavy wrath*] The Good Angel makes no mention of grace or election. His words, addressed to a man whose soul has evidently already been tempted by the necromantic book he is holding, seem less akin to the intervention of Spenser's Una than to the persuasions of Despair: "Is not the measure of thy sinful hire / High heaped up with huge iniquity, / Against the day of wrath, to burden thee?" (*The Faerie Queene* I.ix. 46).
77. *Jove*] The substitution of the supreme god of the pagan Roman pantheon for the Christian God is common in Renaissance humanist texts and in Elizabethan poetry.
83. *India*] a name applied to "both th' Indias of spice and mine" (Donne, "The Sun Rising"); here it seems to refer to the East Indies, as opposed to the Spanish conquests in "the new found world".
84. *orient*] "lustrous; strictly, from the eastern seas" (Jump).
89. *wall...brass*] an aspiration paralleled by Greene's Friar Bacon (*Friar Bacon and Friar Bungay* ii.29) and by Spenser's Merlin (*The Faerie Queene* III.iii.10).
92. *bravely*] splendidly. University regulations forbade students to wear fine clothing.

And chase the Prince of Parma from our land
95 And reign sole king of all our provinces;
Yea, stranger engines for the brunt of war
Than was the fiery keel at Antwerp's bridge
I'll make my servile spirits to invent.
Come, German Valdes and Cornelius,
100 And make me blest with your sage conference!

Enter Valdes and Cornelius.

Valdes, sweet Valdes, and Cornelius,
Know that your words have won me at the last
To practise magic and concealed arts:
Yet not your words only, but mine own fantasy,
105 That will receive no object, for my head
But ruminates on necromantic skill.
Philosophy is odious and obscure;
Both law and physic are for petty wits;
Divinity is basest of the three,
110 Unpleasant, harsh, contemptible and vile;
'Tis magic, magic, that hath ravish'd me.
Then, gentle friends, aid me in this attempt,
And I, that have with concise syllogisms
Gravell'd the pastors of the German church

---

94. *the Prince of Parma*] Alessandro Farnese, Duke of Parma, a grandson of the emperor Charles V and Spanish governor of the Netherlands from 1578 until his death in 1592, was the foremost general of his time; he commanded the force that the Spanish Armada was to have transported across the Channel in 1588 for the invasion of England.
96. *brunt*] assault, onset.
97. *fiery...bridge*] On April 5, 1585 the Netherlanders sent two floating bombs against the pontoon bridge over the river Scheldt which formed part of Parma's siegeworks around Antwerp; one of the "Hell-Burners," as the Spanish called them, reached its target and destroyed part of the bridge, killing many Spanish soldiers. Parma had the bridge rebuilt, and Antwerp subsequently surrendered.
104-6. *Yet...skill*] According to the influential theory of natural magic set out in Marsilio Ficino's *De vita coelitus comparanda* (1489), fantasy or imagination is the chief magical faculty; acting both inside and outside of the body, it links corporeal objects to the incorporeal subject, soul, or mind. Faustus is saying that his ruminations on necromancy block his perceptions of external objects (a category which presumably includes the four chief academic disciplines, as *obiecta intellectionis*).
109. *basest of the three*] "i.e. even baser than the other three" (Greg).

And made the flowering pride of Wittenberg   115
Swarm to my problems as the infernal spirits
On sweet Musaeus when he came to hell,
Will be as cunning as Agrippa was,
Whose shadows made all Europe honor him.

Valdes.

Faustus, these books, thy wit, and our experience   120
Shall make all nations to canonize us.
As Indian Moors obey their Spanish lords,
So shall the subjects of every element
Be always serviceable to us three:
Like lions shall they guard us when we please,   125
Like Almain rutters with their horsemen's staves,
Or Lapland giants trotting by our sides;
Sometimes like women, or unwedded maids,
Shadowing more beauty in their airy brows
Than has the white breasts of the queen of love.   130
From Venice shall they drag huge Argosies,
And from America the golden fleece
That yearly stuffs old Philip's treasury,

---

117. *Musaeus*] the legendary pre-Homeric Greek poet, a pupil of Orpheus, to whom was ascribed the poem on which Marlowe based his *Hero and Leander*. In Virgil's *Aeneid* VI. 666-67, Musaeus is represented as standing in the midst of a crowd of spirits in the underworld, head and shoulders above the rest.

118-19. *Agrippa...Whose shadows*] Henricus Cornelius Agrippa of Nettesheim (1486-1535) distinguished in *De occulta philosophia* III.xlii (*Opera*, i. 437) between two kinds of necromancy: *necyomantia*, the revivifying of corpses by means of a blood sacrifice, and *scyomantia*, in which only the *umbra* or shadow of a dead person is invoked. According to Ficino in his *Theologia Platonica* XVIII. 4, *umbra* is the term applied by the "ancient theologians" (e.g. *Mercurii Trismegisti Pymander* I, and Iamblichus, *De mysteriis Aegyptiis* VI. 4) to the elemental murk (*caligo elementalis*) by which the soul is surrounded, most particularly during this life. The spurious *De occulta philosophia, Liber Quartus* concludes with detailed instructions for the practice of necromancy (see Agrippa, *Opera*, i. 560-61). John Lyly wrote, in the court prologue to *Campaspe*: "Whatsoever we present, we wish it may be thought the dancing of *Agrippa* his shadows, who in the moment they were seen, were of any shape one would conceive..." (ed. Bond, ii. 316).

122. *Indian Moors*] native peoples of the Americas.

123. *subjects*] spirits.

126. *Almain rutters*] German cavalrymen.   *staves*] lances.

129. *shadowing*] harbouring.

133.] An annual plate-fleet shipped gold and silver from the Americas to Spain. Philip II died in 1598.

If learned Faustus will be resolute.

Faustus.

135   Valdes, as resolute am I in this
As thou to live, therefore object it not.

Cornelius.

The miracles that magic will perform
Will make thee vow to study nothing else.
He that is grounded in astrology,

140   Enrich'd with tongues, well seen in minerals,
Hath all the principles magic doth require.
Then doubt not, Faustus, but to be renown'd
And more frequented for this mystery
Than heretofore the Delphian oracle.

145   The spirits tell me they can dry the sea
And fetch the treasure of all foreign wrecks,
Ay, all the wealth that our forefathers hid
Within the massy entrails of the earth.
Then tell me Faustus, what shall we three want?

Faustus.

150   Nothing, Cornelius. O, this cheers my soul!
Come, show me some demonstrations magical,
That I may conjure in some lusty grove
And have these joys in full possession.

Valdes.

Then haste thee to some solitary grove,

155   And bear wise Bacon's and Albanus' works,
The Hebrew Psalter, and New Testament;

---

140. *well seen in minerals*] well versed in the properties of minerals.
148. *massy*] heavy, massive.
155. *wise Bacon's and Albanus's works*] Roger Bacon (c. 1214-94), an English Franciscan philosopher, was reputed also to have been a magician (cf. Robert Greene's play *Friar Bacon and Friar Bungay*); "Albanus" is probably an error for Petrus de Abanus (c. 1250-1316), a physician who was posthumously convicted of sorcery and burned in effigy by the Inquisition.
156. *Psalter, and New Testament*] Ward remarks that the book of Psalms and the opening verses of the Gospel of St. John were thought to be particularly useful in conjurations. For instances of the use of the Psalter and the Bible in divination, see Keith Thomas, *Religion and the Decline of Magic*, pp. 51-52, 139, 254; these books were often also thought to have a protective value: see pp. 48, 83, 590.

And whatsoever else is requisite
We will inform thee ere our conference cease.

Cornelius.
Valdes, first let him know the words of art,
And then, all other ceremonies learn'd,   160
Faustus may try his cunning by himself.

Valdes.
First I'll instruct thee in the rudiments,
And then wilt thou be perfecter than I.

Faustus.
Then come and dine with me, and after meat
We'll canvass every quiddity thereof.   ·   165
For ere I sleep I'll try what I can do;
This night I'll conjure though I die therefore.

Exeunt.

Act I, Scene ii.

Enter two scholars.

1 Sch.
I wonder what's become of Faustus, that was wont to
make our schools ring with *sic probo.*

2 Sch.
That shall we presently know, for see: here comes his
boy.

Enter Wagner.

1 Sch.
How now sirrah, where's thy master?

165. *canvass every quiddity*] discuss every essential particular.

2. sic probo] "Thus I prove."
3. *presently*] at once.
4. *sirrah*] a term of address which expresses the speaker's contempt, or the addressee's social
inferiority, or both.

Wagner.

5   God in heaven knows.

2 Sch.

Why, dost not thou know?

Wagner.

Yes, I know, but that follows not.

1 Sch.

Go to sirrah, leave your jesting, and tell us where he is.

Wagner.

That follows not necessary by force of argument, which
10   you, being licentiate, should stand upon; therefore acknowledge your error and be attentive.

2 Sch.

Why, didst thou not say thou knew'st?

Wagner.

Have you any witness on't?

1 Sch.

Yes sirrah, I heard you.

Wagner.

15   Ask my fellow if I be a thief!

2 Sch.

Well, you will not tell us.

Wagner.

Yes sir, I will tell you; yet if you were not dunces you would
never ask me such a question, for is not he *corpus naturale,*
and is not that *mobile?* Then wherefore should you ask me

10. *licentiate*] licensed by an academic degree to proceed to further studies.

15.] A popular proverbial saying (see Tilley F177). Wagner means that the First Scholar's
support for his companion's statement is worth no more than one thief's testimony to
another's innocence.

17. *dunces*] Renaissance humanists opposed both the hair-splitting complexity of scholastic
logic and the non-classical Latin of scholastic writers. As a result, the name of Johannes
Duns Scotus (d. 1308), one of the most subtle medieval logicians, came to denote sophistical
quibbling and, by extension, stupidity.

18-19. corpus naturale...mobile] Ward explains *corpus naturale seu mobile,* i.e., "a body that
is natural or subject to change," as a scholastic adaptation of Aristotle's statement of the
subject-matter of physics.

such a question? But that I am by nature phlegmatic, slow   20
to wrath and prone to lechery (to love I would say), it were
not for you to come within forty foot of the place of execution—although I do not doubt but to see you both hanged
the next sessions. Thus having triumphed over you, I will set
my countenance like a precisian, and begin to speak thus: 25
Truly, my dear brethren, my master is within at dinner with
Valdes and Cornelius, as this wine if it could speak would
inform your worships; and so the Lord bless you, preserve
you, and keep you, my dear brethren, my dear brethren.

Exit.

1 *Sch.*

Nay then, I fear he is fallen into that damned art, for   30
which they two are infamous through the world.

2 *Sch.*

Were he a stranger, and not allied to me, yet should I
grieve for him. But come, let us go and inform the Rector, and see if he by his grave counsel can reclaim him.

1 *Sch.*

O, but I fear me nothing can reclaim him.   35

2 *Sch.*

Yet let us try what we can do.

Exeunt.

22-23. *place of execution*] the scene of action; in this case the dining-room (Greg). "To do execution" could mean to eat heartily. Wagner at once reverts to the more obvious meaning of the expression.
25. *precisian*] puritan.

Act I, Scene iii.

Enter Faustus to conjure.

Faustus.
    Now that the gloomy shadow of the earth,
    Longing to view Orion's drizzling look,
    Leaps from th'antarctic world unto the sky
    And dims the welkin with her pitchy breath,
5   Faustus, begin thine incantations,
    And try if devils will obey thy hest,
    Seeing thou hast pray'd and sacrific'd to them.
    Within this circle is Jehovah's name,
    Forward and backward anagrammatiz'd,
10   The breviated names of holy saints,
    Figures of every adjunct to the heavens,

---

1. *shadow of the earth*] Macrobius in his *Commentum* I.20.18 writes of "the shadow of the earth which the sun, after setting and progressing into the lower hemisphere, sends out upwards, creating on earth the darkness which is called night..." ("umbra terrae, quam sol post occasum in inferiore hemisphaerio currens sursum cogit emitti, ex qua super terram fit obscuritas quae nox vocatur..."). Qtd. from John Norton-Smith, "Marlowe's *Faustus* (I.iii, 1-4)," *NQ* 25 (1978), 436.

2. *Orion's drizzling look*] The constellation of Orion was associated in classical poetry with winter storms; cf. Virgil's *Aeneid* I. 535 (*nimbosus Orion*), and IV. 52 (*aquosus Orion*).

3. *th'antarctic world*] The thought that Marlowe held "the astonishing view that night comes not from the east but from the southern hemisphere" (Greg) has troubled commentators. But for observers in the northern hemisphere of a geocentric world it is a matter of simple observation that when the sun sets in the west it also sinks into the lower hemisphere or *regio antarctica* from which the shadow of the earth is therefore projected. For parallels to the Macrobius passage noted by Norton-Smith, see Virgil, *Georgics* I. 247-51; also Manilius, *Astronomica* I. 242-45.

4. *welkin*] sky.   *pitchy breath*] Norton-Smith points to a passage in Lucretius, *De rerum natura* VI. 476-79: "...from all rivers and from the earth itself we see clouds and steam rising up, which exhaled hence like breath are carried up in this way, and fill up the sky with their blackness..." ("Praeterea fluviis ex omnibus et simul ipsa / Surgere de terra nebulas aestumque videmus, / Quae velut halitus hinc ita sursum expressa feruntur / Suffunduntque sua caelum caligine...").

9. *anagrammatiz'd*] Cabalist mystics believed that hidden meanings were present in every possible recombination of letters in the Hebrew scriptures; practitioners of Cabalistic magic saw the names of God as containing occult secrets of divine power and knowledge.

10. *breviated*] abbreviated.

11. *adjunct to*] "heavenly body fixed to" (Barnet).

And characters of signs and erring stars
By which the spirits are enforc'd to rise;
Then fear not, Faustus, but be resolute,
And try the uttermost magic can perform.   15
Sint mihi dei Acherontis propitii! Valeat numen triplex
Iehovae! Ignei, aerii, aquatici spiritus salvete! Orientis prin-
ceps Belzebub, inferni ardentis monarcha, et Demogorgon,
propitiamus vos ut appareat et surgat Mephastophilis. Quid
tu moraris? Per Iehovam, Gehennam et consecratam aquam   20
quam nunc spargo, signumque crucis quod nunc facio, et per
vota nostra, ipse nunc surgat nobis dicatus Mephastophilis.

Enter a devil.

I charge thee to return and change thy shape.
Thou art too ugly to attend on me;
Go, and return an old Franciscan friar: 25
That holy shape becomes a devil best.

Exit devil.

I see there's virtue in my heavenly words.
Who would not be proficient in this art?
How pliant is this Mephastophilis,
Full of obedience and humility: 30
Such is the force of magic and my spells!
Now, Faustus, thou art conjurer laureate
That canst command great Mephastophilis!
Quin redis, Mephastophilis, fratris imagine!

Enter Mephastophilis.

12. *characters of signs and erring stars*] diagrams representing the constellations of the zodiac (one Latin term for which was *signa*) and the planets.
16-22.] *Sint...Mephastophilis*] "May the gods of Acheron be propitious to me. Away with the threefold divinity of Jehovah! Hail, spirits of fire, air, and water! Belzebub, Prince of the East, monarch of burning hell, and Demogorgon, we invoke your favor that Mephastophilis may appear and ascend. Why do you delay? By Jehovah, Gehenna, and the holy water which I now sprinkle, by the sign of the cross which I now make, and by our vows, may Mephastophilis himself now rise to serve us!"
27. *virtue*] power; also, ironically, moral virtue.
32. *laureate*] crowned with laurel; of proved distinction.
34. *Quin...imagine*] "Why do you not return, Mephastophilis, in the shape of a friar!"

Meph.

35   Now, Faustus, what wouldst thou have me do?

Faustus.

      I charge thee wait upon me whilst I live
      To do whatever Faustus shall command,
      Be it to make the moon drop from her sphere
      Or the ocean to overwhelm the world.

Meph.

40   I am a servant to great Lucifer,
      And may not follow thee without his leave;
      No more than he commands must we perform.

Faustus.

      Did not he charge thee to appear to me?

Meph.

      No, I came now hither of my own accord.

Faustus.

45   Did not my conjuring speeches raise thee? Speak.

Meph.

      That was the cause, but yet *per accidens*,
      For when we hear one rack the name of God,
      Abjure the Scriptures and his saviour Christ,
      We fly, in hope to get his glorious soul;
50   Nor will we come unless he use such means
      Whereby he is in danger to be damn'd.
      Therefore the shortest cut for conjuring
      Is stoutly to abjure the Trinity,
      And pray devoutly to the prince of hell.

---

38. *to make the moon drop from her sphere*] This and similar feats were ascribed to sorceresses and magicians by various ancient writers: Virgil, *Eclogues* VIII. 69; Horace, *Epodes* V. 45-46 and XVII. 57-58; Ovid, *Metamorphoses* VII. 192 ff.; and Apuleius, *Metamorphoseon (The Golden Ass)* I.iii.

46. *per accidens*] The scholastics distinguished between an efficient cause, i.e., an agent which itself produced an effect, and a cause *per accidens*, which was related to the final effect only in the sense of having provided an occasion for the intervention of some external agent.

47. *rack*] torture.

49. *glorious*] splendid; possibly also boastful (the root meaning of *gloriosus*).

Faustus.
    So Faustus hath already done,   55
    And holds this principle:
    There is no chief but only Belzebub,
    To whom Faustus doth dedicate himself.
    This word "damnation" terrifies not him,
    For he confounds hell in Elysium: 60
    His ghost be with the old philosophers!
    But leaving these vain trifles of men's souls,
    Tell me, what is that Lucifer thy lord?

Meph.
    Arch-regent and commander of all spirits.

Faustus.
    Was not that Lucifer an angel once?   65

Meph.
    Yes Faustus, and most dearly lov'd of God.

Faustus.
    How comes it then that he is prince of devils?

Meph.
    O, by aspiring pride and insolence,
    For which God threw him from the face of heaven.

Faustus.
    And what are you that live with Lucifer?   70

Meph.
    Unhappy spirits that fell with Lucifer,
    Conspir'd against our God with Lucifer,
    And are for ever damn'd with Lucifer.

Faustus.
    Where are you damn'd?

---

60. *confounds hell in Elysium*] identifies hell with Elysium; confuses the two; undoes hell through belief in Elysium. For Homer, Elysium is a place of comfort and perfect happiness reserved for heroes like Menelaus, the son-in-law of Zeus (*Odyssey* IV. 563-69); Virgil identifies it as the home of the righteous dead in the underworld (*Aeneid* VI. 541-42).

Meph.

In hell.

Faustus.

75   How comes it then that thou art out of hell?

Meph.

Why this is hell, nor am I out of it:
Think'st thou that I who saw the face of God
And tasted the eternal joys of heaven
Am not tormented with ten thousand hells
80   In being depriv'd of everlasting bliss?
O Faustus, leave these frivolous demands,
Which strike a terror to my fainting soul.

Faustus.

What, is great Mephastophilis so passionate
For being deprived of the joys of heaven?
85   Learn thou of Faustus manly fortitude
And scorn those joys thou never shalt possess.
Go, bear these tidings to great Lucifer:
Seeing Faustus hath incurr'd eternal death
By desperate thoughts against Jove's deity,
90   Say he surrenders up to him his soul,
So he will spare him four and twenty years,
Letting him live in all voluptuousness,
Having thee ever to attend on me
To give me whatsoever I shall ask,
95   To tell me whatsoever I demand,
To slay mine enemies and aid my friends,
And always be obedient to my will.
Go, and return to mighty Lucifer,

76.] Compare Milton's Satan: "Which way I fly is hell; my self am hell" (*Paradise Lost* IV. 75).
79-80. *ten thousand...bliss*] Jump remarks that "St John Chrysostom, the fourth-century Greek Father, states that ten thousand hells are as nothing in comparison with the loss of celestial bliss. See *Hom. in St Matt.*, xxiii. 9."
83. *passionate*] subject to strong emotion.
91. *So*] on condition that.

And meet me in my study at midnight,
And then resolve me of thy master's mind.   100
Meph.
    I will, Faustus.

Exit.

Faustus.
    Had I as many souls as there be stars
    I'd give them all for Mephastophilis!
    By him I'll be great emperor of the world,
    And make a bridge thorough the moving air   105
    To pass the ocean with a band of men;
    I'll join the hills that bind the Afric shore,
    And make that country continent to Spain,
    And both contributory to my crown;
    The emperor shall not live but by my leave,   110
    Nor any potentate of Germany.
    Now that I have obtain'd what I desire,
    I'll live in speculation of this art
    Till Mephastophilis return again.

Exit.

Act I, Scene iv.

Enter Wagner and the Clown.

Wagner.
    Sirrah boy, come hither.
Clown.
    How, "boy"? Swowns boy, I hope you have seen many

---

105. *thorough*] The distinction between "through" and "thorough", like that between "travail" and "travel", is a modern one; at II.iii. 168, "thoroughly" is spelled "throwly" in A1 and "throughly" in B1.
108. *continent to*] continuous with.

0.1. Clown] a boorish rustic, a fool.
2. *Swowns*] a contraction of "God's wounds".

boys with such pickadevaunts as I have. "Boy," quotha?

Wagner.

    Tell me sirrah, hast thou any comings in?

Clown.

5   Ay, and goings out too, you may see else.

Wagner.

    Alas, poor slave: see how poverty jesteth in his nakedness. The villain is bare, and out of service, and so hungry that I know he would give his soul to the devil for a shoulder of mutton, though it were blood raw.

Clown.

10   How, my soul to the devil for a shoulder of mutton though 'twere blood raw? Not so, good friend: b'urlady I had need have it well roasted, and good sauce to it, if I pay so dear.

Wagner.

    Well, wilt thou serve me, and I'll make thee go like *Qui mihi discipulus*?

Clown.

15   How, in verse?

Wagner.

    No sirrah, in beaten silk and stavesacre.

Clown.

    How, how, knave's acre? Ay, I thought that was all the land his father left him. Do ye hear, I would be sorry to rob you of your living.

---

3. *pickadevaunt*] a short beard trimmed to a point; apparently from the French *piqué devant*, "peaked in front" (although the compound word is unknown in French). In this passage one may suspect an obscene *double entendre*.

4. *comings in*] earnings.

5. *goings out*] expenses; a punning reference to the fact that the Clown is bursting out of his tattered clothes.

11. *b'urlady*] a contraction of "by Our Lady".

13-14. Qui mihi discipulus] "You who are my pupil". The opening words of the *Carmen de moribus*, a didactic poem by William Lily (c.1466-1522) used in Elizabethan grammar schools.

16. *beaten silk*] embroidered silk; with a punning suggestion that Wagner will thrash his servant.   *stavesacre*] a preparation against lice made from the seeds of a plant related to the delphinium.

Wagner.
Sirrah, I say in stavesacre! 20

Clown.
Oho, oho, stavesacre! Why then belike, if I were your man I should be full of vermin.

Wagner.
So thou shalt, whether thou beest with me or no. But sirrah, leave your jesting, and bind yourself presently unto me for seven years, or I'll turn all the lice about 25 thee into familiars, and they shall tear thee in pieces.

Clown.
Do you hear, sir? You may save that labor: they are too familiar with me already, swowns they are as bold with my flesh as if they had paid for my meat and drink.

Wagner.
Well, do you hear, sirrah? Hold, take these guilders. 30

Clown.
Gridirons, what be they?

Wagner.
Why, French crowns.

Clown.
Mass, but for the name of French crowns, a man were as good have as many English counters. And what should I do with these? 35

25. *seven years*] the standard time-period for an apprenticeship or a contract of indentured labor.   *familiars*] Witches and sorcerers were commonly believed to have attendant spirits who took the form of animals.
30-34. *guilders, French crowns, English counters*] Wagner professes to give the Clown Dutch guilders. Observing, it would seem, that the coins have holes punched in them, the Clown mis-hears the word as "gridirons"—whereupon Wagner re-identifies the coins as French crowns. Ormerod and Wortham note that a proclamation of 1587 authorized members of the public to strike holes in French crowns, which in the late 1580s and early 1590s were notoriously debased, and often counterfeit. From the sixteenth until the early nineteenth century, English merchants issued privately minted counters or tokens which circulated without of course having any officially accepted value; "counter" often denoted a debased or counterfeit coin.

Wagner.
> Why now, sirrah, thou art at an hour's warning when-
> soever or wheresoever the devil shall fetch thee.

Clown.
> No, no; here, take your gridirons again.

Wagner.
> Truly, I'll none of them.

Clown.
40   Truly, but you shall.

Wagner.
> Bear witness I gave them him!

Clown.
> Bear witness I give them you again!

Wagner.
> Well, I will cause two devils presently to fetch thee away.
> Baliol, and Belcher!

Clown.
45   Let your Balio and your Belcher come here, and I'll knock
> them, they were never so knocked since they were devils!
> Say I should kill one of them, what would folks say? "Do ye
> see yonder tall fellow in the round slop, he has killed the
> devil": so I should be called "kill-devil" all the parish over.

*Enter two devils, and the clown runs up and down
crying.*

Wagner.
50   Baliol and Belcher, spirits away!

Exeunt.

Clown.
> What, are they gone? A vengeance on them, they have
> vile long nails. There was a he-devil and a she-devil. I'll

---

48. *tall*] fine, handsome.   *round slop*] baggy breeches.

tell you how you shall know them: all he-devils has horns,
and all she-devils has clefts and cloven feet.

Wagner.

Well sirrah, follow me.   55

Clown.

But do you hear: If I should serve you, would you teach
me to raise up Banios and Belcheos?

Wagner.

I will teach thee to turn thyself to anything: to a dog, or
a cat, or a mouse, or a rat, or any thing.

Clown.

How? A Christian fellow to a dog or a cat, a mouse or   60
a rat? No, no, sir. If you turn me into anything, let it be
in the likeness of a little pretty frisking flea, that I may
be here and there and everywhere: O, I'll tickle the pretty
wenches' plackets, I'll be amongst them i'faith!

Wagner.

Well sirrah, come.   65

Clown.

But do you hear, Wagner?

Wagner.

How? Baliol and Belcher!

Clown.

O Lord! I pray sir, let Banio and Belcher go sleep.

Wagner.

Villain, call me Master Wagner, and see that you walk
attentively, and let your right eye be always diametrally   70
fixed upon my left heel, that thou mayest *quasi vestigiis
nostris insistere.*

Exit.

---

57. *Banios*] a pun on "bagnio", a brothel (Kocher).
64. *placket*] pocket in a woman's skirt; metaphorically a woman's genitals.
71-2. quasi vestigiis nostris insistere] "as if walking in our footsteps".

Clown.

God forgive me, he speaks Dutch fustian. Well, I'll follow him, I'll serve him, that's flat.

Exit.

73. *fustian*] bombast, nonsense. Fustian was a coarse cloth made of cotton and flax; the word was metaphorically applied to inflated or inappropriately lofty language.

NOTES TO
ACT I

PROLOGUE

Heading. The...Faustus] *A1*; The Tragedie of *B1*.
1. *Chorus*] *Oxberry*; not in *A1, B1*.
now in] *A1*; in the *B1*.
2. Carthaginians] *A1*; warlicke Carthagens *B1*.
6. vaunt] *B1*; daunt *A1*.
7. Gentlemen] *A1*; Gentles *B1*.
performe] *A1*; now performe *B1*.
9. To patient] *A1*; And now to patient *B1*.
   appeale our plaude] *A1*; appeale *B1*.
11. his parents] *A1*; of parents *B1*.
13. Of] *A1*; At *B1*.   Wittenberg] *B1*; Wertenberg *A1*.
15. soone] *A1*; much *B1*.
16.] *A1*; not in *B1*.
18. whose...disputes] *A1*; and sweetly can dispute *B1*.
19. heauenly] *A1*; th'heauenly *B1*.
22. melting heauens] *A1*; melting, heauens *B1*.
22-23. ouer-throw: / For falling] *B1, Cunningham, Bowers*; ouerthrow. / For falling *A1, Steane, Gill (1971), Pendry and Maxwell*; overthrow; / For, falling *Dyce, Ward, Boas, Jump, Ribner*.
24. now] *B1*; more *A1*.
28.1 Exit] *A1*; not in *B1*.

ACT I Scene i

0.1. *Faustus*] *B1*; *Enter Faustus A1*.
7. *logices*] *B4*; *logicis A1, B1*.
10. that end] *B1*; the end *A1*.
12. *on kai me on*] *Bullen*; *Oncaymaeon A1*; *Oeconomy A2, A3, B1*.   Galen] *A1-3*; and Galen *B1*.
13.] *A1*; not in *B1*.
19.] *A1*; not in *B1*.
22. easde] *A1*; cur'd *B1*.
24. Couldst] *B1*; wouldst *A1*.   men] *A3, B1*; man *A1*.
28. *legatur*] *Dilke*; *legatus A1, B1*.
30. petty] *B1*; pretty *A1*.
31. *Exhereditare*] *Dyce*; *Exhaereditari A1*, *Exhereditari B1*.
33. law] *B1*; Church *A1*.
34. This] *B1*; His *A1*.
36. Too seruile] *B1*; The deuill *A1*.
52. seals] *this edition*; sceanes *A1-3*; not in *B1*; signs *Greg conj.*; schemes *Gill conj.*   and] *A1*; not in *B1*.
55. of omnipotence] *A1*; and omnipotence *B1*.
60.] *A1-3*; not in *B1*.
63. mighty god] *A1*; Demi-god *B1*.
64. tire my] *B1*; Faustus trie thy *A1*.
get] *B1*; gaine *A1*.
70.1. *good...Angell*] *A1*; *Angell and Spirit B1*.

76. treasury] *A1*; treasure *A2, A3, B1*.
78.1. *An[gels]*] *B1*; *not in A1*.
90. Wittenberge] *B1*; Wertenberge *A1*.
91. silk] *Dyce*; skill *A1, B1*.
95. our] *A1*; the *B1*.
97. Antwarpes] *A1*; Anwerpe *B1*.
100.1. *Stage-direction placed as here Tucker Brooke; after line 101 in A1; in right-hand margin at lines 100-101 in B1.*
104-106.] *A1*; *not in B1*.
109-110.] *A1*; *not in B1*.
113. Consissylogismes] *A1*; subtle Sillogismes *A3, B1*.
115. Wittenberg] *B1*; Wertenberge *A1*.
116. Swarme] *A1*; Sworne *B1*.
119. shadowes] *A1*; shadow *B1*.
123. subiects] *A1*; spirits *B1*.
130. has the] *B1*; in their *A1*.
133. stuffes] *A1*; stuff'd *B1*.
140. in] *B1*; *not in A1*.
147. I] *A1*; Yea *B1*.
152. lusty] *A1*; little *A2-3*; bushy *B1*.
167.1. *Exeunt*] *A1*; *Exeunt om. B1*.

ACT I Scene ii

3. presently] *B1*; *not in A1*.   for see here] *A1*; here *B1*.
3.1.] *Stage-direction placed as here in A1; in margin after line 2 in B1.*
6. know] *A1*; know then *B1*.
9. necessary] *A1*; *not in B1*.   which] *B1*; that *A1*.
10. licentiate] *A1*; Licentiats *B1*. vpon] *B1*; vpon't *A1*.
12-15.] *A1*; *not in B1*.
16. Well] *A1*; Then *B1*.
17. Yes sir] *A1*; You are deceiu'd, for *B1*.
18. not he] *A1*; he not *B1*.
23. doubt but] *B1*; doubt *A1*.
27. would] *B1*; it would *A1*.
29. my deare brethren, my deare brethren] *A1*; my deere brethren *B1*.
30-36.] *Prose in A1; the corresponding passage in B1 is in verse.*
30. Nay...art] *A1*; O Faustus, then I feare that which I haue long suspected: / That thou art falne into that damned Art *B1*.
32. and not] *A1*; *not in B1*.
32-33. yet should I grieue for him] *A1*; The danger of his soule would make me

mourne *B1*.
34. and see if hee by] *A1*; It may be *B1*.
36. trie] *A1*; see *B1*.

ACT I Scene iii

0.1. *Enter...conjure*] *A1*; *Thunder. Enter Lucifer and 4 deuils, Faustus to them with this speech B1.*
1. earth] *A1*; night *B1*.
9. Anagramatis'd] *B1*; and Agramithist *A1*.
10. The breuiated] *A1*; Th' abreuiated *B1*.
12. erring] *A1*; euening *B1*.
14. but] *A1*; to *B1*.
15. vttermost] *A1*; vtmost *B1*.
16. *Sint*] *A1*; *Thunder, Sint B1*.
17. *aquatici*] *Tucker Brooke; aquatani A1, B1*.
19. *appareat*] *B1*; *apariat A1. Mephastophilis*] *A1*; *Mephostophilis B1*.
19-20. *Quid tu moraris?*] *Ellis; quod tumeraris A1; Dragon, quod tumeraris B1.*
22. *Mephastophilis*] *A1*; *Mephostophilis B1*.
29. Mephastophilis] *A1*; Mephostophilis *B1*.
32-34.] *A1*; *not in B1*.
32. Now] *Wagner*; No *A1*.
34. redis] *Boas; regis A1*.
34.1. *Mephastophilis*] *A1, B1*.
45. speeches] *A1*; *not in B1*.
46. *accidens*] *B4*; *accident A1, B1*.
53. the Trinitie] *A1*; all godlinesse *B1*.
59. him] *A1*; me *B1*.
60. he confounds] *A1*; I confound *B1*.
61. His] *A1*; My *B1*.
71. fell] *A1*; liue *B1*.
77. who] *A1*; that *B1*.
82. strike] *A1*; strikes *B1*.
83. Mephastophilis] *A1*; Mephostophilis *B1*.
96. ayde] *A1*; to aid *B1*.
103. Mephastophilis] *A1*; Mephostophilis *B1*.
105. thorough] *B5*; through *A1, B1*.
108. Country] *B1*; land *A1*.
112. desire] *A1*; desir'd *B1*.
114. Mephastophilis] *A1*; Mephostophilis *B1*.

Notes to Act I

ACT I Scene iv

1. Sirra...hither] *A1*; Come hither sirra boy *B1*.
2. How...hope] *A1*; Boy? O disgrace to my person: Zounds boy in your face *B1*.
3. such...quotha?] *A1*; with beards I am sure *B1*.
4. Tell me] *A1*; *not in B1*.   any] *A1*; no *B1*.
5. I] *A1*; Yes *B1*.   else] *A1*; sir *B1*.
7. the vilaine is bare, and] *A1*; I know the Villaines *B1*.
10-11. How...burladie] *A1*; Not so neither *B1*.
11. haue] *A1*; to haue *B1*.
12. deere] *A1*; deere, I can tell you *B1*.
13. wel...and Ile] *A1*; Sirra, wilt thou be my man and waite on me? and I will *B1*.
15. How] *A1*; What *B1*.
16. sirra] *A1*; slaue *B1*.
17-22. how, how...vermine] *A1*; Staues-aker? that's good to kill Vermine: then belike if I serue you, I shall be lousy *B1*.
23-25. So...vnto me] *A1*; Why so thou shalt be, whether thou dost it or no: for sirra, if thou dost not presently bind thy selfe to me *B1*.
25. or Ile] *A1*; I'le *B1*.
26. they shal] *A1*; make them *B1*.
27-29. Doe...flesh] *A1*; Nay sir, you may saue your selfe a labour, for they are as familiar with me *B1*.
29. had payd] *A1*; payd *B1*.   drinke] *A1*; drinke, I can tell you *B1*.
30. wel...holde] *A1*; Well sirra, leaue your iesting, and *B1*.
31-35.] *A1*; *in place of these speeches, B1 has* **Clown.** Yes marry sir, and I thanke you to.

36. Why...art] *A1*; So, now thou art to bee *B1*.
37. or] *A1*; and *B1*.
38. No...againe] *A1*; Here, take your Guilders I'le none of 'em *B1*.
39-42.] *A1*; *not in B1*.
43. Well...away] *A1*; Not I, thou art Prest, prepare thy selfe, for I will presently raise vp two deuils to carry thee away *B1*.
44. Baliol and] *A1*; Banio, *B1*.
45-49.] *A1*; *in place of this speech B1 has* Belcher? and Belcher come here, I'le belch him: I am not afraid of a deuill.
49.1. *Enter...crying*] *A1*; *Enter 2 deuils B1*.
50-57. Baliol...Belcheos?] *A1*; *in place of these speeches B1 has* How now sir will you serue me now? **Clown.** I good Wagner take away the deuill then. **Wagner.** Spirits away; now sirra follow me. **Clown.** I will sir; but hearke you Maister, will you teach me this coniuring Occupation?
58. I will] *A1*; I sirra, I'le *B1*.   to any-thing] *A1*; *not in B1*.
60. How?...to] *A1*; *not in B1*.   catte, a] *A1*; Cat, or a *B1*.   rat?] *A1*; rat? O braue Wagner *B1*.
61-68. no...sleepe] *A1*; *not in B1*.
69-71. Villaine...maist] *B1*; Vilaine, call me Maister Wagner, and let thy left eye be diametarily fixt vpon my right heele, with *A1*.
71-72. *vestigiis nostris*] Dyce 2; *vestigias nostras A1, B1*.
72.1.] *A1*; *not in B1*.
73-74. God...flat] *A1*; Well sir, I warrant you *B1*.
74.1. *Exit*] *A1*; *Exeunt B1*.

ACT II

Act II, Scene i.

Enter Faustus in his study.

Faustus.
Now, Faustus, must thou needs be damn'd,
And canst thou not be sav'd.
What boots it then to think of God or heaven?
Away with such vain fancies, and despair,
Despair in God, and trust in Belzebub.   5
Now go not backward: no Faustus, be resolute.
Why waverest thou? O, something soundeth in mine ears:
"Abjure this magic, turn to God again."
Ay, and Faustus will turn to God again.
To God? He loves thee not;   10
The god thou serv'st is thine own appetite,
Wherein is fix'd the love of Belzebub:
To him I'll build an altar and a church,
And offer lukewarm blood of new-born babes!

Enter Good Angel, and Evil.

Good Ang.
Sweet Faustus, leave that execrable art.   15

Faustus.
Contrition, prayer, repentance: what of these?

Good Ang.
O, they are means to bring thee unto heaven.

Evil Ang.
Rather illusions, fruits of lunacy,
That makes men foolish that do trust them most.

---

3. *boots*] avails.
18-19. *illusions, fruits...That makes*] A false concord of a plural subject with a singular verb form is common in the writings of Marlowe and his contemporaries.

Good Ang.

20   Sweet Faustus, think of heaven and heavenly things.

Evil Ang.

No Faustus, think of honor and of wealth.

Exeunt Angels.

Faustus.

Of wealth?
Why, the signory of Emden shall be mine!
When Mephastophilis shall stand by me

25   What God can hurt me? Faustus, thou art safe;
Cast no more doubts. Come, Mephastophilis,
And bring glad tidings from great Lucifer!
Is't not midnight? Come Mephastophilis,
Veni, veni, Mephastophilis!

Enter Mephastophilis.

30   Now tell me, what says Lucifer thy lord?

Meph.

That I shall wait on Faustus whilst he lives,
So he will buy my service with his soul.

Faustus.

Already Faustus hath hazarded that for thee.

Meph.

But now thou must bequeath it solemnly,

35   And write a deed of gift with thine own blood,
For that security craves great Lucifer.
If thou deny it I will back to hell.

---

23. *signory*] lordship, rule.   *Emden*] a prosperous port in north-west Germany which conducted an extensive trade with England.
24-25. *When...me?*] a blasphemous distortion of Romans 8:31: "If God be for us, who can be against us?"
29. Veni, veni, Mephastophilis!] "Come, O come, Mephastophilis!" A blasphemous echo of the Whitsuntide hymn *Veni Creator Spiritus*, which invokes the third person of the Trinity and was used in the liturgy for the consecration of priests; the metrical translation of this hymn in Sternhold and Hopkins's *Wholebooke of Psalms*, a text approved by the Anglican church, retained the title *Veni Creator*. See Celia Barnes, "Matthew Parker's Pastoral Training and Marlowe's *Doctor Faustus*," *CD* 15 (1981), 263-64.

Faustus.
>   Stay Mephastophilis, and tell me,
>   What good will my soul do thy lord?

Meph.
>   Enlarge his kingdom.   40

Faustus.
>   Is that the reason why he tempts us thus?

Meph.
>   *Solamen miseris socios habuisse doloris.*

Faustus.
>   Why, have you any pain that torture others?

Meph.
>   As great as have the human souls of men.
>   But tell me, Faustus, shall I have thy soul?   45
>   And I will be thy slave and wait on thee,
>   And give thee more than thou hast wit to ask.

Faustus.
>   Ay Mephastophilis, I give it thee.

Meph.
>   Then stab thine arm courageously,
>   And bind thy soul, that at some certain day   50
>   Great Lucifer may claim it as his own:
>   And then be thou as great as Lucifer!

Faustus.
>   Lo Mephastophilis, for love of thee
>   I cut mine arm, and with my proper blood
>   Assure my soul to be great Lucifer's,   55
>   Chief lord and regent of perpetual night.
>   View here the blood that trickles from mine arm,
>   And let it be propitious for my wish.

---

42. Solamen...doloris] "It is a comfort to the wretched to have had companions in misfortune." This Latin hexameter appears also in Greene's *Menaphon* (ed. Grosart, vi. 45); the idea, somewhat differently expressed, recurs frequently among medieval writers, and has been traced back to Publilius Syrus and Seneca.
54. *proper*] own.

Meph.
>But Faustus, thou must
60 Write it in manner of a deed of gift.

Faustus.
>Ay, so I will. But Mephastophilis,
>My blood congeals, and I can write no more.

Meph.
>I'll fetch thee fire to dissolve it straight.

Exit.

Faustus.
>What might the staying of my blood portend?
65 Is it unwilling I should write this bill?
>Why streams it not, that I may write afresh?
>"Faustus gives to thee his soul": ah, there it stay'd.
>Why should'st thou not? Is not thy soul thine own?
>Then write again: "Faustus gives to thee his soul."

Enter Mephastophilis with a chafer of coals.

Meph.
70 Here's fire: come Faustus, set it on.

Faustus.
>So: now the blood begins to clear again;
>Now will I make an end immediately.

Meph. [aside]
>O, what will not I do to obtain his soul!

Faustus.
>*Consummatum est*: this bill is ended,
75 And Faustus hath bequeath'd his soul to Lucifer.
>But what is this inscription on mine arm?

60. *deed*] a legally binding document.
65. *bill*] contract.
69.1 chafer] a kind of saucepan or chafing-dish, in this case apparently with a grate over which other dishes could be heated.
74. Consummatum est] "It is finished." According to the gospel of John, but not the synoptic gospels, these were the last words of Jesus on the cross (John 19:30).

Homo fuge! Whither should I fly?
If unto God he'll throw thee down to hell.
My senses are deceiv'd: here's nothing writ.
O yes, I see it plain! Even here is writ   80
Homo fuge; yet shall not Faustus fly.

Meph.

I'll fetch him somewhat to delight his mind.

Exit.

*Enter with devils, giving crowns and rich apparel to
Faustus, and dance, and then [the devils] depart.*

Faustus.

Speak Mephastophilis: what means this show?

Meph.

Nothing, Faustus, but to delight thy mind,
And let thee see what magic can perform.   85

Faustus.

But may I raise such spirits when I please?

Meph.

Ay Faustus, and do greater things than these.

Faustus.

Then there's enough for a thousand souls!
Here Mephastophilis, receive this scroll,
A deed of gift, of body and of soul: 90
But yet conditionally, that thou perform
All articles prescrib'd between us both.

Meph.

Faustus, I swear by hell and Lucifer
To effect all promises between us made.

Faustus.

Then hear me read them.   95

---

77. Homo fuge] "Man, flee!" An allusion to Ps. 139:7-8: "Whither shall I go from thy spirit?
or whither shall I flee from thy presence? If I ascend into heaven, thou art there: if I make
my bed in hell, behold, thou art there."

On these conditions following:
First, that Faustus may be a spirit in form and substance;
Secondly, that Mephastophilis shall be his servant, and at his
command;
100 *Thirdly, that Mephastophilis shall do for him, and bring him*
whatsoever;
Fourthly, that he shall be in his chamber or house invisible;
Lastly, that he shall appear to the said John Faustus at
all times, in what form or shape soever he please;
105 *I, John Faustus of Wittenberg, Doctor, by these presents*
do give both body and soul to Lucifer, Prince of the East,
and his minister Mephastophilis, and furthermore grant
unto them that four and twenty years being expired, and
these articles above written being inviolate, full power to
110 *fetch or carry the said John Faustus, body and soul, flesh,*
blood, or goods, into their habitation wheresover.
By me, John Faustus.

Meph.
Speak Faustus, do you deliver this as your deed?
Faustus.
Ay, take it, and the devil give thee good on't.
Meph.
115 So. Now, Faustus, ask me what thou wilt.
Faustus.
First will I question with thee about hell.
Tell me, where is the place that men call hell?
Meph.
Under the heavens.
Faustus.
Ay, so are all things else; but whereabouts?
Meph.
120 Within the bowels of these elements,
Where we are tortur'd and remain forever.

105. these presents] the legal articles.

Hell hath no limits, nor is circumscrib'd
In one self place, but where we are is hell,
And where hell is there must we ever be;
And to be short, when all the world dissolves   125
And every creature shall be purify'd,
All places shall be hell that is not heaven.

Faustus.
Come, I think hell's a fable.

Meph.
Ay, think so still, till experience change thy mind.

Faustus.
Why, think'st thou then that Faustus shall be damn'd?   130

Meph.
Ay, of necessity, for here's the scroll
Wherein thou hast given thy soul to Lucifer.

Faustus.
Ay, and body too, but what of that?
Think'st thou that Faustus is so fond to imagine
That after this life there is any pain?   135
Tush, these are trifles and mere old wives' tales.

Meph.
But I am an instance to prove the contrary,
For I tell thee I am damn'd, and now in hell.

Faustus.
Nay, and this be hell, I'll willingly be damn'd!
What, sleeping, eating, walking and disputing?   140
But leaving this, let me have a wife, the fairest maid in
Germany, for I am wanton and lascivious, and cannot live
without a wife.

Meph.
How, a wife? I prithee Faustus, talk not of a wife.

Faustus.
Nay, sweet Mephastophilis, fetch me one, for I will have   145

---

123. *self*] single, particular.   134. *fond*] foolish.

one.

Meph.

Well, thou wilt have one. Sit there till I come; I'll fetch thee a wife in the devil's name.

Enter a devil dressed like a woman, with fireworks.

Meph.

Tell, Faustus: how dost thou like thy wife?

Faustus.

150 A plague on her for a hot whore!

Meph.

Tut Faustus, marriage is but a ceremonial toy.
If thou lov'st me, think no more of it.
I'll cull thee out the fairest courtesans
And bring them every morning to thy bed.

155 She whom thine eye shall like, thy heart shall have,
Be she as chaste as was Penelope,
As wise as Saba, or as beautiful
As was bright Lucifer before his fall.
Hold, take this book: peruse it thoroughly.

160 The iterating of these lines brings gold;
The framing of this circle on the ground
Brings whirlwinds, tempests, thunder and lightning.
Pronounce this thrice devoutly to thyself,
And men in armor shall appear to thee,

165 Ready to execute what thou desir'st.

Faustus.

Thanks, Mephastophilis; yet fain would I have a book wherein I might behold all spells and incantations, that I might raise up spirits when I please.

---

151. *toy*] trifle.

156. *Penelope*] the faithful wife of Odysseus.

157. *Saba*] the Queen of Sheba, who in 1 Kings 10:1-13 (see also 2 Chronicles 9:1-12) comes to Jerusalem to test King Solomon's knowledge of God with "hard questions". In the Vulgate text, she is called "regina Saba."

166-79.] This passage appears to be a parodic echo of the apocryphal Wisdom of Solomon 7:17-22.

Meph.
   Here they are in this book.

                    There turn to them.

Faustus.
   Now would I have a book where I might see all characters   170
   and planets of the heavens, that I might know their motions and dispositions.

Meph.
   Here they are too.

                    Turn to them.

Faustus.
   Nay, let me have one book more, and then I have done,
   wherein I might see all plants, herbs, and trees that grow   175
   upon the earth.

Meph.
   Here they be.

Faustus.
   O, thou art deceived.

Meph.
   Tut, I warrant thee.

                    Turn to them.

                    Exeunt.

Act II, Scene ii.

   Enter Robin the ostler with a book in his hand.

Robin.
   O, this is admirable! Here I ha' stolen one of Doctor Faustus'
   conjuring books, and i'faith I mean to search some circles

179. *I warrant thee*] I assure you (that the book contains all that I say it does).

for my own use: now will I make all the maidens in our parish
dance at my pleasure stark naked before me, and so by that
5 means I shall see more than ever I felt, or saw yet.

Enter Rafe, calling Robin.

Rafe.

Robin, prithee come away! There's a gentleman tarries to
have his horse, and he would have his things rubbed and
made clean; he keeps such a chafing with my mistress about
it, and she has sent me to look thee out; prithee come away!

Robin.

10 Keep out, keep out, or else you are blown up, you are
dismembered, Rafe! Keep out, for I am about a roaring
piece of work.

Rafe.

Come, what dost thou with that same book? Thou canst
not read.

Robin.

15 Yes, my master and mistress shall find that I can read:
he for his forehead, she for her private study. She's born
to bear with me, or else my art fails.

Rafe.

Why Robin, what book is that?

Robin.

What book? Why, the most intolerable book for conjur-
20 ing that e'er was invented by any brimstone devil!

Rafe.

Canst thou conjure with it?

3-4.] Ormerod and Wortham suggest that there may be a slanting allusion in these lines to
the orgiastic naked dancing of the witches' sabbath.
11. *roaring*] noisy, riotous. For an account of "the mathematical science of roaring" as practised by Elizabethan and Jacobean bullies and gallants, see Middleton and Rowley, *A Fair
Quarrel* IV.i, iv.
16. *forehead*] A deceived husband or cuckold was said to wear horns on his forehead.
private study] with a quibble, Ormerod and Wortham suggest, on private parts.
17. *to bear with*] to put up with; also (another bawdy quibble) to lie under.

Robin.

I can do all these things easily with it: first, I can make thee drunk with hippocras at any tavern in Europe for nothing; that's one of my conjuring works.

Rafe.

Our master parson says that's nothing.   25

Robin.

True, Rafe. And more, Rafe, if thou hast any mind to Nan Spit our kitchen maid, then turn her and wind her to thine own use, as often as thou wilt, and at midnight.

Rafe.

O brave Robin, shall I have Nan Spit, and to mine own use? On that condition I'll feed thy devil with horse-   30 bread as long as he lives, of free cost.

Robin.

No more, sweet Rafe: let's go and make clean our boots which lie foul upon our hands; and then to our conjuring, in the devil's name!

Exeunt.

Act II, Scene iii.

Enter Faustus in his study, and Mephastophilis.

Faustus.

When I behold the heavens then I repent
And curse thee, wicked Mephastophilis,
Because thou hast depriv'd me of those joys.

---

23. *hippocras*] wine flavoured with spices.
30-31. *horse-bread*] bread made of beans, bran, etc. for horses—but apparently sometimes eaten also by the very poor. See Jonson, *Every Man Out of His Humour* III.ii: "You thread-bare, horse-bread-eating rascals...."

Meph.
      Why Faustus,
5   Think'st thou heaven is such a glorious thing?
      I tell thee 'tis not half so fair as thou
      Or any man that breathes on earth.
Faustus.
      How prov'st thou that?
Meph.
                              'Twas made for man,
      Therefore is man more excellent.
Faustus.
10   If it were made for man, 'twas made for me:
      I will renounce this magic and repent.
                  Enter Good Angel and Evil Angel.

Good Ang.
      Faustus, repent yet, God will pity thee.
Evil Ang.
      Thou art a spirit, God cannot pity thee.
Faustus.
      Who buzzeth in mine ears I am a spirit?
15   Be I a devil, yet God may pity me.
      Ay, God will pity me if I repent.
Evil Ang.
      Ay, but Faustus never shall repent.
                  Exeunt Angels.

Faustus.
      My heart's so harden'd I cannot repent.
      Scarce can I name salvation, faith, or heaven,

---

14. *buzzeth*] whispers.
18. *My heart's so harden'd*] Taking their cue from God's hardening of Pharaoh's heart in Exodus 4:21, 7:3, 13, 10:1, 20, 27, Calvinists understood an impenitent hardness, whether wavering or obdurate, as a condition determined by the will of God. See Calvin, *Institutes* III.xxiii. 1 (ed. McNeill, tr. Battles, ii. 948-49): "God aroused Pharaoh [Rom. 9:17]; then, 'he hardens whom he pleases' [Rom. 9:18]. From this it follows that God's secret plan is the cause of hardening." See also *Institutes* II.iv. 3.

But fearful echoes thunders in mine ears,   20
"Faustus, thou art damn'd!" Then swords and knives,
Poison, guns, halters, and envenom'd steel
Are laid before me to dispatch myself,
And long ere this I should have done the deed
Had not sweet pleasure conquer'd deep despair.   25
Have not I made blind Homer sing to me
Of Alexander's love and Oenon's death?
And hath not he that built the walls of Thebes
With ravishing sound of his melodious harp
Made music with my Mephastophilis?   30
Why should I die, then, or basely despair?
I am resolv'd: Faustus shall ne'er repent.
Come Mephastophilis, let us dispute again,
And reason of divine astrology.
Speak, are there many spheres above the moon?   35
Are all celestial bodies but one globe,
As is the substance of this centric earth?

---

22. *halters*] hangman's nooses.

27. *Alexander's love and Oenon's death*] These are matters which Homer left unsung; Faustus would have been the first to hear them from his lips. In *Iliad* XXIV. 25-30, Homer alludes to the Judgment of Paris (also named Alexandros, as in *Iliad* III. 15 ff.), but does not mention Oenone at all. The tale of Troy, up to the point at which the *Iliad* begins, was filled in by the post-Homeric *Cypria* (of which only fragments now survive); this epic told the familiar story of how Alexandros, a son of King Priam and Queen Hecuba of Troy, was cast out by his parents (for it was prophesied that he should cause the destruction of Troy) and brought up among the shepherds of Mount Ida, where he won the love of Oenone. Asked by Hera, Athena, and Aphrodite to award a golden apple to the most beautiful goddess, he succumbed to Aphrodite's bribe of the love of the fairest woman alive, abandoned Oenone and abducted Helen from Sparta, thus provoking the Trojan War. (See Ovid, *Heroides*, Ep. v, and also George Peele's play *The Arraignment of Paris* [1584].) Quintus Smyrnaeus, whose epic *The Fall of Troy* is a belated (4th c. A.D.) embellishment of Homeric traditions, tells in Book X how Paris, wounded by a poisoned arrow from Philoctetes's bow, could have been healed only by Oenone; after jealously refusing to cure him, she was overwhelmed by grief and remorse, and threw herself onto his funeral pyre. Ormerod and Wortham suggest that Marlowe probably knew the story through such subsequent adaptations as the *Ilias Latina* of Pindarus Thebanus, which "was widely used as a school text in the sixteenth century."

28-29.] Amphion and his brother built the walls of Thebes (*Odyssey* XI. 260-65); the music of Amphion's lyre magically moved huge stones into place (Apollonius Rhodius, *Argonautica* I. 735-41).

34. *astrology*] not clearly distinguished from astronomy until the seventeenth century.

35-62.] The elements (earth, water, air, fire) which make up "the substance of this centric earth" were thought to be concentrically disposed; so also, in the old geocentric cosmology,

Meph.

    As are the elements, such are the heavens,
    Even from the moon unto the empyreal orb,
40   Mutually folded in each other's spheres,
    And jointly move upon one axle-tree
    Whose termine is term'd the world's wide pole.
    Nor are the names of Saturn, Mars, or Jupiter
    Feign'd, but are erring stars.

Faustus.

45   But tell me, have they all one motion, both *situ*
    et tempore?

Meph.

    All jointly move from east to west in four and twenty
    hours upon the poles of the world, but differ in their
    motions upon the poles of the zodiac.

---

were the spheres which governed the motions of those wandering or "erring" stars, the planets. Mephastophilis says there are nine spheres: those of the planets, including the moon and the sun; the firmament, to which the fixed stars are attached; and the empyrean, the outermost and motionless sphere of the universe. (He apparently conflates the *primum mobile*, thought of by some astronomers as a distinct sphere which imparts motion to the heavens, with the firmament.) All of this is utterly commonplace. The systems developed by ancient astronomers were enormously more complex: Eudoxus (4th century B.C.) required twenty-seven, and Ptolemy (2nd century A.D.) more than eighty variously revolving spheres, including epicyclic and eccentric ones, to explain the motions of the planets.

45-46. situ et tempore] "In position and time"; i.e., in the direction of their revolutions around the earth and in the time these take.

49-50, 52. *poles of the world...poles of the zodiac; the double motion of the planets*] The apparent diurnal motion of the planetary spheres "upon one axle-tree" (the northern "termine" of which nearly coincides with the star Polaris) is of course due, in post-Copernican terms, to the earth's rotation upon its axis. The second component of the planets' apparent "double motion" is an effect of the differences between the earth's period of revolution around the sun, and theirs. The periods of planetary revolution given by Faustus correspond for the most part to the then-accepted figures: "Robert Recorde's *Castle of Knowledge* (1556, pp. 572-9), gives them as Saturn 28 years, Jupiter 12 years, Mars 2 years, Venus, Mercury, and, of course, the sun 1 year, and the moon 1 month" (Greg). The actual—as opposed to apparent—periods for the inner planets are of course much less: 7 1/2 and 3 months respectively. The zodiac is a belt of the celestial sphere which contains the paths traced out by the sun, moon, and planets. Extending some eight or nine degrees north and south of the ecliptic (which is the apparent path described by the sun around the celestial sphere), the zodiac is conventionally divided into twelve equal segments named according to the constellations which occupy these spaces. The inclination of the earth's axis of rotation from the perpendicular in relation to the plane of its revolutions around the sun means that the "poles of the zodiac" differ from those of the world.

Faustus.
These slender questions Wagner can decide: 50
Hath Mephastophilis no greater skill?
Who knows not the double motion of the planets?
The first is finish'd in a natural day,
The second thus: Saturn in thirty years,
Jupiter in twelve, Mars in four, the Sun, Venus, and Mer-   55
cury in a year, the Moon in twenty-eight days. Tush, these
are freshmen's suppositions! But tell me, hath every
sphere a dominion or *intelligentia*?

Meph.
Ay.

Faustus.
How many heavens or spheres are there?   60

Meph.
Nine: the seven planets, the firmament, and the empyreal
heaven.

Faustus.
But is there not *coelum igneum, et crystallinum?*

Meph.
No Faustus, they be but fables.

Faustus.
Resolve me then in this one question: Why are not con-   65

---

58. *dominion or* intelligentia] It was widely believed that the planets were moved or guided by angels or intelligences; see Agrippa, *De occulta philosophia* III.xvi; also I.xxii for the divine names and signs of the planetary *intelligentiae*. In III.xvii, Agrippa discusses the pseudo-Dionysius's division of the angels into nine orders, the middle three of which, the Dominions, Virtues and Powers, share in governing the world through their administration of the heavens. In stating that the planets' names are not feigned (43-44), Mephastophilis has already implied that the planets are spiritual agents.
63. coelum igneum, et crystallinum] "a fiery, and a crystalline heaven". The latter was supposed "to account for the 'trepidation of the spheares'" (Donne, 'A Valediction: forbidding mourning'), i.e. the supposed variation in the rate of precession of the equinoxes" (Jump). F.R. Johnson argues that Mephastophilis's refusal to allow moving spheres other than those carrying observable bodies is evidence of Marlowe's alignment with sceptical and empiricist tendencies in Renaissance astronomy. See "Marlowe's 'Imperiall Heaven'," *ELH* 12 (1945), 35-44; and "Marlowe's Astronomy and Renaissance Skepticism," *ELH* 13 (1946), 241-54.

junctions, oppositions, aspects, eclipses all at one time,
but in some years we have more, in some less?

Meph.

    Per inaequalem motum respectu totius.

Faustus.

    Well, I am answered. Now tell me who made the world.

Meph.

70   I will not.

Faustus.

    Sweet Mephastophilis, tell me.

Meph.

    Move me not, Faustus.

Faustus.

    Villain, have I not bound thee to tell me any thing?

Meph.

    Ay, that is not against our kingdom.

75   This is. Thou art damn'd, think thou of hell.

Faustus.

    Think, Faustus, upon God that made the world!

Meph.

    Remember this.

Exit.

Faustus.

    Ay, go accursed spirit to ugly hell:
    'Tis thou hast damn'd distressed Faustus' soul.
    Is't not too late?

Enter Good Angel and Evil Angel.

Evil Ang.

80   Too late.

---

66. *conjunctions, oppositions, aspects*] astrological terms referring respectively to the apparent proximity of two planets, to their positioning on opposite sides of the sky, and to any other angular relation between their positions.

68. Per inaequalem motum respectu totius] "through an unequal motion with respect to the whole".

72. *move*] anger.

Good Ang.
Never too late, if Faustus can repent.

Evil Ang.
If thou repent, devils shall tear thee in pieces.

Good Ang.
Repent, and they shall never raze thy skin.

Exeunt Angels.

Faustus.
Ah Christ, my Saviour,
Seek to save distressed Faustus' soul!   85

Enter Lucifer, Belzebub, and Mephastophilis.

Lucifer.
Christ cannot save thy soul, for he is just;
There's none but I have interest in the same.

Faustus.
O, what art thou that look'st so terribly?

Lucifer.
I am Lucifer, and this is my companion prince in hell.

---

81. *if Faustus can repent*] This condition raises the issue of Calvinist double predestination: if Faustus *is* able to repent, i.e. if he is one of the elect, then it is never too late to do so—but if he is one of the reprobate, and cannot repent, then it is always too late. The B-text's "will repent" appears to be a theologically motivated revision: to say that it is never too late if Faustus will repent is to superimpose upon the question of fact (will he repent?) the suggestion that he can choose to do so. The notion of a will that is anything other than autonomous may seem paradoxical; but so also, to Calvinists, was any notion of human autonomy. As Philippe Du Plessis-Mornay wrote, "God therefore to show his power in our freedom and liberty, hath left our wills to us; and to restrain them from looseness, he hath so ordered them by his wisdom, that he worketh his own will no less by them, than if we had no will at all" (*A Woorke concerning the trewnesse of the Christian Religion*, tr. Sir Philip Sidney and Arthur Golding [1587], p. 221).
83. *raze*] graze.
85. *seek*] According to the Calvinistic orthodoxy of Elizabethan England, the process of salvation had to be initiated by God. Faustus's "seek" suggests that he lacks faith in Christ's ability to save him; the word may also imply that it is primarily up to Christ to save Faustus's soul, and that he has not previously been trying to. The B-text's substitution of "help" removes these implications.
87. *interest in*] a legal claim upon.

Faustus.

90   O Faustus, they are come to fetch away thy soul!

Lucifer.
    We come to tell thee thou dost injure us.
    Thou talk'st of Christ, contrary to thy promise.

Belzebub.
    Thou should'st not think of God.

Lucifer.
                     Think of the devil.

Belzebub.
    And of his dam too.

Faustus.
95   Nor will I henceforth: pardon me in this,
    And Faustus vows never to look to heaven,
    Never to name God or to pray to him,
    To burn his Scriptures, slay his ministers,
    And make my spirits pull his churches down.

Lucifer.
100   So shalt thou show thyself an obedient servant, and we
    will highly gratify thee for it.

Belzebub.
    Faustus, we are come from hell to show thee some pastime.
    Sit down, and thou shalt behold the Seven Deadly Sins ap-
    pear to thee in their own proper shapes and likeness.

Faustus.
105   That sight will be as pleasing unto me as Paradise was to
    Adam, the first day of his creation.

Lucifer.
    Talk not of Paradise, or creation, but mark the show.
    Go, Mephastophilis, fetch them in.

             Enter the Seven Deadly Sins.

98-99.] Compare *The Jew of Malta* V.i. 64-65: "I'll help to slay their children and their wives, / To fire the churches, pull their houses down."

Belzebub.

Now Faustus, question them of their names and dispositions.   110

Faustus.

That shall I soon: what art thou, the first?

Pride.

I am Pride. I disdain to have any parents. I am like to Ovid's
flea, I can creep into every corner of a wench: sometimes like
a periwig I sit upon her brow; next like a necklace I hang
about her neck; then like a fan of feathers I kiss her lips; and   115
then, turning myself to a wrought smock, do what I list. But
fie, what a smell is here? I'll not speak a word more, unless
the ground be perfumed and covered with cloth of arras.

Faustus.

Thou art a proud knave indeed. What art thou, the
second?   120

Covet.

I am Covetousness, begotten of an old churl in an old
leathern bag; and might I have my wish, I would desire that
this house and all the people in it were turned to gold, that
I might lock you up in my good chest. O, my sweet gold!

Faustus.

What art thou, the third?   125

Wrath.

I am Wrath. I had neither father nor mother; I leapt out
of a lion's mouth when I was scarce half an hour old, and
ever since I have run up and down the world with this
case of rapiers, wounding myself when I had nobody to

112-113. *Ovid's flea*] The *Elegia de pulice*, a poem written in imitation of Ovid's amatory
elegies, was wrongly ascribed to him. Jump quotes from it a line addressed to the flea: "Is
quocumque placet; nil tibi, saeve, latet": "You go wherever you wish; nothing, savage, is
hidden from you." See *Poetae latini minores*, ed. N.E. Lemaire (Paris, 1826), vii. 275-78.
(At I.iv. 61-64, the Clown's speech alludes to this same poem.)
118. *cloth of arras*] tapestry fabric of the kind woven at Arras in Flanders; to use it as a
floor covering would be grossly ostentatious.
129. *case*] pair.

130   fight withal. I was born in hell, and look to it: for some
         of you shall be my father.

Faustus.

         What art thou, the fourth?

Envy.

         I am Envy, begotten of a chimney-sweeper and an oyster
         wife. I cannot read, and therefore wish all books were
135   burned; I am lean with seeing others eat. O, that there would
         come a famine through all the world, that all might die, and
         I live alone: then thou should'st see how fat I would be. But
         must thou sit and I stand? Come down, with a vengeance!

Faustus.

         Away, envious rascal! What art thou, the fifth?

Gluttony.

140   Who I, sir? I am Gluttony. My parents are all dead, and the
         devil a penny they have left me, but a bare pension, and that
         buys me thirty meals a day and ten bevers: a small trifle to
         suffice nature. O, I come of a royal parentage: my grandfather
         was a gammon of bacon, my grandmother a hogshead of claret
145   wine. My godfathers were these: Peter Pickleherring and Mar-
         tin Martlemas-beef. O, but my godmother she was a jolly
         gentlewoman, and well-beloved in every good town and city:
         her name was Mistress Margery March-beer. Now, Faustus,
         thou hast heard all my progeny, wilt thou bid me to supper?

Faustus.

150   No, I'll see thee hanged: thou wilt eat up all my victuals.

Gluttony.

         Then the devil choke thee.

133-34. *begotten...wife*] and therefore filthy and foul-smelling.

142. *bevers*] drinks; also light meals or snacks.

145. *Pickleherring*] a clown figure associated (like Jack a Lent and Steven Stockfish) with carnival festivities and popular farces. See C.R. Baskervill, *The Elizabethan Jig*, pp. 47-48, 93, 126-32.

146. *Martlemas-beef*] Martinmas, or St. Martin's day (November 11), was the traditional time to slaughter cattle for the production of salt beef, and therefore also a time for feasting on "green" or unsalted beef.

148. *March-beer*] a strong beer brewed in March.

149. *progeny*] lineage.

Faustus.
Choke thyself, glutton! What art thou, the sixth?

Sloth.
I am Sloth. I was begotten on a sunny bank, where I have lain ever since, and you have done me great injury to bring me from thence. Let me be carried thither again by Gluttony and Lechery. I'll not speak another word for a king's ransom.

155

Faustus.
What are you, mistress minx, the seventh and last?

Lechery.
Who I, sir? I am one that loves an inch of raw mutton better than an ell of fried stock-fish, and the first letter of my name begins with Lechery.

160

Lucifer.
Away, to hell, to hell.

Exeunt the Sins.

Now Faustus, how dost thou like this?

Faustus.
O, this feeds my soul.

Lucifer.
Tut Faustus, in hell is all manner of delight.

Faustus.
O, might I see hell, and return again, how happy were I then!

165

Lucifer.
Thou shalt. I will send for thee at midnight. In mean time,

157. *minx*] hussy, wanton woman.
159. *ell*] a measure of length (equal in England to some forty-five inches), commonly contrasted to an inch, as in "Ye liked...better an inch of your will, than an ell of your thrift" (J. Heywood [1562], qtd. in *OED*, Ell 1.b.).   *stockfish*] unsalted dried fish, sometimes abusively associated with the male organ, as in *1 Henry IV* II.iv. 233: "you bull's pizzle, you stockfish," and more generally with sexual coldness or impotence, as in *Measure for Measure* III.ii. 98: "he was begot between two stockfishes." Compare the words of the female character in a jig (or farcical song and dance routine) dating from c.1570: "I love very well the things that be lickerish / marchpain and quince pie I care for no stockfish" (Baskervill, *The Elizabethan Jig*, p. 416). Gill remarks: "Lechery is saying in effect that she prefers a small amount of virility to a large quantity of impotence."

take this book, peruse it thoroughly, and thou shalt turn
thyself into what shape thou wilt.

Faustus.
170   Great thanks, mighty Lucifer:
This will I keep as chary as my life.

Lucifer.
Farewell, Faustus, and think on the devil.

Faustus.
Farewell, great Lucifer. Come, Mephastophilis.

Exeunt omnes.

171. *chary*] carefully.

NOTES TO
ACT II

ACT II Scene i

1. damnd,] *A1*; damn'd? *B1.*
2. And] *A1*; *not in B1.*
3. of] *A1*; on *B1.*
6. no Faustus] *A1*; Faustus *B1.*
9.] *A1*; *not in B1.*
10. To God?] *A1*; Why *B1.*
10-11. not, / The god] *A1*; *printed as one line in B1.*
14.1. *Enter...Euill*] *A1*; *Enter the two Angels B1. After this stage direction B1 repeats I.i. 75.*
16. these] *B1*; them *A1.*
19. makes men] *A1*; make them *B1.* trust] *A1*; vse *B1.*
21. of wealth] *B1*; wealth *A1.*
21.1. *Ex. An.*] *B1*; *in A1 the stage direction "exeunt" is placed after line 22.*
22. Of] *A1*; *not in B1.*
24. Mephastophilis] *A2, A3*; Mephastophilus *A1*; Mephostophilis *B1.*
25. God] *A1*; power *B1.*   me? Faustus] *B1*; thee Faustus? *A1.*

26. Come Mephastophilis] *A2, A3*; Come Mephastophilus *A1*; Mepho: come *B1.*
28. Mephastophilis] *A2, A3*; Mephastophilus *A1*; Mephostophilis *B1.*
29.] *Mephostophilis B2; Mephastophile A1; Mephostophile B1.*
29.1. *Meph*] *A1*; *Mephosto B1.*
30. me] *B1*; *not in A1.*   sayes] *A1*; saith *B1.*
31. he liues] *B1*; I liue *A1.*
34. now] *B1*; Faustus *B1.*
36. great] *A1*; *not in B1.*
37. wil] *A1*; must *B1.*
38. Mephastophilis] *A2, A3*; Mephastophilus *A1*; Mephostophilis *B1.*
38-39.] *Lineation as in B1; prose in A1.*
41. why] *B1*; *not in A1.*
43. Why] *B1*; *not in A1.*   torture] *B1*; tortures *A1.*   others] *A1*; other *B1.*
48. Mephastophilis] *A2, A3*; Mephastophilus *A1*; Mephostophilis *B1.*   I giue it thee] *A1*; I'le giue it him *B1.*
49. Then stabbe thine] *A1*; Then Faustus stab thy *B1.*

53. Mephastophilis] *A2, A3;* Mephastophilus *A1;* Mephosto *B1.*
53-55.] *Verse as here A1; prose in B1.*
54. I cut mine arme] *A1;* Faustus hath cut his arme *B1.*   my proper] *A1;* his proper *B1.*
55. Assure my] *A1;* assures his *B1.*
57. the] *A1;* this *B1.*
59. thou must] *A1; not in B1.*
60-62. *Verse as here B1; printed as prose in A1.*
61. will] *A1;* do *B1.*   Mephastophilis] *A1;* Mephostophilis *B1.*
67. ah] *A1;* O *B1.*
69.1. *Mephastophilis] A1; Mephostoph B1.*
    a chafer of coles] *A1; the Chafer of Fire B1.*
70. Heres...Faustus] *A1;* See Faustus here is fire *B1.*
73. O] *A1; not in B1.*   Aside] *Dyce; not in A1, B1.*
78. God] *A1;* heauen *B1.*   thee] *A1;* me *B1.*
80. O yes] *B1; not in A1.*   euen heere] *B1;* here in this place A1.
82.2. with] *A1; not in B1. (B1 has "Enter Mephostophilis" after the departure of the devils.)*
82.3. they dance] *B1; and daunce A1.*
83. Speake Mephastophilis, what...shewe?] *A1;* What...shew? speake Mephostophilis *B1.*
84. mind] *B1;* minde withall *A1.*
85. let thee see] *B1;* to shewe thee *A1.*
86. such] *B1;* vp *A1.*
88.] *A1; not in B1.*
89. Here Mephastophilis] *A1;* Then Mephostophilis *B1.*
92. articles prescrib'd] *A1;* Couenants, and Articles *B1.*
94. made] *A1;* both *B1.*
95. them] *A1;* it Mephostophilis *B1.*
98-9. *at his commaund] A1; be by him commanded B1.*
98, 100. *Mephastophilis] A1; Mephostophilis B1.*
104. *forme or shape] A1; shape and forme B1.*
107. *Mephastophilis] A1, B1.*
109. *these Articles aboue written being] B1; the articles aboue written A1.*

110. *or goods] A1; not in B1.*
114. on't] *A1;* of it *B1.*
115. So] *B1; not in A1.*   me] *B1; not in A1.*
116. with] *A1; not in B1.*
119. so...else] *B1; not in A1.*
123. but] *B1;* for *A1.*
124. there] *B1; not in A1.*
125. to be short] *B1;* to conclude *A1.*
128. Come] *A1; not in B1.*
130. thinkst thou then] *A1;* dost thou think *B1.*
132. Wherein] *A1;* In which *B1.*
134-5. fond to imagine, / That] *B1;* fond, / To imagine, that *A1.*
136. Tush] *A1;* No *B1.*
137. But] *B1;* But Faustus *A1.*
138. I tell thee] *B1; not in A1.*   and now] *B1;* and am now *A1.*
139. Nay] *B1;* How? now in hell? nay *A1.*   damn'd] *B1;* damnd here *A1.*
140. sleeping...disputing] *B1;* walking, disputing, &c. *A1.*
141. leauing this] *B1;* leauing off this *A1.*
144-46.] *A1; not in B1.*
147-8. Well...name] *A1;* Well Faustus, thou shalt haue a wife *B1.*
148.1. *Enter...fier workes] A1; He fetches in a woman deuill B1.*
149-50.] *A1; B1 has instead:* Faust. What sight is this? **Meph.** Now Faustus wilt thou haue a wife? **Faust.** Here's a hot whore indeed; no, I'le no wife.
151. Tut Faustus] *A1; not in B1.*
152. If] *A1;* And if *B1.*   no more] *B1;* more *A1.*
156. Be] *A1;* Were *B1.*
159. Hold] *A1;* Here *B1.*   peruse it thorowly] *A1;* and peruse it well *B1.*
162. whirlewindes...lightning] *A1;* Thunder, Whirle-winds, Storme and Lightning *B1.*
164. armour] *A1;* harnesse *B1.*
165. desirst] *A1;* commandst *B1.*
166. Mephastophilis] Mephastophilus *A1;* Mephostophilis *B1.*
166-79.1.] *A1; B1 has instead:* Faust. Thankes Mephostophilis for this sweete booke. / This will I keepe, as chary as my life. *Exeunt.*

179.2. *Exeunt] Ellis; in A1, II.i. is continuous with what in the present edition is identified as II.iii, and II.ii. is placed immediately after the Chorus to IV; in B1, II.i. and II.iii. are separated by eleven lines taken from the Chorus to III (lines 1-6, 20, 22-25).*

ACT II Scene ii

1-34. *] A1; not in B1. In A1, this scene is printed after the Chorus to IV and is followed without a break by a second comic scene which is placed in the present edition as III.ii. In B1, a loosely parallel scene to II.ii. is printed after the pageant of the Seven Deadly Sins (II.iii. in the present edition).*

ACT II Scene iii

0.1. *Enter...Mephostophilis] B1; not in A1, where there is no break between this scene and II.i. In B1, this scene and II.i. are separated by the bizarre expedient of a chorus consisting of lines 1-6, 20, and 22-25 of the Chorus to Act III (which subsequently appears complete in B1).*
2. Mephastophilis] Mephastophilus *A1*; Mephostophilis *B1*.
4. why Faustus] *A1*; 'Twas thine owne seeking Faustus, thanke thy selfe *B1*.
5. Thinkst] *A1*; But think'st *B1*.
6. I tel thee] *A1*; I tell thee Faustus *B1*.
   faire as thou] *A1*; faire / As thou *B1*.
8. 'Twas] *B1*; It was *A1*.
9. therefore is man] *A1*; then he's *B1*.
10. it were] *A1*; Heauen was *B1*.
11.1. *Enter...Angel] A1; Enter the two Angels B1.*
12. Faustus, repent yet,] *A1*; Faustus repent, yet *B1*.
16. Ay] I *A1*; Yea *B1*.
17.1. *Exeunt Angels] exeunt A1; Exit Angels B1.*
18. hearts so] *A1*; heart is *B1*.
20-21.] *A1*; not in B1.
22. Poyson, gunnes] *A1*; Swords, poyson *B1*.
24. done the deed] *B1*; slaine my self *A1*.
30. Mephastophilis] *A1*; Mephostophilis *B1*.
32. nere repent] *A1*; not repent *B1*.
33. Mephastophilis] *A1*; Mephostophilis *B1*.
34. reason] *B1*; argue *A1*.
35. Speake] *B1*; Tel me *A1*.
   Spheares] *B1*; heauens *A1*.
38. heauens] *B1*; spheares *A1*.
39.] *B1*; not in A1.
40. Spheares] *B1*; orbe *A1*.
41. And iontly] *B1*; And Faustus all iointly *A1*.
42. termine] *B1*; terminine *A1*.
44. erring] *A1*; euening *B1*.
45. tell me] *A1*; not in B1.
47. ioyntly] *A1*; not in B1.
50. These slender questions] *B1*; Tush, these slender trifles *A1*.
51. Mephastophilis] *A2, A3*; Mephastophilus *A1*; Mephostophilis *B1*.
53. The] *A1*; That the *B1*.
54. Saturne] *B1*; as Saturne *A1*.
56. Tush] *A1*; not in B1.
57. suppositions] *A1*; questions *B1*.
58. *Intelligentia] B1; Intelligentij A1.*
63-64.] *B1*; not in A1.
65. Resolue me then in this one] *B1*; Well, resolue me in this *A1*.   are not] *B1*; haue wee not *A1*.
69. now] *B1*; not in A1.
71. Mephastophilis] *A2, A3*; Mephastophilus *A1*; Mephostophilis *B1*.
72. Faustus] *B1*; for I will not tell thee *A1*.
73. haue I not] *A1*; haue not I *B1*.
74-75. Kingdome. / This is: Thou art damn'd, think thou of hell] *B1*; kingdome, but this is, / Thinke thou on hell Faustus, for thou art damnd *A1*.
80.1. *Enter...euil Angel] A3; Enter the two Angels B1.*
81. can] *A1*; will *B1*.
82. shall] *A1*; will *B1*.
83.1. *Ex. A.] B1; Exeunt A1.*
84. Ah...Sauiour] *A1*; O Christ my Sauiour, my Sauiour *B1*.
85. seeke] *A1*; Helpe *B1*.
85.1. *Mephastophilis] A2, A3; Mephastophilus A1; Mephostophilis B1.*
88. what] *B1*; who *A1*.   terribly] *B1*; terrible *A1*.

90. away] *A1*; *not in B1*.
91. come] *A1*; are come *B1*.
92. talkst of] *A1*; calst on *B1*.
93. of...of] *A1*; on...on *B1*. *(All of 93-94 is spoken by Lucifer in the A-text, in which Belzebub is a mute throughout.)*
94. of] *A1*; *not in B1*.
95. I] *A1*; Faustus *B1*.   me in] *A1*; him for *B1*.
97-99.] *A1*; *not in B1*.
100-01. So...it] *B1*; Do so, and we will highly gratifie thee *A1*.
102. from hel] *A1*; from hell in person *B1*.
103. behold] *B1*; see al *A1*.
104. appeare to thee] *B1*; appeare *A1*. owne proper shapes and likenesse] *B1*; proper shapes *A1*.
105. pleasing vnto] *A1*; pleasant to *B1*.
107. or] *B1*; nor *A1*.
107-8. marke the shew, go Mephostoph. fetch them in] *B1*; marke this shew, talke of the diuel, and nothing else: come away *A1*.
109. question] *B1*; examine *A1*. names] *B1*; seueral names *A1*.
111. That...soone] *B1*; *not in A1*.
114-15. next...Necke] *B1*; *not in A1*.
115. Then] *B1*; or *A1*.   lippes] *A1*; *not in B1*.
115-16. And...list] *B1*; indeede I doe, what doe I not? *A1*.
117. smell] *B1*; scent *A1*.   a word more] *B1*; an other worde *A1*. *(B1 adds for a Kings ransome, which I take to be an anticipation of II.iii. 156.)*
117-18. vnlesse the ground be] *B1*; except the ground were *A1*.
119. Thou...indeed] *B1*; *not in A1*.
121-22. old leatherne] *A1*; leather *B1*. haue] *A1*; now obtaine *B1*.
122-23. I would desire...turnd] *A1*; this house, you and all, should turne *B1*.
124. vppe...chest] *A1*; safe into my Chest *B1*.
125. What] *A1*; And what *B1*.
126-38.] *In A1, Wrath is the third Sin and Envy the fourth; in B1 the order is reversed.*
127. half] *A1*; *not in B1*.
128. I] *A1*; *not in B1*.   this] *A1*; these *B1*.

129. had no body] *A1*; could get none *B1*.
132.] *A1*; And what art thou the fift? *B1*.
134. were] *A1*; *not in B1*.
136. through] *A1*; ouer *B1*.
139. Away enuious rascall: what] *A1*; Out enuious wretch: But what *B1*.   fift] *A1*; fourth *B1*.
140. who I sir] *A1*; *not in B1*.
141. bare] *A1*; small *B1*.
142. buyes me] *B1*; is *A1*.
143. O] *A1*; *not in B1*.   parentage] *A1*; Pedigree *B1*.   grandfather] *A1*; father *B1*.
144. my grandmother] *A1*; and my mother *B1*.
146. O but my god-mother] *A1*; But my god-mother, O *B1*.   iolly] *A1*; ancient *B1*.
147. and welbeloued...Citie] *A1*; *not in B1*.
148. mistresse] *A1*; *not in B1*.
150. No...victualls] *A1*; Not I *B1*.
153. I am] *A1*; Hey ho; I am *B1*.
153-56. where...Leachery] *A1*; *not in B1*.
156. Ile not] *A1*; hey ho: I'le not *B1*.
157. What] *A1*; And what *B1*.
158. I sir?] *A1*; I I sir? *B1*.
161. Away, to hel, to hel] *A1*; Away to hell, away on piper *B1*. *(In A1, this line lacks any speech prefix.)*
161.1. *exeunt the sinnes*] *A1*; *Ex. the 7 sinnes B1*.
162.] *A1*; *not in B1*.
163. O...soule] *A1*; O how this sight doth delight my soule *B1*.
164. Tut] *A1*; But *B1*.
165. againe] *A1*; againe safe *B1*.
167. Thou] *A1*; Faustus, thou *B1*. I...midnight] *A1*; at midnight I will send for thee *B1*.
167-68. in mean time take this booke, peruse] *A1*; Meane while peruse this booke, and view *B1*.
170. Great] *A1*; *not in B1*.
172. Farewel...diuel] *A1*; Now Faustus farewell *B1*.
173. Mephastophilis] *A1*; Mephostophilis *B1*.
173.1. *exeunt omnes*] *A1*; *Exeunt omnes, seuerall waies B1*.

ACT III

ACT III, CHORUS.

Enter the Chorus [Wagner].

Wagner.

    Learned Faustus,
    To know the secrets of astronomy
    Graven in the book of Jove's high firmament,
    Did mount him up to scale Olympus' top,
5   Where sitting in a chariot burning bright,
    Drawn by the strength of yoked dragons' necks,
    He views the clouds, the planets and the stars,
    The tropic, zones, and quarters of the sky,
    From the bright circle of the horned moon
10   Even to the height of *primum mobile*;
    And whirling round with this circumference
    Within the concave compass of the pole,
    From east to west his dragons swiftly glide,
    And in eight days did bring him home again.
15   Not long he stay'd within his quiet house
    To rest his bones after his weary toil,
    But new exploits do hale him out again,

---

4. *to scale Olympus' top*] i.e. to ascend to the dwelling-place of the gods.

5. *a chariot burning bright*] This fiery chariot is derived from *EFB*, ch. 21, a passage which appears to contain parodic echoes of the vision of the divine chariot-throne in Ezekiel 1:13-28. Mystical (and magical) expositions of this vision were an important component of the Kabbalah, Christian appropriations of which gave added authority to the magical doctrines espoused by figures like Agrippa and the historical Doctor Faustus. See Gershom Scholem, *Kabbalah*, pp. 13-16, 30, and (on the Christian "Cabala"), 196-201.

8. *tropics, zones*] The tropics of Cancer and of Capricorn, the arctic and antarctic circles and the equator divided the celestial sphere into five belts or zones. See Manilius, *Astronomica* I. 561-602.   *quarters*] Traditional astronomy also quartered the celestial sphere with two other circles which passed through its north and south poles: the solstitial colure, which intersects the two tropics at the solstitial points (those at which the ecliptic meets the tropics); and the equinoctial colure, which intersects the equator at the equinoctial points (those at which the ecliptic crosses the equator). See Manilius, *Astronomica* I. 603-32.

And mounted then upon a dragon's back
That with his wings did part the subtle air,
He now is gone to prove cosmography, 20
That measures coasts and kingdoms of the earth,
And as I guess, will first arrive at Rome
To see the Pope, and manner of his court,
And take some part of holy Peter's feast,
The which this day is highly solemniz'd. 25

Exit.

Act III, Scene i.

Enter Faustus and Mephastophilis.

Faustus.
Having now, my good Mephastophilis,
Pass'd with delight the stately town of Trier,
Environ'd round with airy mountain tops,
With walls of flint, and deep entrenched lakes,
Not to be won by any conquering prince; 5
From Paris next, coasting the realm of France,
We saw the river Main fall into Rhine,
Whose banks are set with groves of fruitful vines;
Then up to Naples, rich Campania,
Whose buildings, fair and gorgeous to the eye 10
(The streets straightforth and pav'd with finest brick),

---

19. *subtle*] rarified.
20. *to prove cosmography*] to put geography to the test. Cosmography was sometimes thought of as a science which maps the universe as a whole, thus incorporating geography and astronomy.

2. *Trier*] a city on the Moselle river, capital of an electoral state of the Holy Roman Empire which under the rule of Elector-Archbishop Johann von Schönenburg was subjected during the 1580s and 1590s to a violent wave of witch-hunts (see R. H. Robbins, *The Encyclopaedia of Witchcraft and Demonology*, pp. 514-16).
9. *Campania*] in ancient usage, the plain surrounding the city of Capua; since medieval times, Naples has been the principal city of this region. (In modern Italy the name Campania is applied to a much larger area.)

Quarters the town in four equivalents.
There saw we learned Maro's golden tomb,
The way he cut, an English mile in length,
15   Thorough a rock of stone in one night's space.
From thence to Venice, Padua, and the rest,
In midst of which a sumptuous temple stands,
That threats the stars with her aspiring top.
Thus hitherto hath Faustus spent his time.
20   But tell me now, what resting place is this?
Hast thou, as erst I did command,
Conducted me within the walls of Rome?

Meph.

Faustus, I have, and because we will not be unprovided,
I have taken up his Holiness' privy chamber for our use.

Faustus.

25   I hope his Holiness will bid us welcome.

Meph.

Tut, 'tis no matter, man, we'll be bold with his good cheer.
And now my Faustus, that thou may'st perceive
What Rome containeth to delight thee with,
Know that this city stands upon seven hills
30   That underprop the groundwork of the same;
Just through the midst runs flowing Tiber's stream,
With winding banks that cut it in two parts,

13. *Maro*] Virgil, or Publius Vergilius Maro, died at Naples in 19 B.C. In part because his fourth Eclogue was interpreted as a prophecy of the coming of Christ, he acquired a reputation during the medieval period as a necromancer. His supposed tomb stands on the promontory of Posilipo on the Bay of Naples, at the Naples end of a tunnel, nearly half a mile in length, which cuts through the promontory—and which, as Petrarch wrote, "the insipid masses conclude was made by Virgil with magical incantations" ("quod vulgus insulsum a Virgilio magicis cantaminibus factum putant"; qtd. from *Itinerarium syriacum* by Dyce, p. 91).
14. *way*] road. The tunnel is in fact some seven yards wide.
17-18. *sumptuous temple...That threats the stars*] identified in *EFB* as Saint Mark's in Venice. (The "aspiring top" of line 18 would have to be that of the campanile, which stands at some distance from the church.) The lines added after 18 in B are close to the text of *EFB*, ch. 22, p. 35: "He wondered not a little at...the sumptuous church standing therein called Saint Mark's; how all the pavement was set with coloured stones, and all the roof or loft of the church double gilded over."
24. *privy chamber*] the innermost apartment in a palace, as opposed to more or less public reception rooms.

Over the which four stately bridges lean,
That make safe passage to each part of Rome.
Upon the bridge call'd Ponte Angelo   35
Erected is a castle passing strong,
Within whose walls such stores of ordnance are,
And double cannons, fram'd of carved brass,
As match the days within one complete year—
Besides the gates and high pyramides   40
Which Julius Caesar brought from Africa.

Faustus.
Now, by the kingdoms of infernal rule,
Of Styx, Acheron, and the fiery lake
Of ever-burning Phlegethon, I swear
That I do long to see the monuments   45
And situation of bright splendent Rome.
Come therefore, let's away.

Meph.
Nay Faustus, stay: I know you'd fain see the Pope,
And take some part of holy Peter's feast,
Where thou shalt see a troop of bald-pate friars   50
Whose *summum bonum* is in belly-cheer.

Faustus.
Well, I am content to compass then some sport,
And by their folly make us merriment.
Then charm me, that I may be invisible,
To do what I please   55
Unseen of any whilst I stay in Rome.

35-36.] The papal fortress of Castel San Angelo, which incorporates the ancient mausoleum of the emperor Hadrian, stands at the north end of the bridge.
38. *double cannons*] probably cannons of very large calibre (Jump).
40. *pyramides*] the obelisk brought to Rome from Egypt by the emperor Caligula. It was moved in 1586 to its present site in the Piazza San Pietro. The word is pronounced with four syllables, as in *The Massacre at Paris* ii. 43-46 ("Set me to scale the high pyramides..."); as that passage makes clear, it is singular, not plural.
42-46.] Greg remarks that it is "an extraordinary piece of rhodomontade" for Faustus to swear "by the three rivers of Hades—that he wants to see the sights!"
51. summum bonum] highest good.
52. *compass*] contrive.

[Mephastophilis charms him.]

Meph.
So, Faustus: now
Do what thou wilt, thou shalt not be discern'd.

Sound a sennet. Enter the Pope and the Cardinal of Lorraine to the banquet, with Friars attending.

Pope.
My lord of Lorraine, will't please you draw near?

Faustus.
60   Fall to, and the devil choke you and you spare.

Pope.
How now, who's that which spake? Friars, look about!

Friar.
Here's nobody, if it like your Holiness.

Pope.
My lord, here is a dainty dish was sent me from the Bishop of Milan.

Faustus.
65   I thank you, sir.

[Snatch it.]

Pope.
How now, who's that which snatched the meat from me? Will no man look? My lord, this dish was sent me from the Cardinal of Florence.

Faustus.
You say true, I'll ha'it.

[Snatch it.]

Pope.
70   What, again! My lord, I'll drink to your grace.

58.1. sennet] a flourish on the trumpet to announce a ceremonial entrance.
60. *and you spare*] if you spare.

Faustus.
I'll pledge your grace.

[Snatch it.]

Lorraine.
My lord, it may be some ghost newly crept out of purgatory come to beg a pardon of your Holiness.

Pope.
It may be so. Friars, prepare a dirge to lay the fury of this ghost. Once again, my lord, fall to.   75

The Pope crosseth himself.

Faustus.
What, are you crossing of your self? Well, use that trick no more, I would advise you.

Cross again.

Faustus.
Well, there's the second time. Aware the third, I give you fair warning.

Cross again, and Faustus hits him a box of the ear, and they all run away.

Come on, Mephastophilis, what shall we do?   80
Meph.
Nay, I know not; we shall be cursed with bell, book and candle.
Faustus.
How? Bell, book and candle, candle, book and bell,
Forward and backward, to curse Faustus to hell.

---

74. *dirge*] originally "dirige", the first word of the antiphon at matins in the Office of the Dead ("Dirige, Domine, Deus meus, in conspectu tuo viam meum": "Direct, O Lord, my God, my way in thy sight" [Ps. 5:8]). Hence, as Greg remarks, used correctly here, but incorrectly at line 94 below.
81-82. *bell, book and candle*] At the end of the ritual of excommunication, the bell is tolled, the book closed, and the candle extinguished. As Ward noted, this ritual is confused, both here and in *EFB*, with the office of exorcism.

85   Anon you shall hear a hog grunt, a calf bleat, and an ass bray,
        Because it is Saint Peter's holy day!

Enter all the Friars to sing the dirge.

Friar.
        Come brethren, let's about our business with good devotion.

[They] sing this:

Cursed be he that stole away his Holiness' meat from the table.
Maledicat dominus!
90   *Cursed be he that struck his Holiness a blow on the face.*
Maledicat dominus!
Cursed be he that took Friar Sandelo a blow on the pate.
Maledicat dominus!
Cursed be he that disturbeth our holy dirge.
95   *Maledicat dominus!*
Cursed be he that took away his Holiness' wine.
Maledicat dominus! Et omnes sancti! Amen.

[Faustus and Mephastophilis] beat the Friars and fling
fireworks among them, and so exeunt.

Act III, Scene ii.

Enter Robin and Rafe with a silver goblet.

Robin.
        Come Rafe, did not I tell thee we were for ever made
by this Doctor Faustus' book? *Ecce signum*, here's a
simple purchase for horse-keepers! Our horses shall eat
no hay as long as this lasts.

Enter the Vintner.

89. Maledicat dominus] "May the Lord curse him."

2. Ecce signum] "Behold the proof."

Rafe.
 But Robin, here comes the Vintner.   5
Robin.
 Hush, I'll gull him supernaturally. Drawer, I hope all is
 paid. God be with you; come Rafe.
Vintner.
 Soft, sir: a word with you. I must yet have a goblet paid
 from you ere you go.
Robin.
 I a goblet? Rafe, I a goblet? I scorn you, and you are   10
 but a etc. I a goblet? Search me!
Vintner.
 I mean so, sir, with your favor.

                    [Searches Robin.]

Robin.
 How say you now?
Vintner.
 I must say somewhat to your fellow. You, sir.
Rafe.
 Me, sir? Me, sir! Search your fill! Now, sir, you may be   15
 ashamed to burden honest men with a matter of truth.
Vintner.
 Well, t'one of you hath this goblet about you.
Robin.
 You lie, drawer, 'tis afore me. Sirrah you, I'll teach ye to
 impeach honest men: stand by, I'll scour you for a goblet.
 Stand aside, you had best, I charge you in the name of   20
 Belzebub! Look to the goblet, Rafe.

---

6. *Drawer*] an insult: Robin pretends to mistake the Vintner or innkeeper with his employee
the tapster or drawer who serves the customers.
11. *etc.*] an invitation to the actor to improvise.
16. *a matter of truth*] "charge affecting their reputation for honesty" (Jump).

Vintner.
>What mean you, sirrah?

Robin.
>I'll tell you what I mean.

He reads.

>*Sanctabulorum periphrasticon*—Nay, I'll tickle you,
25   Vintner! Look to the goblet, Rafe. *Polypragmos Bel-*
>*seborams framanto pacostiphos tostu Mephastophilis*, etc.

*Enter Mephastophilis; sets squibs at their backs; they
run about.*

Vintner.
>*O nomine Domine!* What mean'st thou, Robin? Thou
>hast no goblet!

Rafe.
>*Peccatum peccatorum!* Here's thy goblet, good Vintner!

Robin.
30   *Misericordia pro nobis!* What shall I do? Good devil, for-
>give me now, and I'll never rob thy library more!

Meph.
>Monarch of hell, under whose black survey
>Great potentates do kneel with awful fear,
>Upon whose altars thousand souls do lie,
35   How am I vexed with these villains' charms!
>From Constantinople am I hither come
>Only for pleasure of these damned slaves.

Robin.
>How, from Constantinople? You have had a great jour-
>ney, will you take sixpence in your purse to pay for your
40   supper, and be gone?

24-26.] Robin's incantation is gibberish.
26.1. squibs] fireworks.
27-30.] garbled scraps of liturgical Latin.

Meph.

Well villains, for your presumption, I transform thee into
an ape, and thee into a dog, and so be gone!

Exit.

Robin.

How, into an ape? That's brave, I'll have fine sport with
the boys; I'll get nuts and apples enow.

Rafe.

And I must be a dog.   45

Robin.

I'faith, thy head will never be out of the pottage pot.

Exeunt.

N O T E S   T O
A C T   I I I

ACT III CHORUS

0.1. *Enter the Chorus*] *B1*; *enter Wagner
solus A1.*
2. know] *A1*; find *B1. 1 and 2 are a single
line in B1.*
4. him vp] *B1*; himselfe *A1*.
5. Where sitting] *B1*; Being seated *A1*.
6. yoked] *B1*; yoky *A1*.
7-19.] *B1*; *not in A1*.
8. tropics] *Greg*; Tropick *B1*.
21.] *B1*; *not in A1*.
25. The which] *B1*; That to *A1*.
25.1. *Exit*] *B1*; *exit Wagner A1*.

ACT III Scene i

0.1. *Mephastophilis*] *A3*; *Mephostophilus
A1*; *Mephostophilis B1*.
1. Mephostophilis] *A3*; Mephastophilus
A1; Mephostophilis *B1*.
7. Rhine] *A1*; Rhines *B1*.
12.] *A1*; *not in B1*.
15. Thorough] *A1*; Through *B1*.

16. rest] *A1*; East *B1*.
17. midst] *A1*; one *B1*.
18.] *A1*; *B1. After this line B1 adds:*
Whose frame is paued with sundry
coloured stones, / And roof't aloft with
curious worke in gold.
23-24.] *A1*; *B1 has instead:* I haue my
Faustus, and for proofe thereof, / This is
the goodly Palace of the Pope: / And
cause we are no common guests, / I chuse
his priuy chamber for our vse.
26. Tut...cheare] *A1*; All's one, for wee'l
be bold with his Venson *B1*.
27. And] *A1*; But *B1*.
28. containeth...with] *A1*; containes for to
delight thine eyes *B1*.
30. vunderprop] *B1*; vnderprops *A1*.
31-32.] *B1*; *not in A1*.
33. foure] *A1*; two *B1*.
34. make] *B1*; makes *A1*.
35. Ponte] *Dyce*; Ponto *A1, B1*.
37-39. Within...yeare] *A1*; *B1 has instead:*
Where thou shalt see such store of Ordinance, / As that the double Cannons

Notes to Act III

forg'd of brasse, / Do watch [*B2*: match] the number of the daies contain'd, / Within the compasse of one compleat yeare

40. Besides] *A1*; Beside *B1*.
41. Which] *A1*; That *B1*.
43. Acheron] *A1*; of Acheron *B1*.
48. Nay...Pope] *A1*; Nay stay my Faustus: I know you'd see the Pope *B1*.
50-97.02.] *A1*; *see Appendix I for the revised version of this passage that appears in B1.*
54-58.] *Printed as prose in A1.*
56.1.] *Dyce; not in A1.*
58.1. *sennet*] Sonnet *A1*.
69.1, 71.1.] *Not in A1.*

ACT III Scene ii

In A1, III.i. is immediately followed by the Chorus to IV, by the comic scene printed in this edition as II.ii., and (without a break) by this scene. In B1 a loosely parallel cup-stealing scene (for which see Appendix I) is printed, as here, immediately following the Papal banquet.

12.1. *Not in A1.*
26.1. *Mephastophilis*] *A2, A3*; Mephostophilis *A1*.
27. Domine] *A1*; Domini *Dyce*.

31.] *Followed in A1 by the stage direction "Enter to them Meph." and by this speech:* **Meph.** Vanish vilaines, th'one like an Ape, an other like a Beare, the third an Asse, for doing this enterprise. *The scene thus has two distinct endings—a fact which can itself be understood in at least two distinct ways. (a) Lines 26.1.-31 (plus "Vanish vilaines...enterprise") constituted a pre-1602 ending to this scene; lines 32-46 may have been a pre-1602 revision intended to replace the earlier passage in its entirety. (b) Lines 32-46 may have been intended to replace only the single speech "Vanish vilaines...enterprise." Because it requires fewer alterations to the text, I have chosen the second alternative. It is of course possible in either case that lines 32-46 may represent a draft of the 1602 revision—a subsequent version of which appears in the B-text.*
46.1. *exeunt*] *Printed in the margin after line 45 in A1.*

ACT IV

ACT IV, CHORUS.

Enter Chorus.

Chorus.

When Faustus had with pleasure ta'en the view
Of rarest things and royal courts of kings,
He stay'd his course, and so returned home,
Where such as bare his absence but with grief,
I mean his friends and nearest companions,   5
Did gratulate his safety with kind words,
And in their conference of what befell
Touching his journey through the world and air
They put forth questions of astrology,
Which Faustus answer'd with such learned skill   10
As they admir'd and wonder'd at his wit.
Now is his fame spread forth in every land;
Amongst the rest the Emperor is one,
Carolus the Fifth, at whose palace now

---

14. *Carolus the Fifth*] Charles V (1500-1558), King of Spain and Holy Roman Emperor from 1518 and 1519 respectively until his abdication in 1555.

14-15. *at whose palace now / Faustus is feasted*] The historical Doctor Faustus never made an appearance at the imperial court. Contemporary *magi*, however, had connections with the courts both of the emperor Maximilian (Charles V's grandfather and immediate predecessor) and of Charles V. The Abbot Johannes Trithemius (1462-1516), author of the first account, written in 1507, of the historical Doctor Faustus, and himself suspected of practising demonic magic, addressed his *Liber octo quaestionum* (1508) to Maximilian. Several decades later, Martin Luther told of a magician, identified in one report of the conversation as Trithemius, who entertained Maximilian by having demons take on the forms of Alexander the Great and other monarchs (*Tischreden* no. 4450, *WATr* iv. 319). Another humanist *magus*, Henricus Cornelius Agrippa (1486-1535) served Maximilian in diplomatic missions from 1510 or 1511 until at least 1515, and in 1529 was engaged by Margaret of Savoy, regent of the Netherlands, as archivist and historiographer to the emperor Charles V. This appointment was blazoned on the title pages of Agrippa's published works, among them *De incertitudine et vanitate scientiarum et artium atque excellentia verbi dei declamatio* (1530)—which, however, contains harsh criticism both of them "which nowadays be called kings, emperors, and princes" (*Of the Vanitie* [1569], ed. Dunn, ch. 55, p. 170) and also of the vices of royal courts (ch. 68-71). Like his friend and mentor Trithemius, Agrippa was

15   Faustus is feasted 'mongst his noblemen.
       What there he did in trial of his art
       I leave untold, your eyes shall see perform'd.

                 Exit.

Act IV, Scene i.

Enter Emperor, Faustus, and a Knight, with attendants.

Emperor.
      Master Doctor Faustus, I have heard strange report of thy
      knowledge in the black art, how that none in my empire,
      nor in the whole world, can compare with thee for the rare
      effects of magic: they say thou hast a familiar spirit, by
5   whom thou canst accomplish what thou list. This therefore
      is my request: that thou let me see some proof of thy skill,
      that mine eyes may be witnesses to confirm what mine ears
      have heard reported; and here I swear to thee, by the
      honour of mine imperial crown, that whatever thou doest,
10   thou shalt be no ways prejudiced or endamaged.

Knight. [aside]
      I'faith, he looks much like a conjurer.

Faustus.
      My gracious sovereign, though I must confess myself far
      inferior to the report men have published, and nothing
      answerable to the honor of your imperial Majesty, yet for
15   that love and duty binds me thereunto, I am content to
      do whatsoever your Majesty shall command me.

famous for his "shadows" (see note to I.i. 118-19). The historian André Thevet felt it necessary to refute the opinion that Charles V's victories had been won by Agrippa's magic (*Les
vrais pourtraits et vies des hommes illustres* [1584], ii. fol. 542v-543); the same boast, made
on behalf of Doctor Faustus, was refuted by Philipp Melancthon in a lecture given at Wittenberg in the mid-1550s (Palmer and More, p. 103).

10. *endamaged*] harmed.
13-14. *nothing answerable*] quite unequal.
14-15. *for that*] because.

Emperor.
> Then Doctor Faustus, mark what I shall say.
> As I was sometime solitary set
> Within my closet, sundry thoughts arose
> About the honor of mine ancestors: 20
> How they had won by prowess such exploits,
> Got such riches, subdu'd so many kingdoms,
> As we that do succeed, or they that shall
> Hereafter possess our throne shall,
> I fear me, never attain to that degree   25
> Of high renown and great authority;
> Amongst which kings is Alexander the Great,
> Chief spectacle of the world's pre-eminence,
> The bright shining of whose glorious acts
> Lightens the world with his reflecting beams,   30
> As when I hear but motion made of him
> It grieves my soul I never saw the man.
> If therefore thou, by cunning of thine art,
> Canst raise this man from hollow vaults below
> Where lies entomb'd this famous conqueror,   35
> And bring with him his beauteous paramour,
> Both in their right shapes, gesture, and attire
> They us'd to wear during their time of life,
> Thou shalt both satisfy my just desire
> And give me cause to praise thee whilst I live.   40

Faustus.
> My gracious lord, I am ready to accomplish your request,
> so far forth as by art and power of my spirit I am able
> to perform.

Knight. [aside]
> I'faith that's just nothing at all.

---

19. *closet*] study, inner chamber.
28. *pre-eminence*] pre-eminent men.
31. *motion*] mention.

Faustus.

45   But if it like your Grace, it is not in my ability to present
before your eyes the true substantial bodies of those two
deceased princes, which long since are consumed to dust.

Knight. [aside]
Ay, marry Master Doctor, now there's a sign of grace in
you when you will confess the truth.

Faustus.

50   But such spirits as can lively resemble Alexander and his
paramour shall appear before your Grace, in that manner
that they best lived in, in their most flourishing estate, which
I doubt not shall sufficiently content your imperial Majesty.

Emperor.
Go to, Master Doctor, let me see them presently.

Knight.

55   Do you hear, Master Doctor? You bring Alexander and
his paramour before the Emperor?

Faustus.
How then, sir?

Knight.
I'faith, that's as true as Diana turned me to a stag.

Faustus.
No sir, but when Actaeon died, he left the horns for you.

60   Mephastophilis, be gone.

Exit Mephastophilis.

Knight.
Nay, and you go to conjuring, I'll be gone.

Exit Knight.

Faustus.
I'll meet with you anon for interrupting me so. Here they

58-59. *Diana, Actaeon*] Actaeon, a hunter, witnessed the goddess Diana and her nymphs
bathing; the goddess transformed him into a stag and he was torn to pieces by his own dogs.
See Ovid, *Metamorphoses* III. 155-252.
62. *meet with*] get even with.

are, my gracious lord.

Enter Mephastophilis with Alexander and his paramour.

Emperor.
Master Doctor, I heard this lady while she lived had a
wart or mole in her neck. How shall I know whether it   65
be so or no?

Faustus.
Your highness may boldly go and see.

[Emperor does so; then spirits exeunt.]

Emperor.
Sure these are no spirits, but the true substantial bodies
of these two deceased princes.

Faustus.
Will't please your highness now to send for the knight   70
that was so pleasant with me here of late?

Emperor.
One of you call him forth.

Enter the Knight with a pair of horns on his head.

How now, sir knight? Why, I had thought thou had'st been a
bachelor, but now I see thou hast a wife, that not only gives
thee horns but makes thee wear them. Feel on thy head!   75

Knight.
Thou damned wretch and execrable dog,
Bred in the concave of some monstrous rock,
How dar'st thou thus abuse a gentleman?
Villain, I say, undo what thou hast done!

Faustus.
O not so fast, sir; there's no haste but good. Are you   80
remembered how you crossed me in my conference with

---

77. *Bred...rock*] The line is borrowed from *2 Tamburlaine* III.ii. 89: "Fenc'd with the concave
of a monstrous rock".
80. *there's...good*] a common proverb: "No haste but good (speed)." See Tilley H199.

the Emperor? I think I have met with you for it.

Emperor.
Good Master Doctor, at my entreaty release him. He hath done penance sufficient.

Faustus.
85 My gracious lord, not so much for the injury he offered me here in your presence, as to delight you with some mirth, hath Faustus worthily requited this injurious knight; which being all I desire, I am content to release him of his horns. And sir knight, hereafter speak well of scholars. Mephas-
90 tophilis, transform him straight. Now, my good lord, having done my duty, I humbly take my leave.

Emperor.
Farewell, Master Doctor; yet ere you go, expect from me a bounteous reward.

Exeunt Emperor, Knight, and attendants.

Act IV, Scene ii.

Faustus.
Now Mephastophilis, the restless course
That time doth run with calm and silent foot,
Shortening my days and thread of vital life,
Calls for the payment of my latest years.
5 Therefore, sweet Mephastophilis,
Let us make haste to Wittenberg.

Meph.
What, will you go on horseback, or on foot?

Faustus.
Nay, till I am past this fair and pleasant green
I'll walk on foot.

Enter a Horse-courser.

85. *injury*] insult.
93.1.] Faustus and Mephastophilis remain on stage.

Hor.

I have been all this day seeking one Master Fustian; mass,   10
see where he is. God save you, Master Doctor.

Faustus.

What, horse-courser, you are well met.

Hor.

Do you hear, sir? I have brought you forty dollars for
your horse.

Faustus.

I cannot sell him so. If thou lik'st him for fifty, take him.   15

Hor.

Alas sir, I have no more. I pray you, speak for me.

Meph.

I pray you, let him have him. He is an honest fellow, and
he has a great charge, neither wife nor child.

Faustus.

Well, come, give me your money. My boy will deliver him
to you. But I must tell you one thing before you have   20
him: ride him not into the water at any hand.

Hor.

Why sir, will he not drink of all waters?

Faustus.

O yes, he will drink of all waters, but ride him not into
the water. Ride him over hedge or ditch, or where thou
wilt, but not into the water.   25

Hor.

Well, sir, now am I a made man for ever! I'll not leave my
horse for forty. If he had but the quality of hey ding ding,

---

10. *Fustian*] a clownish deformation of "Faustus"; bombast, nonsense.   *mass*] a contraction of "By the Mass".
18. *charge*] burden (of family responsibilities).
21. *at any hand*] under any circumstances.
22. *drink of all waters*] go anywhere (Gill). Compare *Twelfth Night* IV.ii. 57: "I am for all
waters".
26. *leave*] sell.

hey ding ding, I'd make a brave living on him: he has a
buttock so slick as an eel. Well, God-bye sir, your boy will
30   deliver him me. But hark ye sir, if my horse be sick or ill
at ease, if I bring his water to you, you'll tell me what it is?

Faustus.

Away, you villain! What, dost think I am a horse-doctor?

Exit Horse-courser.

What art thou, Faustus, but a man condemn'd to die?
Thy fatal time doth draw to final end;
35   Despair doth drive distrust into my thoughts.
Confound these passions with a quiet sleep:
Tush, Christ did call the thief upon the cross.
Then rest thee, Faustus, quiet in conceit.

Sleeps in his chair.

Enter Horse-courser all wet, crying.

Hor.

Alas, alas, Doctor Fustian, quotha? Mass, Doctor Lopus was
40   never such a doctor: has given me a purgation, has purged me
of forty dollars, I shall never see them more. But yet like an
ass as I was, I would not be ruled by him, for he bade me I
should ride him into no water. Now I, thinking my horse had
some rare quality that he would not have had me know
45   of, I like a venturous youth rid him into the deep pond
at the town's end. I was no sooner in the middle of the
pond, but my horse vanished away, and I sat upon a bottle
of hay, never so near drowning in my life! But I'll seek

29. *God-bye*] a contraction of "God be with you."
31. *water*] urine.
37. *the thief upon the cross*] See Luke 23:43 (which is contradicted, however, by Matt. 27:44).
St. Augustine wrote: "Do not despair—one of the thieves was saved; do not presume—one
of the thieves was damned."
38. *conceit*] state of mind.
39. *Doctor Lopus*] Doctor Roderigo Lopez, a Portuguese marrano and personal physician
to Queen Elizabeth, was accused of attempting to poison the queen, convicted in February
1594 and executed in June (more than a year after Marlowe's death). The allusion indicates
that this scene, in its present form at least, is post-Marlovian.
47. *bottle*] from the French "botte", meaning bundle.

out my doctor, and have my forty dollars again, or I'll
make it the dearest horse. O, yonder is his snipper-snap-   50
per. Do you hear? you, hey-pass, where's your master?

Meph.

Why sir, what would you? You cannot speak with him.

Hor.

But I will speak with him.

Meph.

Why, he's fast asleep; come some other time.

Hor.

I'll speak with him now, or I'll break his glass windows   55
about his ears.

Meph.

I tell thee, he hath not slept this eight nights.

Hor.

And he have not slept this eight weeks I'll speak with him.

Meph.

See where he is, fast asleep.

Hor.

Ay, this is he. God save ye Master Doctor! Master Doc-   60
tor, Master Doctor Fustian, forty dollars, forty dollars for
a bottle of hay!

Meph.

Why, thou seest he hears thee not.

Hor.

So ho, ho! So ho, ho! (*Hallow in his ear.*) No, will you
not wake? I'll make you wake ere I go!   65

   Pull him by the leg, and pull it away.

Alas, I am undone! What shall I do?

50-51. *snipper-snapper*] one who engages in abusive repartee.   *hey-pass*] an expression
used by fairground conjurors or jugglers.
55. *glass windows*] spectacles.
64. *So ho, ho*] a huntsman's cry to direct hounds to the hare (Gill).

Faustus.

    O my leg, my leg! Help, Mephastophilis! Call the officers, my leg, my leg!

Meph.

    Come villain, to the constable.

Hor.

70   O Lord, sir: let me go, and I'll give you forty dollars more.

Meph.

    Where be they?

Hor.

    I have none about me; come to my ostry, and I'll give them you.

Meph.

    Be gone, quickly.

Horse-courser runs away.

Faustus.

    What, is he gone? Farewell he, Faustus has his leg again,
75   and the horse-courser, I take it, a bottle of hay for his labor. Well, this trick shall cost him forty dollars more.

Enter Wagner.

How now, Wagner, what's the news with thee?

Wagner.

    Sir, the Duke of Vanholt doth earnestly entreat your company.

Faustus.

80   The Duke of Vanholt! An honorable gentleman, to whom I must be no niggard of my cunning. Come Mephastophilis, let's away to him.

Exeunt.

72. *ostry*] hostelry, inn.

Act IV, Scene iii.

*Enter to them the Duke, and the Duchess; the Duke
speaks.*

Duke.
Believe me, Master Doctor, this merriment hath much
pleased me.

Faustus.
My gracious lord, I am glad it contents you so well. But it
may be, madam, you take no delight in this. I have heard
that great-bellied women do long for some dainties or   5
other: what is it, madam? Tell me, and you shall have it.

Duchess.
Thanks, good Master Doctor, and for I see your cour-
teous intent to pleasure me, I will not hide from you the
thing my heart desires; and were it now summer, as it is
January, and the dead time of the winter, I would desire   10
no better meat than a dish of ripe grapes.

Faustus.
Alas, madam, that's nothing. Mephastophilis, be gone.

Exit Mephastophilis.

Were it a greater thing than this, so it would content you,
you should have it.

Enter Mephastophilis with the grapes.

Here they be, madam, will't please you taste on them?   15

Duke.
Believe me, Master Doctor, this makes me wonder above
the rest, that being in the dead time of winter, and in the
month of January, how you should come by these grapes.

Faustus.
If it like your Grace, the year is divided into two circles

19-22.] The two "circles" should of course be the northern and southern hemispheres. The
writer who adapted this passage for the stage was at least aware that India and Saba lay to

20   over the whole world, that when it is here winter with us,
       in the contrary circle it is summer with them, as in India,
       Saba, and farther countries in the east; and by means of
       a swift spirit that I have, I had them brought hither, as
       ye see. How do you like them, madam, be they good?

Duchess.

25   Believe me, Master Doctor, they be the best grapes that
       e'er I tasted in my life before.

Faustus.

       I am glad they content you so, madam.

Duke.

       Come, madam, let us in, where you must well reward this
       learned man for the great kindness he hath showed to you.

Duchess.

30   And so I will, my lord, and whilst I live rest beholden for
       this courtesy.

Faustus.

       I humbly thank your Grace.

Duke.

       Come Master Doctor, follow us, and receive your reward.

                           Exeunt.

the east. (Compare *EFB*, ch. 39, p. 59: "...when with us it is winter, in the contrary circle it
is notwithstanding summer, for in India and Saba there falleth or setteth the sun, so that it
is so warm that they have twice a year fruit....") To do him justice, the translator responsible
for *EFB* managed here to trim down an intractably silly passage in his source, the *Historia
von D. Johann Fausten*, ch. 44 (ed. Füssel and Kreutzer, pp. 89-90).
22. *Saba*] the land of the Queen of Sheba, now Yemen; see Milton, *Paradise Lost* IV.
161-63.

NOTES TO
ACT IV

ACT IV CHORUS

Act IV, Chorus. A1; not in B1.

ACT IV Scene i

Act IV, Scene i. A1; see Appendix 1 for the scenes substituted for this one in B1.

17-28.] *Printed as prose in A1, Ormerod and Wortham; verse lineation as here: Dyce, Ward, Tucker Brooke, Kocher, Jump.*

67.1. *Emperor...exeunt*] *This ed.; exit Alex A1.*

93.1. *Exeunt attendants*] *Dyce; exit Emperour A1.*

ACT IV Scene ii

Act IV, Scene ii. A1; see Appendix 1 for the expanded version of this material in

B1. In A1, there is no break between this and the preceding scene.

1-2, 5-9.] *Printed as prose in A1; lineation as here, Dyce.*

6. Wittenberg] Wertenberge *A1.*

26. a made man] *A2, A3;* made man *A1.*

29. god buy] *A1;* God b'wi'ye *Dyce, Ward, Kocher;* good-bye *Ormerod and Wortham.*

32.1. *In A1 the stage direction follows 31.*

33-38. *These lines occur also in B1.*

34. doth drawe to finall] *A1;* drawes to a finall *B1.*

35. into] *B1;* vnto *A1.*

38.1. *Sleeps*] *Sleepe A1.*

44. know] knowne *A1.*

ACT IV Scene iii

Act IV, Scene iii. A1; see Appendix I for the B-version of the Vanholt scene.

ACT V

Act V, Scene i.

Enter Wagner solus.

Wagner.
    I think my master means to die shortly,
    For he hath given to me all his goods;
    And yet methinkes if that death were near
    He would not banquet and carouse and swill
5   Amongst the students, as even now he doth,
    Who are at supper with such belly-cheer
    As Wagner ne'er beheld in all his life.
    See where they come: belike the feast is ended.

Exit.

Enter Faustus with two or three Scholars.

1 Sch.
    Master Doctor Faustus, since our conference about fair
10   ladies, which was the beautiful'st in all the world, we have
    determined with our selves that Helen of Greece was the
    admirablest lady that ever lived. Therefore, Master Doctor,
    if you will do us so much favor as to let us see that peerless
    dame of Greece, whom all the world admires for majesty,
15   we should think ourselves much beholding unto you.

Faustus.
    Gentlemen,
    For that I know your friendship is unfeign'd
    (And Faustus' custom is not to deny
    The just requests of those that wish him well),
20   You shall behold that peerless dame of Greece

---

3. *methinkes*] Modernized spelling would upset the rhythm of this line.

No otherways for pomp and majesty
Than when Sir Paris cross'd the seas with her
And brought the spoils to rich Dardania.
Be silent then, for danger is in words.

Music sounds, and Helen passeth over the stage.

2 Sch.
    Too simple is my wit to tell her praise,   25
    Whom all the world admires for majesty.
3 Sch.
    No marvel though the angry Greeks pursu'd
    With ten years' war the rape of such a queen,
    Whose heavenly beauty passeth all compare.
1 Sch.
    Since we have seen the pride of nature's works,   30
    And only paragon of excellence,

Enter an Old Man.

Let us depart, and for this glorious deed
Happy and blest be Faustus evermore.
Faustus.
    Gentlemen, farewell, the same I wish to you.

Exeunt Scholars.

Old Man.
    Ah Doctor Faustus, that I might prevail   35
    To guide thy steps unto the way of life,
    By which sweet path thou may'st attain the goal
    That shall conduct thee to celestial rest.
    Break heart, drop blood, and mingle it with tears,
    Tears falling from repentant heaviness   40
    Of thy most vile and loathsome filthiness,

23. *Dardania*] Troy, referred to here by the name of the founder of the Trojan dynasty, Dardanus. (Compare Shakespeare, *Troilus and Cressida*, Prologue, line 13: "On Dardan plains".)
28. *rape*] abduction.

The stench whereof corrupts the inward soul
With such flagitious crimes of heinous sins
As no commiseration may expel
45   But mercy, Faustus, of thy Saviour sweet,
Whose blood alone must wash away thy guilt.

Faustus.

Where art thou, Faustus? wretch, what hast thou done?
Damn'd art thou, Faustus, damn'd, despair and die!
Hell claims his right, and with a roaring voice
50   Says, "Faustus, come, thine hour is almost come!"

Enter Mephastophilis, who gives him a dagger.

And Faustus now will come to do thee right.

Old Man.

Ah stay, good Faustus, stay thy desperate steps:
I see an angel hovers o'er thy head,
And with a vial full of precious grace
55   Offers to pour the same into thy soul:
Then call for mercy and avoid despair.

Faustus.

Ah my sweet friend, I feel thy words
To comfort my distressed soul.
Leave me awhile to ponder on my sins.

Old Man.

60   I go, sweet Faustus, but with heavy cheer,
Fearing the ruin of thy hopeless soul.

Exit.

Faustus.

Accursed Faustus, where is mercy now?
I do repent, and yet I do despair:
Hell strives with grace for conquest in my breast;
65   What shall I do to shun the snares of death?

50.1.] There is a similar demonic temptation to suicide in Spenser, *The Faerie Queene* I.ix. 33-54.

Meph.

    Thou traitor, Faustus, I arrest thy soul
    For disobedience to my sovereign lord.
    Revolt, or I'll in piece-meal tear thy flesh!

Faustus.

    I do repent I e'er offended him.
    Sweet Mephastophilis, entreat thy lord   70
    To pardon my unjust presumption,
    And with my blood again I will confirm
    My former vow I made to Lucifer.

Meph.

    Do it then quickly, with unfeigned heart,
    Lest greater danger do attend thy drift.   75

Faustus.

    Torment, sweet friend, that base and crooked age
    That durst dissuade me from thy Lucifer,
    With greatest torments that our hell affords.

Meph.

    His faith is great, I cannot touch his soul.
    But what I may afflict his body with   80
    I will attempt, which is but little worth.

Faustus.

    One thing, good servant, let me crave of thee
    To glut the longing of my heart's desire:
    That I might have unto my paramour
    That heavenly Helen which I saw of late,   85

78.] An echo of Thomas Kyd, *The Spanish Tragedy* (ed. Edwards) II.iii. 48: "With greatest pleasure that our court affords".

85. *heavenly Helen*] The presence of Helen of Troy in the Faustus legend is one sign of that legend's dependence on the patristic legend of Simon Magus, the first-century Gnostic heresiarch and magician. Although in *EFB* Helen's beauty is such that the students "esteem[ed] her rather to be a heavenly than an earthly creature" (ch. 45, p. 65), her appearances there are heavily moralized. But unlike the authors of the *Historia von D. Johann Fausten* and their English translator, Marlowe seems to have been aware of Simon Magus's blasphemous identification of his Helen, a redeemed prostitute, both with Helen of Troy and with the divine Wisdom. Irenaeus (c. 180) states that Simon claimed to be the supreme God, while his companion Helena, whom he had redeemed from prostitution in the city of

Whose sweet embracings may extinguish clean
These thoughts that do dissuade me from my vow,
And keep mine oath I made to Lucifer.

Meph.

Faustus, this, or what else thou shalt desire
90   Shall be perform'd in twinkling of an eye.

Enter Helen.

Faustus.

Was this the face that launch'd a thousand ships
And burnt the topless towers of Ilium?
Sweet Helen, make me immortal with a kiss;
Her lips suck forth my soul, see where it flies!
95   Come Helen, come, give me my soul again;
Here will I dwell, for heaven be in these lips,
And all is dross that is not Helena.

Tyre, "was the first conception of his mind, the mother of all, by whom, in the beginning, he conceived in his mind [the thought] of forming angels and archangels." These subordinate powers, who had subsequently made the world, were ignorant of Simon and jealous of his First Thought, whom they imprisoned in human form, so that "for ages [she] passed in succession from one female body to another, as from vessel to vessel. She was, for example, in that Helen on whose account the Trojan war was undertaken..." (*Against Heresies*, I. 23, tr. Roberts and Rambaut, pp. 87-88). According to the pseudo-Clementine *Recognitions*, Simon asserted that his companion was "Wisdom, the mother of all things, for whom, says he, the Greeks and barbarians contending, were able in some measure to see an image of her; but of herself, as she is, the dweller with the first and only God, they were wholly ignorant" (II. 12, tr. Pratten, Dods and Smith, p. 199).
91. *a thousand ships*] Compare Seneca, *Troades* 26-27 (ed. Miller, i. 126-27): "Spolia populator rapit / Dardania; praedam mille non capiunt rates": "The plunderer hurries away the Dardanian spoils, booty which a thousand ships cannot contain." Tertullian wrote of the Simonian myth: "O hapless Helen, what a hard fate is yours between the poets and the heretics, who have blackened your fame sometimes with adultery, sometimes with prostitution! Only her rescue from Troy is a more glorious affair than her extrication from the brothel. There were a thousand ships to withdraw her from Troy; a thousand pence were probably more than enough to withdraw her from the stews" (*De anima* 34, in *Writings*, tr. Thelwall and Holmes, ii. 493).
92. *Ilium*] Troy.
93-97, 104-5, 110.] Compare the apocryphal Wisdom of Solomon, 7:25-26, 29, 8:2: Wisdom "is the breath of the power of God, and a pure influence flowing from the glory of the Almighty: therefore can no defiled thing fall into her. For she is the brightness of the everlasting light, the unspotted mirror of the power of God, and the image of his goodness. [...] For she is more beautiful than the sun, and above all the order of stars: being compared with the light, she is found before it. [...] I loved her, and sought her out from my youth, I desired to make her my spouse, and I was a lover of her beauty."

Enter Old Man.

I will be Paris, and for love of thee
Instead of Troy shall Wittenberg be sack'd,
And I will combat with weak Menelaus   100
And wear thy colours on my plumed crest;
Yea, I will wound Achilles in the heel
And then return to Helen for a kiss.
O, thou art fairer than the evening air
Clad in the beauty of a thousand stars;   105
Brighter art thou than flaming Jupiter
When he appear'd to hapless Semele,
More lovely than the monarch of the sky
In wanton Arethusa's azur'd arms,
And none but thou shalt be my paramour.   110

Exeunt.

Old Man.

Accursed Faustus, miserable man,
That from thy soul exclud'st the grace of heaven
And fliest the throne of his tribunal seat!

Enter the devils.

Satan begins to sift me with his pride;
As in this furnace God shall try my faith,   115

100.] Book III of Homer's *Iliad* recounts the duel between Alexandros or Paris and
Menelaus. Paris challenged all the best of the Achaeans to single combat, but recoiled in
fear from Menelaus. Having agreed that Helen and her possessions should go to the victor,
Paris was defeated, but saved from death by Aphrodite, who carried him in a mist into his
own bedchamber—where, although shamed in Helen's eyes as in everyone else's, he promptly took her to bed.
107. *hapless Semele*] One of Jupiter's human mistresses, she was persuaded by Juno to ask
him to come to her in the same form in which he embraced Juno in heaven, and was
consumed by fire. See Ovid, *Metamorphoses* III. 259-315.
109. *Arethusa*] a nymph who, bathing in the river Alpheus, aroused the river-god's lust;
fleeing from him, she was transformed into a fountain (see Ovid's *Metamorphoses* V. 577-
641). No classical myth links her with Jupiter or with the sun-god.
114. *sift me*] Compare Christ's words to Peter at the last supper: "Simon, Simon, behold,
Satan hath desired to have you, that he may sift you as wheat" (Luke 22:31, Authorized
Version). Ormerod and Wortham, observing that the Geneva Bible has "winnow" here,
suggest that Marlowe derived "sift" from the Coverdale Bible of 1535.

My faith, vile hell, shall triumph over thee!
Ambitious fiends, see how the heavens smiles
At your repulse, and laughs your state to scorn:
Hence hell, for hence I fly unto my God.

Exeunt.

Act V, Scene ii.

Enter Faustus with the Scholars.

Faustus.
Ah, gentlemen!

1 Sch.
What ails Faustus?

Faustus.
Ah, my sweet chamber-fellow, had I lived with thee, then
had I lived still, but now I die eternally. Look, comes he
5   not, comes he not?

2 Sch.
What means Faustus?

3 Sch.
Belike he is grown into some sickness, by being over-solitary.

1 Sch.
If it be so, we'll have physicians to cure him. 'Tis but a
surfeit, never fear, man.

Faustus.
10   A surfeit of deadly sin, that hath damned both body and
soul.

2 Sch.
Yet Faustus, look up to heaven; remember, God's mercies are infinite.

Faustus.
But Faustus' offence can ne'er be pardoned: the serpent

---

10. *surfeit*] an excessive indulgence in food or drink, and the resulting disorder of the system.

that tempted Eve may be saved, but not Faustus. Ah   15
gentlemen, hear me with patience, and tremble not at my
speeches. Though my heart pants and quivers to remember
that I have been a student here these thirty years, O would
I had never seen Wittenberg, never read book: and what
wonders I have done, all Germany can witness, yea all   20
the world, for which Faustus hath lost both Germany and
the world, yea heaven itself, heaven the seat of God, the
throne of the blessed, the kingdom of joy, and must remain
in hell for ever—hell, ah, hell, for ever! Sweet friends, what
shall become of Faustus, being in hell for ever?   25

3 Sch.

Yet Faustus, call on God.

Faustus.

On God, whom Faustus hath abjured? on God, whom Faustus hath blasphemed? Ah my God, I would weep, but the
devil draws in my tears. Gush forth blood instead of tears,
yea life and soul! Oh, he stays my tongue; I would lift up   30
my hands, but see, they hold them, they hold them!

All.

Who, Faustus?

Faustus.

Lucifer and Mephastophilis. Ah, gentlemen, I gave them
my soul for my cunning.

All.

God forbid!   35

Faustus.

God forbade it indeed, but Faustus hath done it: for the vain
pleasure of four and twenty years hath Faustus lost eternal
joy and felicity. I writ them a bill with mine own blood, the
date is expired, the time will come, and he will fetch me!

1 Sch.

Why did not Faustus tell us of this before, that divines   40

34. *cunning*] knowledge.
38. *bill*] deed.

might have prayed for thee?

Faustus.

Oft have I thought to have done so, but the devil threatened to tear me in pieces if I named God, to fetch both body and soul if I once gave ear to divinity, and now
45 'tis too late: gentlemen, away, lest you perish with me.

2 Sch.

O what may we do to save Faustus?

Faustus.

Talk not of me, but save yourselves, and depart.

3 Sch.

God will strengthen me, I will stay with Faustus.

1 Sch.

Tempt not God, sweet friend, but let us into the next
50 room, and there pray for him.

Faustus.

Ay, pray for me, pray for me; and what noise soever ye hear, come not unto me, for nothing can rescue me.

2 Sch.

Pray thou, and we will pray that God may have mercy upon thee.

Faustus.

55 Gentlemen, farewell. If I live till morning, I'll visit you; if not, Faustus is gone to hell.

All.

Faustus, farewell.

Exeunt Scholars.

The clock strikes eleven.

Faustus.

Ah Faustus,
Now hast thou but one bare hour to live,
60 And then thou must be damn'd perpetually.

Stand still, you ever-moving spheres of heaven,
That time may cease, and midnight never come!
Fair nature's eye, rise, rise again, and make
Perpetual day, or let this hour be but a year,
A month, a week, a natural day,   65
That Faustus may repent, and save his soul.
O lente lente currite noctis equi!
The stars move still, time runs, the clock will strike,
The devil will come, and Faustus must be damn'd.
O, I'll leap up to my God: who pulls me down?   70
See, see where Christ's blood streams in the firmament:
One drop would save my soul, half a drop! Ah, my Christ,
Ah rend not my heart for naming of my Christ,
Yet will I call on him, oh spare me Lucifer!
Where is it now? 'tis gone,   75
And see where God stretcheth out his arm
And bends his ireful brows!
Mountains and hills, come, come, and fall on me
And hide me from the heavy wrath of God.
No, no?   80
Then will I headlong run into the earth.
Earth, gape! O no, it will not harbor me.

61-69.] Compare *Edward II* V.i. 64-70: "Continue ever, thou celestial sun, / Let never silent night possess this clime; / Stand still, you watches of the element, / All times and seasons rest you at a stay, / That Edward may be still fair England's king. / But day's bright beams doth vanish fast away, / And needs I must resign my wished crown."

67. O lente...equi] "O gallop slowly, slowly, you horses of the night!" Faustus is quoting from Ovid, *Amores* I.xiii. 40. The tone of Ovid's request to Aurora to hold back her horses so that he can remain longer in bed with his beloved is deliberately frivolous. In this passage, he tells the goddess she has left Tithonus' bed because he is old, but in other circumstances would behave differently: "At si quem mavis Cephalum complexa teneres, / Clamares 'lente currite, noctis equi!'"—lines which Marlowe translated thus, in *All Ovids Elegies*: "But heldst thou in thine arms some Cephalus, / Then wouldst thou cry, stay night and run not thus." The playfully erotic associations of this line make it especially poignant in the present context.

71.] Compare *2 Tamburlaine* V.iii. 48-50: "Come let us march against the powers of heaven, / And set black streamers in the firmament / To signify the slaughter of the gods."

73.] This line, addressed to Lucifer, echoes one spoken by Edward II to his lover Gaveston: "Rend not my heart with thy too piercing words" (*Edward II* I.iv. 117).

78-79.] This is a recurrent motif in apocalyptic writings, e.g. Luke 23:30: "Then shall they begin to say to the mountains, Fall on us; and to the hills, Cover us"; Revelation 6:16: "And said to the mountains and rocks, Fall on us, and hide us from the face of him that sitteth on the throne, and from the wrath of the Lamb". See also Hosea 10:8.

You stars that reign'd at my nativity,
Whose influence hath allotted death and hell,
85   Now draw up Faustus like a foggy mist
Into the entrails of yon laboring cloud,
That when you vomit forth into the air
My limbs may issue from your smoky mouths,
So that my soul may but ascend to heaven.

The watch strikes.

90   Ah, half the hour is past: 'twill all be past anon.
Oh God, if thou wilt not have mercy on my soul,
Yet for Christ's sake, whose blood hath ransom'd me,
Impose some end to my incessant pain:
Let Faustus live in hell a thousand years,
95   A hundred thousand, and at last be sav'd.
O, no end is limited to damned souls.
Why wert thou not a creature wanting soul?
Or why is this immortal that thou hast?
Ah, Pythagoras' metempsychosis, were that true
100   This soul should fly from me, and I be chang'd
Unto some brutish beast.
All beasts are happy, for when they die
Their souls are soon dissolv'd in elements,
But mine must live still to be plagu'd in hell.

83-89.] Having aspired initially to "rend the clouds" (I.i. 60) and to beget himself in divine form (I.i. 63-64), Faustus now begs to undergo a bizarrely literalized reversal of the process of rebirth that was central to Renaissance Hermetic-Cabalistic magic. The bargain proposed—of resorption into a dismembering womb and of the regurgitation and dispersal of his body in exchange for the salvation of his soul—is the most violent expression of despair in the play.

89.1. watch] clock.

96. *no end is limited to damned souls*] i.e. damnation is endless. But "end" here suggests purpose and finality as well as temporal conclusiveness. Faustus, who challenged "the end of every art" (I.i. 4) and set out to transgress the limits fixed by his human state and his despair, here seems to recognize an absence of limit (and a corresponding emptying out of purposefulness and temporality) as the defining conditions of damnation. See Edward A. Snow, "Marlowe's *Doctor Faustus* and the Ends of Desire", in Alvin Kernan, ed., *Two Renaissance Mythmakers: Christopher Marlowe and Ben Jonson* (Baltimore: Johns Hopkins UP, 1977), pp. 70-110.

99. *metempsychosis*] the doctrine of the transmigration of souls.

Curst be the parents that engender'd me;   105
No Faustus, curse thyself, curse Lucifer
That hath depriv'd thee of the joys of heaven!

The clock striketh twelve.

O it strikes, it strikes, now body, turn to air
Or Lucifer will bear thee quick to hell!

Thunder and lightning.

O soul, be changed into little water drops   110
And fall into the ocean, ne'er be found;
My God, my God, look not so fierce on me!

Enter devils.

Adders and serpents, let me breathe awhile!
Ugly hell gape not, come not Lucifer,
I'll burn my books, ah Mephastophilis!   115

Exeunt with him.

EPILOGUE.

Enter Chorus.

Chorus.
Cut is the branch that might have grown full straight,
And burned is Apollo's laurel bough
That sometime grew within this learned man:
Faustus is gone, regard his hellish fall,

---

109. *quick*] alive.
114.] Edward A. Snow remarks of II.i. 26-29 and of this line that "The same erotic energy charges both utterances, and the later one is the genuine consummation of the earlier one as well as its ironic inversion" ("Marlowe's *Doctor Faustus* and the Ends of Desire," p. 72).

5   Whose fiendful fortune may exhort the wise
    Only to wonder at unlawful things,
    Whose deepness doth entice such forward wits
    To practice more than heavenly power permits.

Exit.

Terminat hora diem, terminat Author opus.

6. *Only to wonder*] to be content with wondering.
8.2.] "The hour ends the day; the author ends his work."

NOTES TO
ACT V

ACT V Scene i

0.1. *enter Wagner solus*] *A1*; *Thunder and lightning: Enter deuils with couer'd dishes; Mephostophilis leades them into Faustus Study: Then enter Wagner B1.*

1-8.] *A1*; *in place of which B1 has the following, printed as prose:* I think my Maister means to die shortly, he hath made his will, & giuen me his wealth, his house, his goods, & store of golden plate; besides two thousand duckets ready coin'd: I wonder what he meanes, if death were nie, he would not frolick thus: hee's now at supper with the schollers, where ther's such belly-cheere, as Wagner in his life nere saw the like: and see where they come, belike the feast is done.

8.1. *Exit*] *B1*; *not in A1.*

8.2. *Enter Faustus with*] *A1*; *Enter Faustus, Mephostophilis, and B1.*

9. Maister Doctor] *A1*; Doctor *B1.*

13. so much] *B1*; that *A1.*

16-23.] *verse in B1*; *printed as prose in A1.*

18. and...denie] *A1*; It is not Faustus custome to deny *B1.*

21. otherwaies] *A1*; otherwise *B1.* and maiestie] *A1*; or Maiesty B1.

24.1. *Musicke...Stage*] *A1*; *Musicke sound, Mephosto brings in Hellen, she passeth ouer the stage...* *B1.*

25-46.] *A1*; *see Appendix 1 for the substantially different parallel passage in B1.*

48.] *A1*; *not in B1.*

49. claimes his] *B1*; calls for *A1.*

50. almost] *B1*; *not in A1.*

50.1. *Enter...dagger*] *Mepha. giues him a dagger A1*; *Meph....dagger B1. A1 gives no indication as to when Mephastophilis enters; in B1 he is onstage throughout this scene.*

51. now] *B1*; *not in A1.*

52. Ah] *A1*; O *B1.*

53. houers] *A1*; houer *B1.*

57. Ah my sweete] *A1*; O *B1.*

60. I...cheare] *A1*; Faustus I leaue thee, but with griefe of heart *B1.*

61. ruine] *A1*; enemy *B1.*   hopelesse] *A1*; haplesse *B1.*

Notes to Act V

61.1. Exit] *B1*; *not in A1*.
62. where...now] *A1*; wretch what hast thou done *B1*.
69.] *B1*; *not in A1*.
70. Mephastophilis] *A1*; Mephasto *B1*.
73. My] *A1*; The *B1*.
74. quickely] *A1*; Faustus *B1*.
75. danger] *A1*; dangers *B1*.
76. crooked age] *A1*; aged man *B1*.
78. torments] *A1*; torment *B1*.
86. imbracings] *A1*; embraces *B1*. cleane] *A1*; cleare *B1*.
88. mine oath] *A1*; my vow *B1*.
89. Faustus...desire] *A1*; This, or what else my Faustus shall desire *B1*.
90.1. enter Helen] *A1*; Enter Hellen againe, passing ouer betweene two Cupids *B1*.
94. sucke] *B1*; suckes *A1*.
96. be] *A1*; is *B1*.
97.1. enter old man] *A1*; *not in B1*.
99. Wittenberg] *B1*; Wertenberge *A1*.
104. euening] *A1*; euenings *B1*.
111-19.1.] *A1*; not in *B1*.

ACT V Scene ii

Act IV, Scene ii. See Appendix 1 for the twenty-five line passage with which the B-text's version of this scene begins.
0.1. Enter...Schollers] *A1*.
1. Ah] *A1*; Oh *B1*.
4. I die] *A1*; must dye *B1*.   looke] *A1*; Looke sirs *B1*.
6. what meanes Faustus] *A1*; *1*. O my deere Faustus what imports this feare? / *2*. Is all our pleasure turn'd to melancholy? *B1*.
7. Belike...by] *A1*; *3*. He is not well with *B1*.
8. to cure him] *A1*; and Faustus shall bee cur'd *B1*.
9. surffet, neuer feare man] *A1*; surfet sir, feare nothing *B1*.
12-13. remember gods mercies are] *A1*; and remember mercy is *B1*.
14-15. But...Faustus] *Printed as verse in A1 and B1*.
15. Ah] *A1*; O *B1*.
16. heare me] *A1*; heare *B1*.
17. pants and quiuers] *A1*; pant & quiuer *B1*.

19. Wittenberg] *B1*; Wertenberge *A1*.
24, 28. ah] *A1*; O *B1*.
33. Lucifer] *A1*; Why Lucifer *B1*. Ah] *A1*; O *B1*.
35. God] *A1*; O God *B1*.
36. the vaine] *B1*; vaine *A1*.
39. the time wil come] *A1*; this is the time *B1*.
43-44. fetch both] *A1*; fetch me *B1*.
46. may] *B1*; shal *A1*.   saue] *B1*; *not in A1*.
50. there] *A1*; *not in B1*.
57.2.] *The striking of the clock is preceded in B1 by a passage of almost fifty lines in which Faustus is addressed in turn by Mephostophilis and by the Good and Bad Angels; for this passage, see Appendix 1.*
58. Ah] *A1*; O *B1*.
70. my God] *A1*; heauen *B1*.
71-72. See...Christ] *A1*; *B1 substitutes* One drop of bloud will saue me; oh my Christ
73. Ah] *A1*; *not in B1*.
76-77. And see...browes] *A1*; *B1 substitutes* And see a threatning Arme, an angry Brow.
79. God] *A1*; heauen *B1*.
80. No no,] *A1*; No? *B1*. *In A1 and B1 80 and 81 are a single line.*
82. Earth gape] *A1*; Gape earth *B1*.
89. So...heauen] *A1*; But let my soule mount, and ascend to heauen *B1*.
89.1.] *B1*; *in A1 this same stage direction follows* Ah, halfe the houre is past
90. Ah] *A1*; O *B1*. *A1 begins a new line after "past".*
91-92. Oh God...ransomd me] *A1*; *B1 substitutes* O, if my soule must suffer for my sinne
96. O] *A1*; *not in B1*.
99. Ah] *A1*; Oh *B1*.
101. Vnto] *A1*; Into *B1*.
101-2.] *Lineation as in B1; printed as one line in A1*.
108. O] *A1*; *not in B1*.
109.1, 112.1.] *A1*; *B1 substitutes, after* 111, *the stage direction* "Thunder, and enter the deuils."
110. little] *A1*; small *B1*.
112. My God, my God] *A1*; O mercy heauen *B1*.

Notes to Act V

115. ah Mephastophilis] *A1*; oh Mephostophilis *B1*.
115.1.] *This stage direction is followed in B1 by nineteen lines spoken by the three Scholars; see Appendix 1.*

EPILOGUE

1. *Chorus*] *Dyce; not in A1, B1.*
8.2. *Terminat... Opus*] *Followed in A1 by a printer's device bearing the words "Such as I make / Such will I take," and in B1 by by the single word "Finis."*

APPENDIX 1

(a) 1616 text: Act I, Scene iv.

Enter Wagner and the Clown.

Wagner.
  Come hither, sirrah boy.

Clown.
  Boy? O disgrace to my person! Zounds, boy in your face:
  you have seen many boys with beards, I am sure.

Wagner.
  Sirrah, hast thou no comings in?

Clown.
  Yes, and goings out too, you may see, sir. 5

Wagner.
  Alas, poor slave; see how poverty jests in his nakedness.
  I know the villain's out of service, and so hungry that I
  know he would give his soul to the devil for a shoulder
  of mutton, though it were blood raw.

Clown.
  Not so neither: I had need to have it well roasted, and 10
  good sauce to it, if I pay so dear, I can tell you.

Wagner.
  Sirrah, wilt thou be my man and wait on me? and I will
  make thee go like *Qui mihi discipulus.*

Clown.
  What, in verse?

Wagner.

15   No slave, in beaten silk and stavesacre.

Clown.

Stavesacre? That's good to kill vermin: then belike if I serve you, I shall be lousy.

Wagner.

Why, so thou shalt be, whether thou dost it or no. But sirrah, if thou dost not presently bind thyself to me for

20   seven years, I'll turn all the lice about thee into familiars and make them tear thee in pieces.

Clown.

Nay sir, you may save yourself a labor, for they are as familiar with me as if they paid for their meat and drink, I can tell you.

Wagner.

25   Well, sirrah, leave your jesting, and take these guilders.

Clown.

Yes, marry sir, and I thank you too.

Wagner.

So, now thou art to be at an hour's warning whensoever and wheresoever the devil shall fetch thee.

Clown.

Here, take your guilders: I'll none of 'em!

Wagner.

30   Not I, thou art pressed. Prepare thyself, for I will present-ly raise up two devils to carry thee away: Banio, Belcher!

Clown.

Belcher? And Belcher come here, I'll belch him; I am not afraid of a devil.

Enter two devils.

Wagner.

How now, sir, will you serve me now?

Clown.

35   Ay, good Wagner, take away the devil then.

Wagner.
Spirits, away! Now sirrah, follow me.

Clown.
I will, sir. But hark you master, will you teach me this conjuring occupation?

Wagner.
Ay sirrah, I'll teach thee to turn thyself to a dog, or a cat, or a mouse, or a rat, or anything.   40

Clown.
A dog, or a cat, or a mouse, or a rat? O brave Wagner!

Wagner.
Villain, call me Master Wagner, and see that you walk attentively, and let your right eye be always diametrally fixed upon my left heel, that thou maist *quasi vestigiis nostris insistere.*   45

Clown.
Well sir, I warrant you.

Exeunt.

(b) 1616 text: Act II, Scene iii.

Enter the Clown [Robin].

Robin.
What, Dick, look to the horses there till I come again. I have gotten one of Doctor Faustus' conjuring books, and now we'll have such knavery as't passes.

Enter Dick.

Dick.
What, Robin, you must come away and walk the horses.

3. *as't passes*] as beats everything (Boas).

Robin.

5   I walk the horses? I scorn't, 'faith, I have other matters
       in hand; let the horses walk themselves and they will. [*He
       attempts to read*] A, *per se*, a; t, h, e, the; o *per se*, o; deny
       orgon, gorgon. Keep further from me, O thou illiterate
       and unlearned ostler.

Dick.

10   'Snails, what hast thou got there, a book? Why, thou
       can'st not tell ne'er a word on't.

Robin.

       That thou shalt see presently. Keep out of the circle, I
       say, lest I send you into the ostry with a vengeance.

Dick.

       That's like, 'faith! You had best leave your foolery, for
15   an my master come he'll conjure you, 'faith.

Robin.

       My master conjure me? I'll tell thee what, an my master
       come here, I'll clap as fair a pair of horns on's head as
       e'er thou sawest in thy life.

Dick.

       Thou need'st not do that, for my mistress hath done it.

Robin.

20   Ay, there be of us here that have waded as deep into
       matters as other men, if they were disposed to talk.

Dick.

       A plague take you! I thought you did not sneak up and
       down after her for nothing. But I prithee tell me, in good
       sadness, Robin, is that a conjuring book?

---

7. *A*, per se, *a; t, h, e, the; o* per se, *o*] A by itself spells a; t, h, e, spells the; o by itself spells
o.

7-8. *deny orgon, gorgon*] a valiant attempt at the name "Demogorgon," which appeared in
Faustus's invocation at I.iii. 18.

10. *'Snails*] a contraction of "by God's nails," and thus an oath which, like "Zounds" or
"Swowns," refers to Christ's crucifixion.

12. *presently*] at once.

13. *ostry*] hostelry, inn.

15. *an*] if.

23-24. *in good sadness*] seriously speaking.

Robin.

    Do but speak what thou't have me to do, and I'll do't. If   25
thou't dance naked, put off thy clothes, and I'll conjure
thee about presently. Or if thou't go but to the tavern
with me, I'll give thee white wine, red wine, claret wine,
sack, muscadine, malmsey and whippincrust, hold-belly-
hold, and we'll not pay one penny for it.   30

Dick.

    O brave! prithee let's to it presently, for I am as dry as a dog.

Robin.

    Come then, let's away.

Exeunt.

(c) 1616 text: Act III, Scenes i-iii.

Act III, Scene i, lines 44-199 (1616 text).

*A conflated text can be established without much difficulty
for the first fifty-one lines of this scene, in which the 1604
and 1616 texts parallel one another quite closely. At line
52, however, the two texts diverge: the greater part of the
1616 text beyond this point in the play is evidently constituted by the additions for which Henslowe paid in 1602.
(Some of the defects of the 1604 text may also be traceable
to the 1602 revision.)*

Faustus.

    Now, by the kingdoms of infernal rule,

28. *claret*] a term used until the early seventeenth century to distinguish wine of a deep
yellow or reddish colour from white and red wines; subsequently applied to red wines, now
exclusively those of the Bordeaux region.
29. *sack*] a class of light-coloured wines imported from Spain and the Canaries.   *muscadine*] muscatel, a strong sweet wine.
29. *malmsey*] a strong sweet wine, originally Greek; later applied to similar wines from Spain,
Madeira and elsewhere.   *whippincrust*] an ignorant distortion of "hippocras," wine
flavored with spices.
29-30. *hold-belly-hold*] a belly-full.

45 Of Styx, of Acheron, and the fiery lake
 Of ever-burning Phlegethon, I swear
 That I do long to see the monuments
 And situation of bright splendent Rome.
 Come therefore, let's away.

Meph.

50 Nay stay, my Faustus; I know you'd see the Pope,
 And take some part of holy Peter's feast,
 The which in state and high solemnity
 This day is held through Rome and Italy
 In honor of the Pope's triumphant victory.

Faustus.

55 Sweet Mephostophilis, thou pleasest me;
 Whilst I am here on earth, let me be cloy'd
 With all things that delight the heart of man.
 My four and twenty years of liberty
 I'll spend in pleasure and in dalliance,

60 That Faustus' name, whilst this bright frame doth stand,
 May be admired through the furthest land.

Meph.

 'Tis well said, Faustus. Come then, stand by me,
 And thou shalt see them come immediately.

Faustus.

 Nay stay, my gentle Mephostophilis,

65 And grant me my request, and then I go.
 Thou know'st within the compass of eight days
 We view'd the face of heaven, of earth and hell.

45-46. *Styx, Acheron, Phlegethon*] the three rivers of Hades.

48. *situation*] lay-out.

50-53. *Nay...Italy*] These lines echo the last three lines of the Chorus to Act III (which appear both in A1 and in B1).

60-61.] Rhyming couplets (of which there is only one in the entire A-text, at II.i. 89-90) are one of the distinctive features of the B-text additions.

66-72. *Thou...beheld*] While it may echo the Chorus to Act III, 1-14, this passage is more distinctly derived from *EFB* ch. xxi. Compare, e.g., lines 67-70 with *EFB* ch. xxi, p. 33: "...and as I came down I looked upon the world and the heavens...and me thought that the whole length of the earth was not a span long...."

Appendix 1: Act III scene i, 68-86

So high our dragons soar'd into the air
That looking down the earth appear'd to me
No bigger than my hand in quantity.   70
There did we view the kingdoms of the world,
And what might please mine eye I there beheld.
Then in this show let me an actor be,
That this proud Pope may Faustus' cunning see.

Meph.
    Let it be so, my Faustus, but first stay   75
And view their triumphs as they pass this way,
And then devise what best contents thy mind,
By cunning in thine art to cross the Pope
Or dash the pride of this solemnity,
To make his monks and abbots stand like apes   80
And point like antics at his triple crown,
To beat the beads about the friars' pates
Or clap huge horns upon the cardinals' heads,
Or any villainy thou canst devise,
And I'll perform it, Faustus. Hark, they come: 85
This day shall make thee be admir'd in Rome.

**Enter the Cardinals and bishops, some bearing
crosiers, some the pillars; monks and friars, singing
their procession. Then the Pope, and Raymond, King
of Hungary, with Bruno led in chains.**

76. *triumphs*] processions celebrating a victory; also public festivities, spectacles or pageants.
81. *antics*] grotesques.
86.2. crosier] an episcopal crook.   pillar] a devotional emblem commemorating the
flagellation of Christ; George Cavendish reports in his *Life and Death of Cardinal Wolsey*
that the cardinal's many attendants included "two pillar-bearers".
86.3. procession] a litany or office sung in a religious procession.   the Pope] Addressed
as "Pope Adrian" in line 123 of this scene, he is not named in *EFB* or in the A-text. Adrian
VI (1522-23) was a contemporary of the historical Doctor Faustus, but much of the action
of this scene is derived from the account in John Foxe's *Acts and Monuments of these Latter
Days* (or *Book of Martyrs*) of the conflict between Adrian IV (1154-59) and his successor
Alexander III with the emperor Frederic Barbarossa.
86.3-4. Raymond, King of Hungary; Bruno] Neither of these are historical figures. A "Saxon
Bruno" was pope as Gregory V (996-99); the predicament of the B-text's Bruno may reflect
the fact that the Hermetic philosopher Giordano Bruno, who was in England from 1583 to
1585, and who lectured at Wittenberg (in Saxony) from 1586 to 1588, was burned at the
stake in Rome in 1600.

Pope.
> Cast down our footstool.

Raymond.
> Saxon Bruno, stoop,
> Whilst on thy back his Holiness ascends
> Saint Peter's chair and state pontifical.

Bruno.
90
> Proud Lucifer, that state belongs to me;
> But thus I fall to Peter, not to thee.

Pope.
> To me and Peter shalt thou groveling lie,
> And crouch before the papal dignity.
> Sound trumpets, then, for thus Saint Peter's heir
95
> From Bruno's back ascends Saint Peter's chair.

A flourish while he ascends.

> Thus, as the gods creep on with feet of wool
> Long ere with iron hands they punish men,
> So shall our sleeping vengeance now arise
> And smite with death thy hated enterprise.
100
> Lord Cardinals of Florence and Padua,

87-89.] These lines imitate a famous sequence in *1 Tamburlaine*. Having ordered his followers to "Bring out my footstool" (IV.ii. 1), the Scythian tyrant commands Bajazeth, the "Turkish emperor" (III.i. 22), to "Fall prostrate on the low disdainful earth, / And be the footstool of great Tamburlaine, / That I may rise into my royal throne" (IV.ii.13-15).

89. *state pontifical*] papal throne. Postpositive constructions of this kind, usually placed at the end of a line, are a recurrent feature both of Samuel Rowley's play *When You See Me You Know Me* (printed 1605) and of the B-text additions. See Greg, ed., *Marlowe's "Doctor Faustus" 1604-1616: Parallel Texts*, pp. 133-34. One such construction also appears in the A-text: "demonstrations magical" (I.i. 151).

92-95, 133-40.] These passages have no basis in *EFB*, but are derived from Foxe's *Acts and Monuments*. Foxe tells how Adrian IV "bluster[ed] and thunder[ed] agnot Frederic, the emperor" (ed. Pratt, ii. 189). When the next pope was elected, Frederic set up an anti-pope, but Alexander III forced the emperor into submission, and made him kneel before him: "The proud pope, setting his foot upon the emperor's neck, said the verse of the psalm, 'Super aspidem et basiliscum ambulabis, et conculcabis leonem et draconem:' that is, 'Thou shalt walk upon the adder and on the basilisk, and shalt tread down the lion and the dragon.' To whom the emperor answering again, said, 'Non tibi sed Petro:' that is, 'Not to thee, but to Peter.' The pope again, 'Et mihi et Petro;' 'Both to me and to Peter.' The emperor...held his peace" (ii. 195-96). See L. M. Oliver, "Rowley, Foxe, and the *Faustus* Additions," *MLN* 60 (1945), 391-94.

96-97.] a variant form of the proverb: "God comes with leaden (woolen) feet but strikes with iron hands." See Tilley, G182.

Go forthwith to our holy consistory,
And read amongst the statutes decretal
What, by the holy council held at Trent,
The sacred synod hath decreed for him
That doth assume the papal government   105
Without election and a true consent.
Away, and bring us word with speed.

1 Card.
We go, my lord.

Exeunt Cardinals.

Pope.
Lord Raymond— [*They converse together.*]

Faustus.
Go, haste thee, gentle Mephostophilis: 110
Follow the cardinals to the consistory,
And as they turn their superstitious books
Strike them with sloth and drowsy idleness,
And make them sleep so sound that in their shapes
Thy self and I may parley with this Pope,   115
This proud confronter of the Emperor,
And in despite of all his holiness
Restore this Bruno to his liberty
And bear him to the states of Germany.

Meph.
Faustus, I go.

Faustus.
                        Dispatch it soon: 120
The Pope shall curse that Faustus came to Rome.

Exeunt Faustus and Mephostophilis.

---

101. *consistory*] i.e. meeting place of the papal consistory or senate.
102. *statutes decretal*] that part of canon law which is constituted by the decrees of the popes on matters of doctrine or policy. "Decretal" is evidently understood here as embracing also the decisions of church councils.
103. *council held at Trent*] The Council of Trent sat, with interruptions, from 1545 to 1563.
104. *synod*] general council of the church.

Bruno.

Pope Adrian, let me have some right of law;
I was elected by the Emperor.

Pope.

We will depose the Emperor for that deed,
125   And curse the people that submit to him.
Both he and thou shalt stand excommunicate
And interdict from Church's privilege
And all society of holy men:
He grows too proud in his authority,
130   Lifting his lofty head above the clouds,
And like a steeple over-peers the Church.
But we'll pull down his haughty insolence,
And as Pope Alexander, our progenitor,
Trod on the neck of German Frederick,
135   Adding this golden sentence to our praise,
"That Peter's heirs should tread on emperors,
And walk upon the dreadful adder's back,
Treading the lion and the dragon down,
And fearless spurn the killing basilisk";
140   So will we quell that haughty schismatic,
And by authority apostolical
Depose him from his regal government.

Bruno.

Pope Julius swore to princely Sigismund,
For him and the succeeding popes of Rome,
145   To hold the emperors their lawful lords.

Pope.

Pope Julius did abuse the Church's rites,
And therefore none of his decrees can stand.

---

127. *interdict*] authoritatively cut off.

133. *progenitor*] here used in a figurative sense to mean "predecessor."

139. *basilisk*] a mythical reptile whose glance was said to be fatal; it seems appropriate in this context that the Greek word from which "basilisk" is derived means "kinglet."

143-45.] another instance of the blithe disregard for history that characterizes the B-text additions. Julius I lived in the fourth century; Julius II and III were popes respectively from 1503 to 1513, and from 1550 to 1555; the German emperor Sigismund lived from 1368 to 1437.

Is not all power on earth bestow'd on us?
And therefore, though we would, we cannot err.
Behold this silver belt, whereto is fix'd   150
Seven golden keys fast seal'd with seven seals,
In token of our seven-fold power from heaven
To bind or loose, lock fast, condemn, or judge,
Resign, or seal, or whatso pleaseth us.
Then he, and thou, and all the world shall stoop,   155
Or be assured of our dreadful curse
To light as heavy as the pains of hell.

Enter Faustus and Mephostophilis, like the Cardinals.

Meph.
Now tell me, Faustus, are we not fitted well?

Faustus.
Yes Mephostophilis, and two such cardinals
Ne'er served a holy pope as we shall do.   160
But whilst they sleep within the consistory
Let us salute his reverend Fatherhood.

Raymond.
Behold, my lord, the cardinals are return'd.

Pope.
Welcome, grave fathers; answer presently,
What have our holy council there decreed   165
Concerning Bruno and the Emperor,
In quittance of their late conspiracy
Against our state and papal dignity?

Faustus.
Most sacred patron of the Church of Rome,
By full consent of all the synod   170
Of priests and prelates it is thus decreed:

---

151. *keys*] of St. Peter.
154. *resign*] "The word here, in its contrast with 'seal', seems to have almost the meaning
of the Latin 'resignare', unseal" (Boas).
157. *light*] alight: to settle on, fall upon (*OED* II. 6, 7).
167. *quittance*] requital for.

That Bruno and the German Emperor
Be held as lollards and bold schismatics
And proud disturbers of the Church's peace;
175   And if that Bruno by his own assent,
Without enforcement of the German peers,
Did seek to wear the triple diadem
And by your death to climb Saint Peter's chair,
The statutes decretal have thus decreed:
180   He shall be straight condemn'd of heresy,
And on a pile of faggots burnt to death.

Pope.

It is enough. Here, take him to your charge
And bear him straight to Ponte Angelo,
And in the strongest tower enclose him fast.
185   Tomorrow, sitting in our consistory
With all our college of grave cardinals,
We will determine of his life or death.
Here, take his triple crown along with you
And leave it in the Church's treasury.
190   Make haste again, my good lord cardinals,
And take our blessing apostolical.

Meph.

So, so: was never devil thus bless'd before.

Faustus.

Away, sweet Mephostophilis, be gone;
The cardinals will be plagu'd for this anon.

Exeunt Faustus and Mephostophilis [with Bruno].

---

173. *lollard*] a name of contempt given in the fourteenth century to followers of Wyclif; subsequently synonymous with "heretic."
176. *without enforcement of*] without having been compelled by.
183. *Ponte Angelo*] See III.i. 35-36, where the castle is said to stand on the bridge; the Castel San Angelo (which incorporates the ancient mausoleum of the emperor Hadrian) in fact stands at the north end of the bridge.
186. *college*] the name given to the pope's council, constituted by the cardinals of the church.
190. *again*] i.e. to return.

Pope.
> Go presently and bring a banquet forth   195
> That we may solemnize Saint Peter's feast,
> And with Lord Raymond, King of Hungary,
> Drink to our late and happy victory.
> > > *Exeunt.*

Act III, Scene ii (1616 text).

> *A sennet while the banquet is brought in, and then*
> *enter Faustus and Mephostophilis in their own shapes.*

Meph.
> Now Faustus, come prepare thyself for mirth:
> The sleepy cardinals are hard at hand
> To censure Bruno, that is posted hence,
> And on a proud-paced steed as swift as thought
> Flies o'er the Alps to fruitful Germany,   5
> There to salute the woeful Emperor.

Faustus.
> The Pope will curse them for their sloth to-day,
> That slept both Bruno and his crown away!
> But now, that Faustus may delight his mind
> And by their folly make some merriment,   10
> Sweet Mephostophilis, so charm me here
> That I may walk invisible to all,
> And do whate'er I please, unseen of any.

Meph.
> Faustus, thou shalt; then kneel down presently,
> > *Whilst on thy head I lay my hand*   15
> > *And charm thee with this magic wand.*
> > *First wear this girdle, then appear*
> > *Invisible to all are here:*

0.1. sennet] a flourish on the trumpet to signal a ceremonial entrance.

        The planets seven, the gloomy air,
20   *Hell, and the Furies' forked hair,*
        Pluto's blue fire, and Hecate's tree,
        With magic spells so compass thee
        That no eye may thy body see.
      So Faustus, now for all their holiness
25   Do what thou wilt, thou shalt not be discern'd.

Faustus.

      Thanks Mephostophilis; now friars, take heed
      Lest Faustus make your shaven crowns to bleed.

Meph.

      Faustus, no more: see where the Cardinals come.

        Enter Pope and all the lords.
        Enter the Cardinals with a book.

Pope.

      Welcome lord Cardinals; come, sit down.
30   Lord Raymond, take your seat. Friars, attend,
      And see that all things be in readiness
      As best beseems this solemn festival.

1 Card.

      First may it please your sacred Holiness
      To view the sentence of the reverend synod
35   Concerning Bruno and the Emperor?

Pope.

      What needs this question? Did I not tell you,
      Tomorrow we would sit i'the consistory
      And there determine of his punishment?
      You brought us word, even now, it was decreed
40   That Bruno and the cursed Emperor

20. *forked hair*] suggested by the forked tongues of the snakes that formed the hair of the Furies (Greg).

21. *Pluto's blue fire*] the sulphurous flames of hell.   *Hecate's tree*] Possibly the gallows-tree, since Hecate was said to appear on moonlit nights at cross-roads (hence her other name "Trioditis," or in Latin, "Trivia"), accompanied by the dogs of the Styx and crowds of the dead. Boas suggests the reading "three," in allusion to Hecate's triform deity.

Were by the holy council both condemn'd
For loathed lollards, and base schismatics:
Then wherefore would you have me view that book?

1 Card.
Your Grace mistakes, you gave us no such charge.

Raymond.
Deny it not: we all are witnesses   45
That Bruno here was late deliver'd you
With his rich triple crown to be reserv'd
And put into the Church's treasury.

Ambo Cardinals.
By holy Paul we saw them not!

Pope.
By Peter you shall die   50
Unless you bring them forth immediately!
Hale them to prison, lade their limbs with gyves.
False prelates, for this hateful treachery
Curs'd be your souls to hellish misery.

[Exeunt attendants with the two Cardinals.]

Faustus.
So, they are safe: now Faustus, to the feast;   55
The Pope had never such a frolic guest.

Pope.
Lord Archbishop of Rheims, sit down with us.

Bish.
I thank your Holiness.

Faustus.
Fall to, the devil choke you an you spare!

44. *no such charge*] An odd denial: the Pope has made no mention of his instructions to
the Cardinals, or of his having entrusted Bruno to them. Several lines may be missing;
alternatively, this discontinuity may be due to the writer's carelessness.
49.] Ambo] both.
52. *gyves*] fetters.

Pope.
60   Who's that spoke? Friars, look about.
Lord Raymond, pray fall to; I am beholding
To the Bishop of Milan for this so rare a present.

Faustus.
I thank you, sir.

[Snatch it.]

Pope.
How now? who snatch'd the meat from me?
65   Villains, why speak you not?
My good lord Archbishop, here's a most dainty dish
Was sent me from a cardinal in France.

Faustus.
I'll have that too.

[Snatch it.]

Pope.
What lollards do attend our Holiness
70   That we receive such great indignity?
Fetch me some wine.

Faustus.
Ay, pray do, for Faustus is a-dry.

Pope.
Lord Raymond, I drink unto your Grace.

Faustus.
I pledge your Grace.

[Snatch it.]

Pope.
75   My wine gone too? Ye lubbers, look about
And find the man that doth this villainy,
Or by our sanctitude you all shall die!
I pray, my lords, have patience at this troublesome banquet.

Archbishop.
Please it your Holiness, I think it be some ghost crept

out of purgatory, and now is come unto your Holiness 80
for his pardon.

Pope.

It may be so;
Go then, command our priests to sing a dirge
To lay the fury of this same troublesome ghost.

[The Pope crosseth himself.]

Faustus.

How now? must every bit be spiced with a cross? 85
Nay then, take that!

[Faustus hits him a box of the ear.]

Pope.

O, I am slain, help me my lords!
O come and help to bear my body hence;
Damn'd be this soul forever for this deed.

Exeunt the Pope and his train.

Meph.

Now Faustus, what will you do now? for I can tell you, 90
you'll be cursed with bell, book, and candle.

Faustus.

Bell, book and candle; candle, book and bell,
Forward and backward, to curse Faustus to hell!

Enter the Friars with bell, book and candle for the dirge.

1 Friar.

Come brethren, let's about our business with good devotion. 95

---

83. *dirge*] originally "dirige," the first word of the antiphon at matins in the Office of the Dead ("Dirige, Domine, Deus meus, in conspectu tuo viam meum": "Direct, O Lord, my God, my way in thy sight" [Ps. 5:8]). Hence, as Greg remarks, used correctly here, but incorrectly at line 102 below.
91. *bell, book, and candle*] At the end of the ritual of excommunication, the bell is tolled, the book closed, and the candle extinguished. As Ward noted, this ritual is confused, both here and in *EFB*, with the office of exorcism.

[Sing this:]

Cursed be he that stole his Holiness' meat from the table.
    Maledicat Dominus.
Cursed be he that struck his Holiness a blow on the face.
    Maledicat Dominus.
100 Cursed be he that took Friar Sandelo a blow on the pate.
    Maledicat Dominus.
Cursed be he that disturbeth our holy dirge.
    Maledicat Dominus.
Cursed be he that took away his Holiness' wine.
105   *Maledicat Dominus.*

**[Faustus and Mephostophilis] beat the friars,
fling fireworks among them, and Exeunt.**

Act III, Scene iii (1616 Text).

Enter Clown [Robin] and Dick, with a cup.

Dick.
    Sirrah Robin, we were best look that your devil can
    answer the stealing of this same cup, for the vintner's boy
    follows us at the hard heels.
Robin.
    'Tis no matter, let him come: an he follows us, I'll so
5   conjure him as he was never conjured in his life, I warrant
    him. Let me see the cup.

Enter Vintner.

Dick.
    Here 'tis. Yonder he comes; now Robin, now or never
    show thy cunning.

---

3. *at the hard heels*] hard at heel, closely.
4. *an*] if.

Vintner.

O, are you here? I am glad I have found you. You are a
couple of fine companions! Pray, where's the cup you   10
stole from the tavern?

Robin.

How, how? we steal a cup? Take heed what you say: we
look not like cup-stealers, I can tell you.

Vintner.

Never deny't, for I know you have it, and I'll search you.

Robin.

Search me? Ay, and spare not—hold the cup, Dick.   15
Come, come; search me, search me.

Vintner.

[*To Dick*] Come on, sirrah; let me search you now.

Dick.

Ay, ay; do, do—hold the cup, Robin. I fear not your sear-
ching; we scorn to steal your cups, I can tell you.

Vintner.

Never outface me for the matter, for sure the cup is be-   20
tween you two.

Robin.

Nay, there you lie: 'tis beyond us both.

Vintner.

A plague take you! I thought 'twas your knavery to take
it away. Come, give it me again.

Robin.

Ay, much! when, can you tell? Dick, make me a circle, and   25
stand close at my back, and stir not for thy life. Vintner,
you shall have your cup anon—say nothing Dick! O, per
se, o; Demogorgon, Belcher and Mephostophilis!

Enter Mephostophilis.

---

20. *outface me*] brazen it out.
22. *beyond us both*] Robin has perhaps thrown it up into the air.

Meph.

   You princely legions of infernal rule,
30   How am I vexed by these villains' charms!
   From Constantinople have they brought me now,
   Only for pleasure of these damned slaves.

[Exit Vintner.]

Robin.

   By lady sir, you have had a shrewd journey of it: will it
   please you to take a shoulder of mutton to supper, and
35   a tester in your purse, and go back again?

Dick.

   Ay, I pray you heartily sir, for we called you but in jest,
   I promise you.

Meph.

   To purge the rashness of this cursed deed,
   First be thou turned to this ugly shape:
40   For apish deeds transformed to an ape.

Robin.

   O brave, an ape! I pray sir, let me have have the carrying
   of him about to show some tricks.

Meph.

   And so thou shalt: be thou transformed to a dog, and
   carry him upon thy back. Away, be gone!

Robin.

45   A dog? that's excellent: let the maids look well to their
   porridge-pots, for I'll into the kitchen presently. Come
   Dick, come.

Exeunt the two clowns.

Meph.

   Now with the flames of ever-burning fire

---

33. *shrewd*] tiresome.
35. *tester*] a sixpence.

I'll wing myself, and forthwith fly amain
Unto my Faustus, to the Great Turk's court.   50

Exit.

(d) 1616 Text: Act IV, Scenes i-vi.

Act IV, Scene i (1616 text).

Enter Martino and Frederick at several doors.

Martino.
    What ho, officers, gentlemen:
    Hie to the presence to attend the Emperor.
    Good Frederick, see the rooms be voided straight.
    His Majesty is coming to the hall;
    Go back, and see the state in readiness.   5

Frederick.
    But where is Bruno, our elected Pope,
    That on a fury's back came post from Rome?
    Will not his Grace consort the Emperor?

Martino.
    O yes, and with him comes the German conjurer,
    The learned Faustus, fame of Wittenberg,   10
    The wonder of the world for magic art;
    And he intends to show great Carolus
    The race of all his stout progenitors,
    And bring in presence of his Majesty
    The royal shapes and warlike semblances   15
    Of Alexander and his beauteous paramour.

Frederick.
    Where is Benvolio?

3. *voided straight*] cleared at once.
8. *consort*] accompany.

Martino.
>Fast asleep, I warrant you.
>He took his rouse with stoups of Rhenish wine
20 >So kindly yesternight to Bruno's health
>That all this day the sluggard keeps his bed.

Frederick.
>See, see: his window's ope; we'll call to him.

Martino.
>What ho, Benvolio!

Enter Benvolio above at a window, in his nightcap,
buttoning.

Benvolio.
>What a devil ail you two?

Martino.
25 >Speak softly sir, lest the devil hear you!
>For Faustus at the court is late arriv'd,
>And at his heels a thousand furies wait
>To accomplish whatsoe'er the doctor please.

Benvolio.
>What of this?

Martino.
30 >Come leave thy chamber first, and thou shalt see
>This conjurer perform such rare exploits
>Before the Pope and royal Emperor
>As never yet was seen in Germany.

Benvolio.
>Has not the Pope enough of conjuring yet?
35 >He was upon the devil's back late enough,
>And if he be so far in love with him
>I would he would post with him to Rome again.

---

19. *took his rouse*] drank heavily, caroused. The line echoes *Hamlet* I.iv. 8-10: "The King doth wake tonight and takes his rouse, / Keeps wassail, and the swagg'ring upspring reels, / And as he drains his draughts of Rhenish down...."
32. *Pope*] i.e. Bruno.

Frederick.
Speak, wilt thou come and see this sport?
Benvolio.

Not I.

Martino.
Wilt thou stand in thy window and see it then?
Benvolio.
Ay, and I fall not asleep i'the mean time.   40
Martino.
The Emperor is at hand, who comes to see
What wonders by black spells may compass'd be.
Benvolio.
'Well, go you attend the Emperor.
        [Exeunt Frederick and Martino.]

I am content for this once to thrust my head out at a window,
for they say if a man be drunk overnight the devil cannot hurt   45
him in the morning. If that be true, I have a charm in my head
shall control him as well as the conjurer, I warrant you.

*A sennet. Charles the German Emperor, Bruno, Saxony,
Faustus, Mephostophilis, Frederick, Martino, and
attendants.*

Emp.
Wonder of men, renown'd magician,
Thrice learned Faustus, welcome to our court.
This deed of thine in setting Bruno free   50
From his and our professed enemy
Shall add more excellence unto thine art
Than if by powerful necromantic spells
Thou couldst command the world's obedience.
Forever be belov'd of Carolus;   55
And if this Bruno thou hast late redeem'd
In peace possess the triple diadem
And sit in Peter's chair, despite of chance,

Thou shalt be famous through all Italy,
60   And honor'd of the German Emperor.

Faustus.

These gracious words, most royal Carolus,
Shall make poor Faustus to his utmost power
Both love and serve the German Emperor
And lay his life at holy Bruno's feet.
65   For proof whereof, if so your Grace be pleas'd,
The doctor stands prepar'd by power of art
To cast his magic charms, that shall pierce through
The ebon gates of ever-burning hell
And hale the stubborn furies from their caves
70   To compass whatsoe'er your Grace commands.

Benvolio.

Blood, he speaks terribly! But for all that I do not greatly
believe him: he looks as like a conjurer as the Pope to
a costermonger.

Emp.

Then Faustus, as thou late didst promise us,
75   We would behold that famous conqueror,
Great Alexander, and his paramour,
In their true shapes and state majestical,
That we may wonder at their excellence.

Faustus.

Your Majesty shall see them presently.
80   Mephostophilis, away,
And with a solemn noise of trumpets' sound
Present before this royal Emperor
Great Alexander and his beauteous paramour.

Meph.

Faustus, I will.

[Exit.]

---

73. *costermonger*] one who sells apples in the open street.

Benvolio.

Well, Master Doctor, an your devils come not away quickly,   85
you shall have me asleep presently: zounds, I could eat my self
for anger to think I have been such an ass all this while, to
stand gaping after the devil's governor, and can see nothing.

Faustus.

I'll make you feel something anon, if my art fail me not.—
My lord, I must forewarn your Majesty   90
That when my spirits present the royal shapes
Of Alexander and his paramour
Your Grace demand no questions of the King,
But in dumb silence let them come and go.

Emp.

Be it as Faustus please, we are content.   95

Benvolio.

Ay, ay, and I am content too: and thou bring Alexander
and his paramour before the Emperor, I'll be Actaeon
and turn myself into a stag.

Faustus.

And I'll play Diana and send you the horns presently.

*Sennet. Enter at one door the Emperor Alexander, at the
other Darius; they meet, Darius is thrown down;
Alexander kills him, takes off his crown, and offering to
go out, his paramour meets him; he embraceth her and
sets Darius' crown upon her head; and coming back,
both salute the Emperor, who leaving his state, offers to
embrace them, which Faustus seeing suddenly stays
him. Then trumpets cease, and music sounds.*

Faustus.

My gracious Lord, you do forget yourself: 100

97. *Actaeon*] a hunter who came upon the goddess Diana and her nymphs bathing; the
goddess transformed him into a stag and he was torn to pieces by his own dogs. See Ovid,
Metamorphoses III. 155-252.
99.1-2. *Alexander, Darius*] Alexander the Great defeated Darius, the emperor of Persia, at
the battles of Issus and Arbela (333 and 331 B.C.); Darius was killed by his followers in 330
B.C. to prevent his capture.

These are but shadows, not substantial.

Emp.
O, pardon me, my thoughts are ravish'd so
With sight of this renowned Emperor
That in mine arms I would have compass'd him.
105 But Faustus, since I may not speak to them
To satisfy my longing thoughts at full,
Let me this tell thee: I have heard it said
That this fair lady, whilst she liv'd on earth,
Had on her neck a little wart or mole;
110 How may I prove that saying to be true?

Faustus.
Your Majesty may boldly go and see.

Emp.
Faustus, I see it plain,
And in this sight thou better pleasest me
Than if I gain'd another monarchy.

Faustus.
115 Away, be gone!

Exit show.

See, see, my gracious lord: what strange beast is yon, that
thrusts his head out at window?

Emp.
O wondrous sight: see, Duke of Saxony,
Two spreading horns most strangely fastened
120 Upon the head of young Benvolio!

Saxony.
What, is he asleep, or dead?

Faustus.
He sleeps, my Lord, but dreams not of his horns.

Emp.
This sport is excellent: we'll call and wake him.
What ho, Benvolio!

Benvolio.
> A plague upon you! let me sleep awhile.   125

Emp.
> I blame thee not to sleep much, having such a head of
> thine own.

Saxony.
> Look up Benvolio, 'tis the Emperor calls.

Benvolio.
> The Emperor! Where? O zounds, my head!

Emp.
> Nay, and thy horns hold, 'tis no matter for thy head, for   130
> that's armed sufficiently.

Faustus.
> Why, how now, sir knight; what, hanged by the horns?
> This is most horrible; fie, fie, pull in your head for shame,
> let not all the world wonder at you.

Benvolio.
> Zounds Doctor, is this your villainy?   135

Faustus.
> O say not so, sir: the doctor has no skill,
> No art, no cunning to present these lords
> Or bring before this royal Emperor
> The mighty monarch, warlike Alexander.
> If Faustus do it, you are straight resolv'd   140
> In bold Actaeon's shape to turn a stag.
> And therefore my Lord, so please your Majesty,
> I'll raise a kennel of hounds shall hunt him so
> As all his footmanship shall scarce prevail
> To keep his carcase from their bloody fangs.   145
> Ho, Belimote, Argiron, Asterote!

Benvolio.
> Hold, hold! Zounds, he'll raise up a kennel of devils I
> think, anon. Good my lord, entreat for me; 'sblood, I am
> never able to endure these torments.

125. *A plague upon you*] He has not recognized the Emperor's voice.

Emp.

150   Then, good Master Doctor,
      Let me entreat you to remove his horns;
      He has done penance now sufficiently.

Faustus.

      My gracious lord, not so much for injury done to me as to
      delight your Majesty with some mirth hath Faustus justly re-
155   quited this injurious knight, which being all I desire, I am
      content to remove his horns. Mephostophilis, transform him;

      [Mephostophilis removes the horns.]

      and hereafter, sir, look you speak well of scholars.

Benvolio.

      Speak well of ye? 'Sblood, and scholars be such cuckold-
      makers to clap horns of honest men's heads o'this order,
160   I'll ne'er trust smooth faces and small ruffs more. But an
      I be not revenged for this, would I might be turned to a
      gaping oyster, and drink nothing but salt water.

Emp.

      Come Faustus, while the Emperor lives,
      In recompense of this thy high desert
165   Thou shalt command the state of Germany
      And live belov'd of mighty Carolus.

                    Exeunt omnes.

Act IV, Scene ii (1616 text)

Enter Benvolio, Martino, Frederick, with soldiers.

Martino.

      Nay sweet Benvolio, let us sway thy thoughts
      From this attempt against the conjurer.

---

155. *injurious*] insulting, offensive.
159. *o'this order*] in this manner.
160. *smooth faces and small ruffs*] "beardless scholars in academical garb" (Boas).

Benvolio.
Away, you love me not to urge me thus.
Shall I let slip so great an injury,
When every servile groom jests at my wrongs,   5
And in their rustic gambols proudly say,
"Benvolio's head was grac'd with horns today"?
O, may these eyelids never close again
Till with my sword I have that conjurer slain!
If you will aid me in this enterprise   10
Then draw your weapons and be resolute;
If not, depart: here will Benvolio die,
But Faustus' death shall quit my infamy.

Frederick.
Nay, we will stay with thee, betide what may,
And kill that doctor if he come this way.   15

Benvolio.
Then gentle Frederick, hie thee to the grove
And place our servants and our followers
Close in an ambush there behind the trees.
By this, I know, the conjurer is near;
I saw him kneel and kiss the Emperor's hand   20
And take his leave, laden with rich rewards.
Then soldiers, boldly fight: if Faustus die,
Take you the wealth, leave us the victory.

Frederick.
Come soldiers, follow me unto the grove;
Who kills him shall have gold and endless love.   25

Exit Frederick with the soldiers.

Benvolio.
My head is lighter than it was by th'horns,

---

4. *let slip*] overlook.
13. *quit*] repay.
18. *close*] hidden.
19. *by this*] by this time, by now.

But yet my heart's more ponderous than my head
And pants until I see that conjurer dead.

Martino.
Where shall we place ourselves, Benvolio?

Benvolio.
30   Here will we stay to bide the first assault.
O, were that damned hell-hound but in place,
Thou soon shouldst see me quit my foul disgrace.

Enter Frederick.

Frederick.
Close, close: the conjurer is at hand,
And all alone comes walking in his gown;
35   Be ready then and strike the peasant down.

Benvolio.
Mine be that honor, then: now sword, strike home:
For horns he gave, I'll have his head anon.

Enter Faustus with the false head.

Martino.
See, see: he comes.

Benvolio.
               No words: this blow ends all;
Hell take his soul, his body thus must fall!

[Strikes.]

Faustus.
40   Oh!

Frederick.
Groan you, Master Doctor?

Benvolio.
Break may his heart with groans! Dear Frederick, see;
Thus will I end his griefs immediately.

43. *griefs*] sufferings.

Martino.
> Strike with a willing hand: his head is off.

Benvolio.
> The devil's dead: the furies now may laugh.   45

Frederick.
> Was this that stern aspect, that awful frown,
> Made the grim monarch of infernal spirits
> Tremble and quake at his commanding charms?

Martino.
> Was this that damned head whose heart conspir'd
> Benvolio's shame before the Emperor?   50

Benvolio.
> Ay, that's the head; and here the body lies,
> Justly rewarded for his villainies.

Frederick.
> Come, let's devise how we may add more shame
> To the black scandal of his hated name.

Benvolio.
> First on his head, in quittance of my wrongs,   55
> I'll nail huge forked horns, and let them hang
> Within the window where he yok'd me first,
> That all the world may see my just revenge.

Martino.
> What use shall we put his beard to?

Benvolio.
> We'll sell it to a chimney-sweeper: it will wear out ten   60
> birchen brooms, I warrant you.

Frederick.
> What shall his eyes do?

46-50. *Was this...Emperor?*] This double echo of the most famous line in the play ("Was this the face that launched a thousand ships...?" [V.i. 91]) provides one indication of the derivative and secondary nature of these B-version passages.
57. *yok'd*] held fast, as though in a yoke.

Benvolio.
We'll put out his eyes, and they shall serve for buttons
to his lips, to keep his tongue from catching cold.

Martino.
65   An excellent policy! And now sirs, having divided him,
what shall the body do?

[Faustus gets up.]

Benvolio.
Zounds, the devil's alive again!

Frederick.
Give him his head, for God's sake!

Faustus.
Nay, keep it: Faustus will have heads and hands,
70   Ay, all your hearts to recompense this deed.
Knew you not, traitors, I was limited
For four and twenty years to breathe on earth?
And had you cut my body with your swords,
Or hew'd this flesh and bones as small as sand,
75   Yet in a minute had my spirit return'd
And I had breath'd a man made free from harm.
But wherefore do I dally my revenge?
Asteroth, Belimoth, Mephostophilis!

Enter Mephostophilis and other devils.

Go horse these traitors on your fiery backs
80   And mount aloft with them as high as heaven;
Thence pitch them headlong to the lowest hell!
Yet stay: the world shall see their misery,
And hell shall after plague their treachery.
Go Belimoth, and take this caitiff hence
85   And hurl him in some lake of mud and dirt;
Take thou this other, drag him through the woods
Amongst the pricking thorns and sharpest briars,
Whilst with my gentle Mephostophilis
This traitor flies unto some steepy rock,

That rolling down may break the villain's bones   90
As he intended to dismember me.
Fly hence, dispatch my charge immediately.

Frederick.
Pity us, gentle Faustus, save our lives!

Faustus.
Away!

Frederick.
He must needs go that the devil drives.

Exeunt spirits with the knights.

Enter the ambushed soldiers.

1 Sold.
Come sirs, prepare yourselves in readiness,   95
Make haste to help these noble gentlemen;
I heard them parley with the conjurer.

2 Sold.
See where he comes: dispatch, and kill the slave.

Faustus.
What's here? an ambush to betray my life!
Then Faustus, try thy skill. Base peasants, stand!   100
For lo, these trees remove at my command
And stand as bulwarks 'twixt yourselves and me
To shield me from your hated treachery.
Yet to encounter this your weak attempt,
Behold, an army comes incontinent.   105

*Faustus strikes the door, and enter a devil playing on
a drum; after him another bearing an ensign, and
divers with weapons; Mephostophilis with fireworks;
they set upon the soldiers and drive them out.*

[Exit Faustus.]

94. *He...drives*] a common proverb. See Tilley, D 278.
101 *remove*] shift their position.
105. *incontinent*] without delay.
105.1. door] i.e. of the stage.

Act IV, Scene iii (1616 text).

Enter at several doors Benvolio, Frederick, and Martino, their heads and faces bloody and besmeared with mud and dirt, all having horns on their heads.

Martino.
What ho, Benvolio!

Benvolio.
                      Here! What, Frederick, ho!

Frederick.
O help me, gentle friend; where is Martino?

Martino.
Dear Frederick, here,
Half-smother'd in a lake of mud and dirt
5   Through which the furies dragg'd me by the heels.

Frederick.
Martino, see: Benvolio's horns again!

Martino.
O misery! How now, Benvolio?

Benvolio.
Defend me, heaven; shall I be haunted still?

Martino.
Nay, fear not, man: we have no power to kill.

Benvolio.
10   My friends transformed thus: O hellish spite,
Your heads are all set with horns.

Frederick.
You hit it right, it is your own you mean:
Feel on your head.

Benvolio.
              Zounds, horns again!

Martino.
Nay, chafe not, man, we all are sped.

14. *sped*] done for.

Benvolio.
What devil attends this damn'd magician,   15
That, spite of spite, our wrongs are doubled?
Frederick.
What may we do that we may hide our shames?
Benvolio.
If we should follow him to work revenge,
He'd join long asses' ears to these huge horns
And make us laughing stocks to all the world.   20
Martino.
What shall we then do, dear Benvolio?
Benvolio.
I have a castle joining near these woods,
And thither we'll repair and live obscure
Till time shall alter these our brutish shapes.
Sith black disgrace hath thus eclips'd our fame,   25
We'd rather die with grief than live with shame.

                    Exeunt omnes.

Act IV, Scene iv (1616 text).

        Enter Faustus, and the Horse-courser, and
                Mephostophilis.

Hor.
I beseech your worship accept of these forty dollars.
Faustus.
Friend, thou canst not buy so good a horse for so small
a price. I have no great need to sell him, but if thou like
him for ten dollars more, take him, because I see thou
hast a good mind to him.   5
Hor.
I beseech you sir, accept of this. I am a very poor man,

16. *spite of spite*] despite everything.   *doubled*] a trisyllable.
25. *sith*] since.

and have lost very much of late by horseflesh, and this
bargain will set me up again.

Faustus.

Well, I will not stand with thee; give me the money. Now
10   sirrah, I must tell you that you may ride him o'er hedge
and ditch, and spare him not, but do you hear? in any
case, ride him not into the water.

Hor.

How sir, not into the water? Why, will he not drink of
all waters?

Faustus.

15   Yes, he will drink of all waters, but ride him not into the
water: o'er hedge and ditch, or where thou wilt, but not
into the water. Go, bid the ostler deliver him unto you,
and remember what I say.

Hor.

I warrant you, sir. O joyful day, now am I a made man
20   for ever!

Exit.

Faustus.

What art thou, Faustus, but a man condemn'd to die?
Thy fatal time draws to a final end;
Despair doth drive distrust into my thoughts.
Confound these passions with a quiet sleep:
25   Tush, Christ did call the thief upon the cross.
Then rest thee, Faustus, quiet in conceit.

He sits to sleep.

Enter the Horse-courser, wet.

Hor.

O what a cozening doctor was this! I riding my horse into the
water, thinking some hidden mystery had been in the horse, I

---

25. *Tush...cross*] See note to IV.ii. 37 of the A-version text.

had nothing under me but a little straw, and had much ado to
escape drowning. Well, I'll go rouse him, and make him give me   30
my forty dollars again. Ho, sirrah Doctor, you cozening scab!
Master Doctor, awake, and rise, and give me my money again,
for your horse is turned to a bottle of hay. Master Doctor!

He pulls off his leg.

Alas, I am undone, what shall I do? I have pulled off his leg!

Faustus.

O help, help, the villain hath murdered me!   35

Hors.

Murder or not murder, now he has but one leg I'll outrun
him, and cast this leg into some ditch or other.

[Exit.]

Faustus.

Stop him, stop him, stop him!—Ha, ha, ha: Faustus hath
his leg again, and the horse-courser a bundle of hay for
his forty dollars!   40

Enter Wagner.

How now, Wagner, what news with thee?

Wagner.

If it please you, the Duke of Vanholt doth earnestly
entreat your company, and hath sent some of his men to
attend you with provision fit for your journey.

Faustus.

The Duke of Vanholt's an honorable gentleman, and one   45
to whom I must be no niggard of my cunning. Come away!

Exeunt.

---

33. *bottle*] bundle.

Act IV, Scene v (1616 text).

Enter Clown [Robin], Dick, Horse-courser, and a carter.

Carter.
> Come, my masters, I'll bring you to the best beer in
> Europe. What ho, hostess! Where be these whores?

Enter Hostess.

Hostess.
> How now, what lack you? What, my old guests, welcome!

Clown.
> Sirrah Dick, dost thou know why I stand so mute?

Dick.
5 > No Robin, why is't?

Clown.
> I am eighteen pence on the score. But say nothing; see
> if she have forgotten me.

Hostess.
> Who's this, that stands so solemnly by himself? What, my
> old guest!

Clown.
10 > O hostess, how do you? I hope my score stands still.

Hostess.
> Ay, there's no doubt of that, for methinks you make no
> haste to wipe it out.

Dick.
> Why hostess, I say, fetch us some beer.

Hostess.
> You shall presently: look up into th' hall there, ho!

Exit.

---

14. *Look...ho!*] The hostess is summoning her staff. Jump notes a parallel construction in *I Henry IV* II.iv. 37-38: "Look down into the Pomgarnet, Ralph".

Dick.

Come sirs, what shall we do now till mine hostess comes?   15

Carter.

Marry sir, I'll tell you the bravest tale how a conjuror served me. You know Doctor Fauster?

Hor.

Ay, a plague take him! Here's some on's have cause to know him. Did he conjure thee too?

Carter.

I'll tell you how he served me. As I was going to Wittenberg   20
t'other day with a load of hay, he met me and asked me what he should give me for as much hay as he could eat. Now sir, I thinking that a little would serve his turn, bade him take as much as he would for three farthings. So he presently gave me my money and fell to eating, and as I am a cursen man,   25
he never left eating till he had eat up all my load of hay.

All.

O monstrous: eat a whole load of hay!

Clown.

Yes, yes, that may be, for I have heard of one that has eat a load of logs.

Hor.

Now sirs, you shall hear how villainously he served me. I went   30
to him yesterday to buy a horse of him, and he would by no means sell him under forty dollars; so sir, because I knew him to be such a horse as would run over hedge and ditch and never tire, I gave him his money. So when I had my horse, Doctor Fauster bade me ride him night and day and spare   35
him no time. "But," quoth he, "in any case ride him not into the water." Now sir, I, thinking the horse had had some rare quality that he would not have me know of, what did I but rid him into a great river, and when I came just in the midst my

---

17, 35. *Fauster*] a clownish corruption of "Faustus"; one which reappears in the nursery rhyme about Doctor Foster.
24. *farthing*] a small copper coin, worth one-quarter of a penny.
25. *cursen*] a deformation of "christen" or "Christian".

40   horse vanished away, and I sat straddling upon a bottle of hay.

All.

        O brave doctor!

Hor.

        But you shall hear how bravely I served him for it. I went
me home to his house, and there I found him asleep; I
kept a hallowing and whooping in his ears, but all could
45   not wake him. I, seeing that, took him by the leg and
never rested pulling till I had pulled me his leg quite off,
and now 'tis at home in mine hostry!

Clown.

        And has the doctor but one leg, then? That's excellent, for
one of his devils turned me into the likeness of an ape's face.

Carter.

50   Some more drink, hostess.

Clown.

        Hark you, we'll into another room and drink awhile, and
then we'll go seek out the doctor.

                          Exeunt omnes.

Act IV, Scene vi (1616 text).

       Enter the Duke of Vanholt, his Dutchess, Faustus, and
            Mephostophilis; [also a servant].

Duke.

        Thanks, Master Doctor, for these pleasant sights.
Nor know I how sufficiently to recompense your great
deserts in erecting that enchanted castle in the air,
The sight whereof so delighted me
5   As nothing in the world could please me more.

Faustus.

        I do think myself, my good lord, highly recompensed in that

---

41, 42. *brave...bravely*] worthy, worthily.

it pleaseth your Grace to think but well of that which Faustus hath performed. But gracious lady, it may be that you have taken no pleasure in those sights; therefore I pray you tell me, what is the thing you most desire to have? 10
Be it in the world, it shall be yours. I have heard that great-bellied women do long for things are rare and dainty.

Lady.

True, Master Doctor, and since I find you so kind, I will make known unto you what my heart desires to have; and were it now summer, as it is January, a dead time of the winter, I 15
would request no better meat than a dish of ripe grapes.

Faustus.

This is but a small matter. Go Mephostophilis, away!

Exit Mephostophilis.

Madam, I will do more than this for your content.

Enter Mephostophilis again with the grapes.

Here: now taste ye these. They should be good,
For they come from a far country, I can tell you. 20

Duke.

This makes me wonder more than all the rest, that at this time of the year, when every tree is barren of his fruit, from whence you had these ripe grapes.

Faustus.

Please it your Grace, the year is divided into two circles over the whole world, so that when it is winter with us, in 25
the contrary circle it is likewise summer with them, as in India, Saba, and such countries that lie far east, where they have fruit twice a year. From whence, by means of a swift spirit that I have, I had these grapes brought, as you see.

Lady.

And trust me, they are the sweetest grapes that e'er I tasted. 30

24-27.] See note to IV.iii, 19-22 in the A-version text.

The Clowns bounce at the gate within.

Duke.

What rude disturbers have we at the gate?

Go, pacify their fury, set it ope,

And then demand of them what they would have.

They knock again, and call out to talk with Faustus.

Servant.

Why, how now, masters, what a coil is there!

35   What is the reason you disturb the Duke?

Dick.

We have no reason for it, therefore a fig for him!

Servant.

Why, saucy varlets, dare you be so bold?

Hor.

I hope, sir, we have wit enough to be more bold than welcome.

Servant.

It appears so: pray be bold elsewhere,

And trouble not the Duke.

Duke.

40   What would they have?

Servant.

They all cry out to speak with Doctor Faustus.

Carter.

Ay, and we will speak with him.

Duke.

Will you, sir? Commit the rascals.

Dick.

Commit with us? he were as good commit with his father

30.1. bounce] to knock, or thump.
34. *coil*] tumult, noisy disturbance.
36. *a fig*] an expression of contempt, probably accompanied here by an obscene gesture (of closing the hand with the thumb thrust between the first and second fingers, or of thrusting the thumb into the mouth).
43. *Commit the rascals*] Take them to prison.
44. *commit with*] engage in sexual intercourse with.

as commit with us.   45
Faustus.
I do beseech your Grace, let them come in;
They are good subject for a merriment.
Duke.
Do as thou wilt, Faustus, I give thee leave.
Faustus.
I thank your Grace.

Enter the Clown, Dick, Carter, and Horse-courser.

                    Why, how now, my good friends?
'Faith, you are too outrageous. But come near,   50
I have procur'd your pardons; welcome all!
Clown.
Nay sir, we will be welcome for our money, and we will
pay for what we take. What ho, give's half a dozen of
beer here, and be hanged!
Faustus.
Nay, hark you, can you tell me where you are?   55
Carter.
Ay marry, can I: we are under heaven.
Servant.
Ay, but sir sauce-box, know you in what place?
Hor.
Ay, ay, the house is good enough to drink in. Zounds,
fill us some beer, or we'll break all the barrels in the
house and dash out your brains with your bottles.   60
Faustus.
Be not so furious; come, you shall have beer.
My lord, beseech you give me leave a while;
I'll gage my credit 'twill content your Grace.
Duke.
With all my heart, kind Doctor. Please thyself:
Our servants and our court's at thy command.   65

Faustus.
I humbly thank your Grace. Then fetch some beer.

[Exit Mephostophilis.]

Hor.
Ay marry, there spake a doctor indeed, and 'faith I'll drink a health to thy wooden leg for that word.

Faustus.
My wooden leg? What dost thou mean by that?

Carter.
70   Ha, ha, ha! Dost hear him, Dick? He has forgot his leg.

Hor.
Ay, ay, he does not stand much upon that.

Faustus.
No, faith, not much upon a wooden leg.

Carter.
Good Lord, that flesh and blood should be so frail with your worship! Do you not remember a horse-courser you
75   sold a horse to?

Faustus.
Yes, I remember I sold one a horse.

Carter.
And do you remember you bid he should not ride him into the water?

Faustus.
Yes, I do very well remember that.

Carter.
80   And do you remember nothing of your leg?

Faustus.
No, in good sooth.

Carter.
Then I pray, remember your curtsy.

---

71. *stand much upon*] with a quibble on the figurative sense "attach much importance to".
80, 82. *leg...curtsy*] The Carter is playing on the metaphorical sense of "leg" as "bow".

Faustus.
> I thank you, sir.

> *[Bows.]*

Carter.
> 'Tis not so much worth. I pray you tell me one thing.

Faustus.
> What's that?   85

Carter.
> Be both your legs bedfellows every night together?

Faustus.
> Wouldst thou make a Colossus of me, that thou askest
> me such questions?

Carter.
> No truly, sir, I would make nothing of you; but I would
> fain know that.   90

> *Enter Hostess with drink.*

Faustus.
> Then I assure thee certainly they are.

Carter.
> I thank you, I am fully satisfied.

Faustus.
> But wherefore dost thou ask?

Carter.
> For nothing, sir; but methinks you should have a wooden
> bedfellow of one of 'em.   95

Hor.
> Why, do you hear, sir, did not I pull off one of your legs
> when you were asleep?

Faustus.
> But I have it again now I am awake: look you here, sir.

84. *'Tis...worth*] Faustus's bow hasn't helped the Carter tell whether or not he has a wooden
leg.
87. *Colossus*] gigantic statue. The legs of the Colossus at Rhodes were said to have straddled
the entrance to the harbor.

All.

O horrible! Had the doctor three legs?

Carter.

100 Do you remember, sir, how you cozened me and eat up my load of—

Faustus charms him dumb.

Dick.

Do you remember how you made me wear an ape's—

[Faustus charms him dumb.]

Hor.

You whoreson conjuring scab, do you remember how you cozened me with a ho—

[Faustus charms him dumb.]

Clown.

105 Ha'you forgotten me? You think to carry it away with your "Hey-pass" and "Re-pass". Do you remember the dog's fa—

[Faustus charms him dumb.] Exeunt Clowns.

Hostess.

Who pays for the ale? Hear you, Master Doctor, now you have sent away my guests, I pray who shall pay me for my a—

[Faustus charms her dumb.] Exit Hostess.

Lady.

My lord, we are much beholding to this learned man.

Duke.

110 So are we, Madam, which we will recompense
With all the love and kindness that we may.
His artful sport drives all sad thoughts away.

Exeunt.

(e) 1616 text: Non-parallel passages in Act V.

Act V, Scene i, lines 25-64 (1616 text).

For the first twenty-four lines of this scene, the A and B texts parallel one another quite closely. After the appearance of Helen, however, the two texts diverge. The scholars' speeches in B are several lines shorter, and the Old Man's intervention is quite differently conceived. In B the Old Man does not re-enter, and the judgment of Faustus expressed in his last speech (which appears in A only) is replaced in B by the moralistic additions to V.ii.

Music sounds; Mephostophilis brings in Helen; she passeth over the stage.

2 Sch.

 Was this fair Helen, whose admired worth   25
 Made Greece with ten years' wars afflict poor Troy?

3 Sch.

 Too simple is my wit to tell her worth,
 Whom all the world admires for majesty.

1 Sch.

 Now we have seen the pride of nature's work,
 We'll take our leaves, and for this blessed sight 30
 Happy and blest be Faustus evermore.

Exeunt Scholars.

Faustus.

 Gentlemen, farewell, the same wish I to you.

Enter an Old Man.

25-26. *Was...Troy?*] Another anticipation (as in B-version, IV.ii. 46-50.) of the first two lines of Faustus's speech to Helen. Greg remarks that "poor Troy" has "a feebly sentimental effect that, to us at least, is almost comic." Compare "poor Faustus" (B version, IV.i. 62).

Old Man.
> O gentle Faustus, leave this damned art,
> This magic, that will charm thy soul to hell
35 > And quite bereave thee of salvation.
> Though thou hast now offended like a man,
> Do not persever in it like a devil:
> Yet, yet, thou hast an amiable soul,
> If sin by custom grow not into nature:
40 > Then, Faustus, will repentance come too late,
> Then thou art banish'd from the sight of heaven;
> No mortal can express the pains of hell.
> It may be this my exhortation
> Seems harsh and all unpleasant; let it not,
45 > For, gentle son, I speak it not in wrath
> Or envy of thee, but in tender love
> And pity of thy future misery,
> And so have hope that this my kind rebuke,
> Checking thy body, may amend thy soul.

Faustus.
50 > Where art thou, Faustus? wretch, what hast thou done!
> Hell claims his right, and with a roaring voice
> Says, "Faustus, come, thine hour is almost come!"

> *Mephostophilis gives him a dagger.*

> And Faustus now will come to do thee right.

Old Man.
> O stay, good Faustus, stay thy desperate steps!

---

37. *persever*] accented on the second syllable.
38-39. *Yet...nature*] i.e. Your soul is still worthy of love so long as sin does not through force of habit become your nature. These lines are strongly Augustinian in tone. St. Augustine explained the soul's vacillation between opposing wills, the mind's monstrous inability to command itself to will one thing, in terms of the contrary pulls of truth and of custom (*Confessions* VIII.ix. 21). He had himself been bound by the chains of custom or habit: "The enemy, from his control of my will, had made a chain to bind me fast. For from a perverse act of will, desire had grown; and when desire is satisfied, custom is forged; and custom not resisted becomes necessity..." (*Confessions* VIII.v. 10). This sort of custom, "created for the soul by its own act of sin" (*Acta contra Fortunatum Manichaeum* 22), also becomes part of our nature, as a matter both of the pleasure derived from the memory of past sins and also of the increasing ease with which they are repeated.
49. *Checking*] reproving.

I see an angel hover o'er thy head,   55
And with a vial full of precious grace
Offers to pour the same into thy soul:
Then call for mercy, and avoid despair.

Faustus.
O friend, I feel thy words to comfort my distressed soul;
Leave me awhile to ponder on my sins.   60

Old Man.
Faustus, I leave thee, but with grief of heart,
Fearing the enemy of thy hapless soul.

                        Exit.

Faustus.
Accursed Faustus: wretch, what hast thou done?
I do repent, and yet I do despair [....]

Act V, Scene ii, first addition (1616 text).

*The B-version of the last scene of the play contains two
added passages. In the first of these, the same demonic
trinity that answered Faustus's appeal to Christ (in II.iii of
this edition) arrives to witness his final hours, and Faustus
talks briefly with Wagner about his will. The second passage, inserted between Faustus's confession to the Scholars
and his last soliloquy, consists of a final incitement to
despair from Mephostophilis, followed by the moralizing
interventions of the Good and Bad Angels.*

Thunder. Enter Lucifer, Belzebub, and Mephostophilis.

0.1.] As in I.iii (where A's stage direction "Enter Faustus to conjure" is replaced in B by
"Thunder. Enter Lucifer and four devils, Faustus to them with this speech"), the B-text
introduces a second, demonic audience, which in the former scene at least remains invisible
to Faustus.

Lucifer.
    Thus from infernal Dis do we ascend
    To view the subjects of our monarchy,
    Those souls which sin seals the black sons of hell,
    'Mong which as chief, Faustus, we come to thee,
5   Bringing with us lasting damnation
    To wait upon thy soul; the time is come
    Which makes it forfeit.
Meph.
                 And this gloomy night
    Here in this room will wretched Faustus be.
Bel.
    And here we'll stay
10 To mark him how he doth demean himself.
Meph.
    How should he but in desperate lunacy?
    Fond worldling, now his heart-blood dries with grief;
    His conscience kills it, and his laboring brain
    Begets a world of idle fantasies
15 To overreach the devil: but all in vain,
    His store of pleasures must be sauc'd with pain.
    He and his servant Wagner are at hand;
    Both come from drawing Faustus' latest will.
    See where they come.

        Enter Faustus and Wagner.

Faustus.
20 Say Wagner, thou hast perus'd my will;
    How dost thou like it?
Wagner.
              Sir, so wondrous well
    As in all humble duty I do yield
    My life and lasting service for your love.

1. *Dis*] a name given to Pluto and, by transference, to the underworld over which he rules.
18-24.] This discussion of Faustus's will is redundant (Wagner has already said all that need be said at the outset of V.i), and also dramatically clumsy, since it obliges Faustus to move from calmness to a state of panic within two lines.

Enter the Scholars.

Faustus.
Gramercies, Wagner. Welcome, gentlemen.

[Exit Wagner.]

1 Sch.
Now, worthy Faustus, methinks your looks are chang'd.   25

Faustus.
Oh gentlemen!

2 Sch.
What ails Faustus?

Faustus.
Ah my sweet chamber-fellow, had I liv'd with thee,
Then had I liv'd still, but now must die eternally.
Look sirs, comes he not, comes he not?   30

1 Sch.
O my dear Faustus, what imports this fear?

2 Sch.
Is all our pleasure turn'd to melancholy?

3 Sch.
He is not well with being over solitary.

2 Sch
If it be so, we'll have physicians, and Faustus shall be
cured.   35

3 Sch.
'Tis but a surfeit, sir, fear nothing.

---

24. *Gramercies*] thank you.
24-26. *Welcome...Oh gentlemen!*] This would make dramatic sense if it were assumed that
the writers responsible for the B-version intended Faustus at this point to see the devils,
who yet remain invisible to his companions. However, line 30 makes such an assumption
impossible. The dramatic awkwardness of the B-version at this point is one sign of its secondary nature.

Act V, Scene ii, second addition (1616 text).

In order to facilitate comparisons with the 1604 version of this scene, the line numbers in this passage have been made to correspond with those of the present A-version edition; there is no connection between these numbers and the lineation of any B-version edition of the play.

Faustus.

56   Gentlemen, farewell. If I live till morning, I'll visit you; if not, Faustus is gone to hell.

All.

     Faustus, farewell.

Exeunt Scholars.

Meph.

     Ay Faustus, now thou hast no hope of heaven;
60   Therefore despair, think only upon hell,
     For that must be thy mansion, there to dwell.

Faustus.

     O thou bewitching fiend, 'twas thy temptation
     Hath robb'd me of eternal happiness!

Meph.

     I do confess it, Faustus, and rejoice;
65   'Twas I that, when thou wert i'the way to heaven,
     Damm'd up thy passage: when thou took'st the book
     To view the scriptures, then I turn'd the leaves
     And led thine eye.
     What, weep'st thou? 'tis too late, despair, farewell;
70   Fools that will laugh on earth must weep in hell!

Exit.

Enter the Good Angel and the Bad Angel at several doors.

70.2. several] different.

Good.
　O Faustus, if thou hadst given ear to me,
　Innumerable joys had follow'd thee;
　But thou didst love the world.

Bad.
　　　　　　　　　　　Gave ear to me,
　And now must taste hell's pains perpetually.

Good.
　O what will all thy riches, pleasures, pomps,　　　75
　Avail thee now?

Bad.
　　　　　　　　Nothing but vex thee more,
　To want in hell, that had on earth such store.

　　　Music while the throne descends.

Good.
　O, thou hast lost celestial happiness,
　Pleasures unspeakable, bliss without end.
　Hadst thou affected sweet divinity,　　　　　80
　Hell or the devil had had no power on thee.
　Hadst thou kept on that way, Faustus, behold
　In what resplendent glory thou hadst sat
　In yonder throne, like those bright shining saints,
　And triumph'd over hell; that hast thou lost,　　85
　And now, poor soul, must thy good angel leave thee:
　The jaws of hell are open to receive thee.

　　Exit. [The throne ascends.]
　　Hell is discovered.

Bad.
　Now, Faustus, let thine eyes with horror stare

77.1.] The throne would have been let down from the theatre's "heavens" by means of ropes and pulleys.
80. *affected*] been drawn to, preferred, loved.
87.2. Hell is discovered] perhaps by the drawing of a curtain to reveal a painted backcloth; or perhaps by the uncovering of a trap with smoke rising from it.

Into that vast perpetual torture-house:
90   There are the furies, tossing damned souls
On burning forks; their bodies broil in lead.
There are live quarters broiling on the coals,
That ne'er can die; this ever-burning chair
Is for o'er tortur'd souls to rest them in.
95   These that are fed with sops of flaming fire
Were gluttons and lov'd only delicates,
And laugh'd to see the poor starve at their gates.
But yet all these are nothing: thou shalt see
Ten thousand tortures that more horrid be.

Faustus.

100   O, I have seen enough to torture me!

Bad.

Nay, thou must feel them, taste the smart of all;
He that loves pleasure must for pleasure fall.
And so I leave thee, Faustus, till anon,
Then wilt thou tumble in confusion.

Exit.

Act V, Scene iii (1616 text).

Enter the Scholars.

1 Sch.

Come gentlemen, let us go visit Faustus,
For such a dreadful night was never seen:
Since first the world's creation did begin,
Such fearful shrieks and cries were never heard.
5   Pray heaven the doctor have escap'd the danger.

2 Sch.

O help us heaven! See, here are Faustus' limbs
All torn asunder by the hand of death!

3 Sch.

The devils whom Faustus serv'd have torn him thus,

104.1.] This stage direction is followed by the striking of the clock and by Faustus's last soliloquy.

For 'twixt the hours of twelve and one methought
I heard him shriek and call aloud for help,   10
At which self time the house seem'd all on fire
With dreadful horror of these damned fiends.

2 Sch.

Well gentlemen, though Faustus' end be such
As every Christian heart laments to think on,
Yet for he was a scholar once admir'd   15
For wondrous knowledge in our German schools
We'll give his mangled limbs due burial,
And all the students, cloth'd in mourning black,
Shall wait upon his heavy funeral.

Exeunt.

19. *wait upon*] to observe; also to accompany on its way.   *heavy*] sad, sorrowful.

NOTES TO
APPENDIX 1

ACT I Scene iv (1616 text)

1-46.] *B1; for collations and notes see the A-version text of this scene.*

ACT II Scene iii (1616 text)

1. *Robin.*] *Dyce; not in B1.*
6-7. *He...read*] *Not in B1.*

ACT III Scene i (1616 text)

52. in state and] *B2; this day with B1.*
74, 78. cunning] *B4; comming B1.*
100. Florence] *conj. Greg; France B1.*
151. keys] *conj. Oxberry, Boas; seales B1.*
183. Ponte] *Dyce; Ponto B1.*

ACT III Scene ii (1616 text)

0.2. *Mephostophilis*] *Mephastophilis B1.*
11. Mephostophilis] *Mephasto B1.*
54.1. *Exeunt...Cardinals*] *Dyce; not in B1.*
63.1, 68.1, 74.1.] *This stage direction occurs in A1 (at III.i. 65.1 only), but not in B1.*
79. *Archbishop*] *Dyce; Bish. B1.*
84.1, 86.1, 94.1.] *Borrowed from A1 (III.i. 75.1, 79.1, and 87.1); not in B1.*
98. on the face] *A1, B2; the face B1.*
100. tooke] *A1; strucke B1.*

ACT III Scene iii (1616 text)

29. You...Rule] *B1. A revision, most probably, of the parallel lines in A1*

("Monarch of hel, vnder whose blacke suruey / Great Potentates do kneele with awful feare, / Vpon whose altars thousand soules do lie" [III.ii. 32-34]), *which were no doubt felt to be shocking.*
32.1. *Exit Vintner] Dyce; not in B1.*

ACT IV Scene i (1616 text)

43.1. *Exeunt...Martino] Not in B1, which prints "Exit" at 47.1. Dyce's emendation of the B1 stage direction to "Exeunt Frederick and Martino" has been accepted by most subsequent editors—many of whom follow Cunningham in starting a new scene with the Emperor's entrance. Gill (1971) prefers to assume that Frederick and Martino remain on stage.*
72. like a] *B2*; like *B1.*
84.1. *Exit] Dyce; not in B1.*
99.1. *dore] B2; not in B1.*
102. ravish'd so] *Greg*; so rauished *B1.*
156. Mephostophilis] Mephastophilis *B1.*
156.1. *Mephostophilis...horns] Dyce; not in B1.*

ACT IV Scene ii (1616 text)

27. heart's] *B2*; heart *B1.*
39.1. *Strikes] Dyce; not in B1.*
62. his] *B2* ; *not in B1.*
66.1. *Faustus gets up] Robinson; not in B1.*
70. Ay, all] *Oxberry*; I call *B1.*
105.5. *Exit Faustus] Boas; not in B1.*

ACT IV Scene iii (1616 text)

12-13. *The line breaks occur after "right" and "head" in B1.*
13. Zounds] *B2*; 'Zons *B1.*
24. these] *B2*; this *B1.*

ACT IV Scene iv (1616 text)

37.1. *Exit] Oxberry; not in B1.*

ACT IV Scene v (1616 text)

17, 35. Fauster] *B1*; Faustus *B2.*
37. rare] *B2; not in B1.*

ACT IV Scene vi (1616 text)

1-112.1.] *B1. Lines 1-30 are loosely parallel to IV.iii in the A-text; for collation of the two passages, see the A-version text.*
0.2. *also a servant] Not in B1. A servant is required at line 32, and speaks at line 34.*
3-4. air, / The sight] Aire: the / Sight *B1.*
30.1. *Clowns bounce] Dyce; Clowne bounce B1; bounceth B3.*
34. *Servant.] A Seruant. B1.*
58. Zounds] Zons *B1.*
66.1. *Exit Mephostophilis] Not in B1. Most editors ignore the need for a stage direction here; Kirschbaum goes overboard with "To servants, some of whom exeunt. Mephostophilis also exit."*
77. ride him] *B2*; ride *B1.*
82. curtsy] curtesie *B1. The word means "courtesy" in the abstract as well as "curtsy" (an obeisance now understood as an exclusively feminine gesture, but in the early seventeenth century equated with "making a leg".*
83.1. *Bows] Kirschbaum; not in B1.*
102.1, 104.1, 106.1, 108.1. *Faustus...dumb] Not in B1.*

ACT V Scene i (lines 25-64; 1616 text)

24.1. *sounds] A1; sound B1. Mephostophilis...she] B1; and Helen A1.*
25-26. Was...Troy?] *B1; not in A1. These lines replace a speech which in A follows the lines given in B to 3 Scholar:* No maruel tho the angry Greekes pursude / With tenne yeares warre the rape of such a queene, / Whose heauenly beauty passeth all compare.
29. Now] *B1*; Since *A1.* worke] *B1*; workes *A1.*
30. Wee'l...sight] *B1;* And onely Paragon of excellence, / Let vs depart, and for this glorious deed *A1.*
31.1. *Exeunt Schollers] In B1 this stage direction is placed in the margin after line 31; in A1 it follows the next line.*
32. wish I] *B1*; I wish *A1.*
32.1. *Enter an old Man] B1; placed in A1 in the margin beside the two lines which*

Notes to Appendix 1

in *B1* are replaced by line 30.

33-49. O gentle...soule] *B1; not in A1.*

50. Where...done?] *B1, A1. Followed in A1 by* Damnd art thou Faustus, damnd, dispaire and die.

51. claimes his] *B1;* calls for *A1.*

52. almost] *B1; not in A1.*

52.1. *Meph. giues him a dagger] Placed in B1 in the margin beside lines 51-53; in A1 in the margin beside the latter two lines only.*

53. now] *B1; not in A1.*

54. O] *B1;* Ah *A1.*

55. houer] *B1;* houers *A1.*

59. O...feel] *B1;* Ah my sweete friend, I feele *A1.*

61. Faustus...heart] *B1;* I goe sweete Faustus, but with heauy cheare *A1.*

62. enemy] *B1;* ruine *A1.*   haplesse] *B1;* hopelesse *A1.*

62.1. *Exit] B1; not in A1.*

63. wretch...done?] *B1;* where is mercie now? *A1.*

64. *The rest of the scene after this line is quite closely parallel in the A- and B-texts, except that in B the Old Man does not re-enter, and B therefore lacks the last nine lines of the scene in A.*

ACT V Scene ii (first addition; 1616 text)

1-25.] *B1; not in A1.*

23.1. *Enter the scholers] B1; the scene in A1 begins with the stage direction "Enter Faustus with the Schollers" and Faustus's exclamation* Ah Gentlemen! *(=B version, V.ii. 26).*

24.1. *Exit Wagner] Oxberry; not in B1.*

26. Oh] *B1;* Ah *A1.*

28-29.] *Verse as here in B1; printed as prose in A1.*

29. must dye] *B1;* I die *A1.*

30. Looke sirs] *B1;* looke *A1.*

31-32. O...melancholy?] *B1;* 2 Sch: what means Faustus? *A1.*

33. He...solitarie] *B1;* Belike he is growne into some sickenesse, by being ouer solitary. *A1.*

34-35. and...cur'd] *B1;* to cure him *A1.*

36. sir, feare nothing] *B1;* neuer feare man *A1. From this point until the departure of the Scholars, A and B are closely parallel.*

ACT V Scene ii (second addition; 1616 text)

56-58.1.] *B1, A1.*

59-104.1.] *B1; not in A1.*

70. must] *B2;* most *B1.*

83. sat] *Cunningham;* set *B1;* sit *B2.*

87.1. *The throne ascends] Dyce; not in B1.*

ACT V Scene iii (1616 text)

1-19.1. *B1; this scene does not appear in A1.*

APPENDIX 2

Excerpts from *The Historie of the damnable life, and deserved death of Doctor John Faustus* (London, 1592).

The principal passages of the English Faustbook drawn upon in the A-version of Marlowe's play and in the B-text revisions are reproduced here, in modernized form, and with obvious misprints silently corrected. To facilitate comparisons, I have indicated the passages in Marlowe's *Doctor Faustus* which correspond to these excerpts.

Doctor Faustus, **Prologue, 11-27; I.i; I.iii.**

EFB, Chap. 1. John Faustus, born in the town of Rhode, lying in the province of Weimar in Germ[any], his father a poor husbandman and not [able] well to bring him up: but having an uncle at Wittenberg, a rich man and without issue, took this J. Faustus from his father and made him his heir, in so much that his father was no more troubled with him, for he remained with his uncle at Wittenberg, where he was kept at the university in the same city to study divinity. But Faustus, being of a naughty mind and otherwise addicted, applied not his studies, but took himself to other exercises: the which his uncle oftentimes hearing, rebuked him for it, as Eli oft times rebuked his children for sinning against the Lord: even so this good man labored to have Faustus apply his study of divinity, that he might come to the knowledge of God and his laws. But it is manifest that many virtuous parents have wicked children, as Cain, Reuben, Absolom and such like have been to their parents: so this Faustus having godly parents, and seeing him to be of a toward wit, were very desirous to bring him up in those virtuous studies, namely, of divinity: but he gave himself secretly to study necromancy and conjuration, in so much that few or none could perceive his profession.

But to the purpose: Faustus continued at study in the university, and was by the Rectors and sixteen Masters afterwards examined how he had profited in his studies; and being found by them that none for his time were able to argue with him in divinity, or for the excellency of his wisdom to compare with him, with one consent they made him Doctor of Divinity. But Doctor Faustus, within short time after he had obtained his degree, fell into such fantasies and deep cogitations that he was marked of many, and of the most part of the students was called the Speculator; and sometime he would throw the scriptures from him as though he had no care of his former profession: so that he began a very ungodly life, as hereafter more at large may appear; for the old proverb saith, Who can hold that will away? So who can hold Faustus from the devil, that seeks after him with all his endeavor? For he accompanied himself with divers that were seen in those devilish arts, and that had the Chaldean, Persian, Hebrew, Arabian, and Greek tongues, using figures, characters, conjurations, incantations, with many other ceremonies belonging to these infernal arts, as necromancy, charms, soothsaying, witchcraft, enchantment, being delighted with their books, words, and names so well that he studied day and night therein: in so much that he could not abide to be called doctor of divinity, but waxed a worldly man, and named himself an astrologian, and a mathematician: and for a shadow sometimes a physician, and did great cures, namely with herbs, roots, waters, drinks, receipts, and clisters. And without doubt he was passing wise, and excellent perfect in the holy scriptures: but he that knoweth his master's will and doth it not, is worthy to be beaten with many stripes. It is written, No man can serve two masters, and Thou shalt not tempt the Lord thy God: but Faustus threw all this in the wind, and made his soul of no estimation, regarding more his worldly pleasure than the joys to come: therefore at the day of judgment there is no hope of his redemption.

EFB, Chap. 2.   You have heard before, that all Faustus' mind was set to study the arts of necromancy and conjuration, the which exercise he followed day and night: and taking to him the wings of an eagle, thought to fly over the whole world, and to know the secrets of heaven and earth; for his speculation was so wonderful, being expert in using his *vocabula*, figures, characters, conjurations, and other ceremonial actions, that in all the haste he put in practice to bring the devil before him. And taking his way to a thick wood near to Wittenberg, called in the German tongue *Spisser Waldt*..., he came into the same wood towards evening into a cross way, where he made with a wand a circle in the dust, and within that many more circles and characters: and thus he passed away the time, until it was nine or ten of the clock in the night, then began Doctor Faustus to call for Mephostophiles the spirit, and to charge him in the name of Beelzebub to appear there personally without any long stay: then presently the devil began so great a rumor in the wood, as if heaven and earth would have come together with wind, the trees bowing their tops to the ground; then fell the devil to bleat as if the whole wood had been full of lions, and suddenly about the circle ran the devil as if a thousand wagons had been running together on paved stones. After this at the four corners of the wood it thundered horribly, with such lightnings as if the whole world, to his seeming, had been on fire. Faustus all this while half amazed at the devil's so long tarrying, and doubting whether he were best to abide any more such horrible conjurings, thought to leave his circle and depart; whereupon the devil made him such music of all sorts, as if the nymphs themselves had been in place: whereat Faustus was revived and stood stoutly in his circle aspecting his purpose, and began again to conjure the spirit Mephostophiles in the name of the prince of devils to appear in his likeness: whereat suddenly over his head hanged hovering in the air a mighty dragon: then calls Faustus again after his devilish manner, at which there was a monstrous cry in the wood, as if hell had been open, and all the tormented souls crying to God for mercy; presently not three fathom above his head fell a flame in manner of a lightning, and changed itself into a globe: yet Faustus feared it not, but did persuade himself that the devil should give him his request before he would leave.... Faustus, vexed at the spirit's so long tarrying, used his charms with full purpose not to depart before he had his intent, and crying on Mephostophiles the spirit, suddenly the globe opened and sprang up in height of a man: so burning a time, in the end it converted to the shape of a fiery man. This pleasant beast ran about the circle a great while, and lastly appeared in manner of a grey friar, asking Faustus what was his request. Faustus commanded that the next morning at twelve of the clock he should appear to him at his house, but the devil would in no wise grant. Faustus began again to conjure him in the name of Beelzebub, that he should fulfil his request: whereupon the spirit agreed, and so they departed each one his way.

EFB, Chap. 3. Doctor Faustus having commanded the spirit to be with him, at his hour appointed he came and appeared in his chamber, demanding of Faustus what his desire was: then began Doctor Faustus anew with him to conjure him that he should be obedient unto him, and to answer him certain articles, and to fulfil them in all points.

1 That the spirit should serve him and be obedient unto him in all things that he asked of him from that hour until the hour of his death.

2 Farther, any thing that he desired of him he should bring it to him.

3 Also, that in all Faustus his demands or interrogations the spirit should tell him nothing but that which is true.

Hereupon the spirit answered and laid his case forth, that he had no power of himself, until he had first given his prince (that was ruler over him) to understand thereof, and to know if he could obtain so much of his lord: Therefore speak farther that I may do thy whole desire to my prince: for it is not in my power to fulfil without his leave....

Doctor Faustus upon this arose where he sat, and said, I will have my request, and yet I will not be damned. The spirit answered, Then shalt thou want thy desire, and yet art thou mine notwithstanding: if any man would detain thee it is in vain, for thine infidelity hath confounded thee.

Hereupon spake Faustus: Get thee hence from me, and take Saint Valentine's farewell and Crisam with thee, yet I conjure thee that thou be here at evening, and bethink thyself on that I have asked thee, and ask thy prince's counsel therein. Mephostophiles the spirit, thus answered, vanished away, leaving Faustus in his study, where he sat pondering with himself how he might obtain his request of the devil without loss of his soul: yet fully he was resolved in himself rather than to want his pleasure, to do whatsoever the spirit and his lord should condition upon.

EFB, Chap. 10. ...Here Faustus said: But how came thy lord and master Lucifer to have so great a fall from heaven? Mephostophiles answered: My lord Lucifer was a fair angel, created of God as immortal, and being placed in the seraphins, which are above the cherubins, he would have presumed unto the throne of God, with intent to have thrust God out of his seat. Upon this presumption the Lord cast him down headlong, and where before he was an angel of light, now dwells he in darkness....

EFB, Chap. 13. ...Faustus, my lord Lucifer (so called now, for that he was banished out of the clear light of heaven) was at the first an angel of God; he sat on the cherubins, and saw all the wonderful works of God, yea he was so of God ordained for shape, pomp, authority, worthiness, and dwelling, that he far exceeded all the other creatures of God, yea our gold and precious stones: and so illuminated, that he far surpassed the brightness of the sun and all other stars: wherefore God placed him on the cherubins, where he had a kingly office, and was always before God's seat, to the end he might be the more perfect in all his beings: but when he began to be high-minded, proud, and so presumptuous that he would usurp the seat of his Majesty, then was he banished out from amongst the heavenly powers...

Doctor Faustus, **II.i. 30-158.**

EFB, Chap. 4. Faustus continuing in his devilish cogitations, never moving out of the place where the spirit left him (such was his fervent love to the devil), the night approaching, this swift flying spirit appeared to Faustus, offering himself with all submission to his service, with full authority from his prince to do whatsoever he would request, if so be Faustus would promise to be his: This answer I bring thee, and an answer must thou make by me again, yet will I hear what is thy desire, because thou hast sworn me to be here at this time. Doctor Faustus gave him this answer, though faintly (for his soul's sake): That his request was none other but to become a devil, or at least a limb of him, and that the spirit should agree unto these articles as followeth.

1 That he might be a spirit in shape and quality.
2 That Mephostophiles should be his servant, and at his commandment.
3 That Mephostophiles should bring him any thing, and do for him whatsoever.
4 That at all times he should be in his house, invisible to all men, except only to himself, and at his commandment to show himself.
5 Lastly, that Mephostophiles should at all times appear at his command, in what form or shape soever he would.

Upon these points the spirit answered Doctor Faustus, that all this should be granted him and fulfilled, and more if he would agree unto him upon certain articles as followeth.

First, that Doctor Faustus should give himself to his lord Lucifer, body and soul.
Secondly, for confirmation of the same, he should make him a writing, written with his own blood.
Thirdly, that he would be an enemy to all Christian people.
Fourthly, that he would deny his Christian belief.
Fifthly, that he let not any man change his opinion, if so be any man should go about to dissuade or withdraw him from it.

Further, the spirit promised Faustus to give him certain years to live in health and pleasure, and when such years were expired, that then Faustus should be fetched away, and if he should hold these articles and conditions, then he should have all whatsoever his heart would wish or desire; and that Faustus should quickly perceive himself to be a spirit in all manner of actions whatsoever. Hereupon Doctor Faustus his mind was so inflamed that he forgot his soul, and promised Mephostophiles to hold all things as he had mentioned them: he thought the devil was not so black as they use to paint him, nor hell so hot as the people say, etc.

EFB, Chap. 5. ...After a while, Faustus promised Mephostophiles to write and make his obligation, with full assurance of the articles in the chapter before rehearsed. A pitiful case (Christian reader), for certainly this letter or obligation was found in his house after his most lamentable end, with all the rest of his damnable practices used in his whole life. Therefore I wish all Christians to take an example by this wicked Faustus, and to be comforted in Christ, contenting themselves with that vocation whereunto it hath pleased God to call them, and not to esteem the vain delights of this life, as did this unhappy Faustus, in giving his soul to the devil: and to confirm it the more assuredly, he took a small penknife, and pricked a vein in his left hand, and for certainty thereupon were seen on his hand these words written, as if they had been written with blood, *ô homo fuge*: whereat the spirit vanished, but Faustus continued in his damnable mind, and made his writing as followeth.

EFB, Chap. 6. *How Doctor Faustus set his blood in a saucer on warm ashes, and writ as followeth.*

I Johannes Faustus, Doctor, do openly acknowledge with mine own hand, to the greater force and strengthening of this letter, that siththence I began to study and speculate the course and order of the elements, I have not found through the gift that is given me from above any such learning and wisdom that can bring me to my desires: and for that I find that men are unable to instruct me any farther in the matter, now have I, Doctor John Faustus, unto the hellish prince of Orient and his messenger Mephostophiles, given both body and soul, upon such condition that they shall learn me, and fulfil my desire in all things, as they have promised and vowed unto me, with due obedience unto me, according to the articles mentioned between us.

Further, I covenant and grant them by these presents, that at the end of 24 years next ensuing the date of this present letter...I give them full power to do with me at their pleasure, to rule, to send, fetch, or carry me or mine, be it either body, soul, flesh, blood, or goods, into their habitation, be it wheresoever: and hereupon, I defy God and his Christ, all the host of heaven, and all living creatures that bear the shape of God, yea all that lives; and again I say it, and it shall be so. And to the more strengthening of this writing, I have written it with mine own hand and blood....

EFB, Chap. 7. [Faustus is treated to a series of magical spectacles in which spirits assume the forms of animals, and is given a sack of gold and another of silver.] Lastly, was heard by Faustus all manner instruments of music..., the which so ravished his mind, that he thought he had been in another world, forgot both body and soul, in so much that he was minded never to change his opinion concerning that which he had done. Hereat came Mephostophiles into the hall to Faustus, in apparel like unto a friar, to whom Faustus spake: Thou hast done me a wonderful pleasure in showing me this pastime; if thou continue as thou hast begun, thou shalt win my heart and soul, yea and have it. Mephostophiles answered, This is nothing, I will please thee better: yet that thou maist know my power and all, ask what thou wilt request of me, that shalt thou have, conditionally hold thy promise, and give me thy hand-writing: at which words, the wretch thrust forth his hand, saying, Hold thee, there hast thou my promise: Mephostophiles took the writing....

EFB, Chap 11. The night following, after Faustus his communication had with Mephostophiles as concerning the fall of Lucifer, Doctor Faustus dreamed that he had seen a part of hell: but in what manner it was, or in what place he knew not: whereupon he was greatly troubled in mind, and called unto him Mephostophiles his spirit, saying to him, My Mephostophiles, I pray thee resolve me in this doubt: what is hell, what substance is it of, in what place stands it, and when was it made? Mephostophiles answered: My Faustus, thou shalt know that before the fall of my lord Lucifer there was no hell, but even then was hell ordained: it is of no substance, but a confused thing...: in this confused hell is nought to find but a filthy, sulphurish, firie, stinking mist or fog.... Further, we devils know not how God hath laid the foundation of our hell, nor whereof it is: but to be short with thee, Faustus, we know that hell hath neither bottom nor end.

EFB, Chap. 9. Doctor Faustus continued thus in his epicurish life day and night, and believed not that there was a God, hell, or devil: he thought that body and soul died together, and had quite fogotten divinity or the immortality of his soul, but stood in his damnable heresy day and night. And bethinking himself of a wife, called

Mephostophiles to counsel; which would in no wise agree, demanding of him if he would break the covenant made with him, or if he had forgot it. Hast not thou (quoth Mephostophiles) sworn thyself an enemy to God and all creatures? To this I answer thee, thou canst not marry; thou canst not serve two masters, God, and my prince: for wedlock is a chief institution ordained of God, and that hast thou promised to defy, as we do all, and that hast thou also done: and moreover thou hast confirmed it with thy blood: persuade thyself that what thou dost in contempt of wedlock, it is all to thine own delight. Therefore, Faustus, look well about thee, and bethink thyself better, and I wish thee to change thy mind: for if thou keep not what thou hast promised in thy writing, we will tear thee in pieces like the dust under thy feet.... But shortly, and that within two hours after, Faustus called his spirit, which came in his old manner like a friar. Then Faustus said unto him, I am not able to resist nor bridle my fantasy, I must and will have a wife, and I pray thee give thy consent to it. Suddenly upon these words came such a whirlwind about the place, that Faustus thought the whole house would come down; all the doors in the house flew off the hooks: after all this, his house was full of smoke, and the floor covered over with ashes: which when Doctor Faustus perceived, he would have gone up the stairs: and flying up, he was taken and thrown into the hall, that he was not able to stir hand nor foot: then round about him ran a monstrous circle of fire, never standing still, that Faustus fried as he lay, and thought there to have been burned. Then cried he out to his spirit Mephostophiles for help, promising him he would live in all things as he had vowed in his handwriting. Hereupon appeared unto him an ugly devil, so fearful and monstrous to behold, that Faustus durst not look on him. The devil said, What wouldst thou have, Faustus? how likest thou thy wedding? what mind art thou in now? Faustus answered, he had forgot his promise, desiring him of pardon, and he would talk no more of such things. The devil answered, Thou wert best so to do, and so vanished.

After appeared unto him his friar Mephostophiles with a bell in his hand, and spake to Faustus: It is no jesting with us; hold thou that which thou hast vowed, and we will perform as we have promised: and more than that, thou shalt have thy heart's desire of what woman soever thou wilt, be she alive or dead, and so long as thou wilt, thou shalt keep her by thee.

These words pleased Faustus wonderful well, and repented himself that he was so foolish to wish himself married, that might have any woman in the whole city brought to him at his command; the which he practised and persevered in a long time.

EFB, Chap. 10. Doctor Faustus living in all manner of pleasure that his heart could desire, continuing in his amorous drifts, his delicate fare, and costly apparel, called on a time his Mephostophiles to him: which being come, brought with him a book in his hand of all manner of devilish and enchanted arts, the which he gave Faustus, saying: Hold, my Faustus, work now thy heart's desire....

Doctor Faustus, **II.iii.**

EFB, Chap. 18. Doctor Faustus...called unto him Mephostophiles his spirit, saying:...when I confer *Astronomia* and *Astrologia*, as the mathematicians and ancient writers have left in memory, I find them to vary and very much to disagree: wherefore I pray thee to teach me the truth in this matter.

EFB, Chap. 19. Doctor Faustus revolving with himself the speeches of his spirit, he became so woeful and sorrowful in his cogitations that he thought himself already frying in the hottest flames of hell; and lying in his muse, suddenly there appeared unto him his spirit, demanding what things so grieved and troubled his conscience.... To whom Faustus answered, I have taken thee unto me as a servant to do me service, and thy service will be very dear unto me; yet I cannot have any diligence of thee farther than thou list thyself, neither dost thou in any thing as it becometh thee. The spirit replied, My Faustus, thou knowest that I was never against thy commandments as yet, but ready to serve and resolve thy questions; although I am not bound unto thee in such respects as concern the hurt of our kingdom, yet was I always willing to answer thee, and so I am still: therefore, my Faustus, say on boldly, what is thy will and pleasure? At which words, the spirit stole away the heart of Faustus, who spake in this sort: Mephostophiles, tell me how and after what sort God made the world, and all the creatures in them, and why man was made after the image of God? The spirit, hearing this, answered: Faustus, thou knowest that all this is in vain for thee to ask. I know that thou art sorry for that thou hast done, but it availeth thee not, for I will tear thee in thousands of pieces if thou change not thine opinions, and hereat he vanished away. Whereat Faustus, all sorrowful for that he had put forth such a question, fell to weeping and to howling bitterly, not for his sins towards God, but for that the devil was departed from him so suddenly, and in such a rage. And being in this perplexity, he was suddenly taken in such an extreme cold, as if he should have frozen in the place where he sat, in which the greatest devil in hell appeared unto him, with certain of his hideous and infernal company in the most ugliest shapes that it was possible to think upon, and traversing the chamber round about where Faustus sat, Faustus thought to himself, Now are they come for me though my time be not come, and that because I have asked such questions of my servant Mephostophiles: at whose cogitations, the chiefest devil, which was his lord unto whom he gave his soul, that was Lucifer, spake in this sort: Faustus, I have seen thy thoughts, which are not as thou hast vowed unto me, by virtue of this letter, and showed him the obligation that he had written with his own blood; wherefore I am come to visit thee and to show thee some of our hellish pastimes, in hope that will draw and confirm thy mind a little more steadfast unto us. Content, quoth Faustus, go to, let me see what pastime you can make.

[There follows a pageant, not of the Seven Deadly Sins, but of grotesquely shaped devils, the last of whom, Mephostophiles, appears first as a dragon, and then transforms himself into the shape of a friar, "saying, Faustus, what wilt thou?"] Saith Faustus, I will that thou teach me to transform myself in like sort as thou and the rest have done: then Lucifer put forth his paw, and gave Faustus a book, saying, Hold, do what thou wilt, which he looking upon, straightways changed himself into a hog, then into a worm, then into a dragon, and finding this for his purpose, it liked him well. Quoth he to Lucifer, And how cometh it that all these filthy forms are in the world? Lucifer answered, They are ordained of God as plagues unto men, and so shalt thou be plagued (quoth he), whereupon came scorpions, wasps, emmets, bees, and gnats, which fell to stinging and biting him...; wherefore he cried for help, saying, Mephostophiles my faithful servant, where art thou, help, help I pray thee! Hereat his spirit answered nothing, but Lucifer himself said, Ho ho ho, Faustus, how likest thou the creation of the world? And incontinent it was clear again, and the devils and all the filthy cattle were vanished; only Faustus was left alone, seeing nothing, but hearing the sweetest music that ever he heard before, at which he was so ravished with delight that he forgot the fears he was in before: and it repented him that he had seen no more of their pastime.

EFB, Chap. 20. ...on a time he called his spirit Mephostophiles, and said unto him, Bring thou hither unto me thy lord Lucifer, or Belial. He brought him (notwithstanding) one that was called Beelzebub, the which asked Faustus his pleasure. Quoth Faustus, I would know of thee if I may see hell and take a view thereof. That thou shalt (said the devil), and at midnight I will fetch thee.

Doctor Faustus, **Act III, Chorus.**

EFB, Chap. 21. [This chapter takes the form of a letter written by Faustus to a friend.] I being once laid on my bed, and could not sleep for thinking on my calendar and practice, I marveled with myself how it were possible that the firmament should be known and so largely written of men, or whether they write true or false, by their own opinions or supposition, or by due observations and true course of the heavens. Behold, being in these my muses, suddenly I heard...a groaning voice which said, Get up, the desire of thy heart, mind, and thought shalt thou see...and behold, there stood a wagon, with two dragons before it to draw the same, and all the wagon was of a light burning fire.... Hereupon I got me into the wagon, so that the dragons carried me upright into the air...on the Tuesday went out, and on Tuesday seven-nights following I came home again, that is, eight days, in which time I slept not.... And farther, my good schoolfellow, I was thus nigh the heavens, where me thought every planet was but as half the earth..., and as I came down I looked upon the world and the heavens, and me thought that the earth was enclosed in comparison with the firmament, as the yolk of an egg within the white, and me thought that the whole length of the earth was not a span long....

Doctor Faustus, **III.i.**

EFB, Chap. 22. ...All these kingdoms, provinces, and countries he passed in 25 days, in which time he saw very little that delighted his mind: wherefore he took a little rest at home, and burning in desire to see more at large, and to behold the secrets of each kingdom, he set forward again on his journey upon his swift horse Mephostophiles, and came to Trier, for that he chiefly desired to see this town, and the monuments thereof; but there he saw not many wonders, except one fair palace that belonged unto the bishop, and also a mighty large castle that was built of brick, with three walls and three great trenches, so strong that it was impossible for any prince's power to win it...from whence he departed to Paris, where he liked well the academy; and what place or kingdom soever fell in his mind, the same he visited. He came from Paris to Mentz, where the river of Maine falls into the Rhine; notwithstanding he tarried not long there, but went to Campania in the kingdom of Neapolis, in which he saw an innumerable sort of cloisters, nunneries, and churches, great and high houses of stone, the streets fair and large, and straight forth from one end of the town to the other as a line, and all the pavement of the city was of brick, and the more it rained in the town, the fairer the streets were; there saw he the tomb of Virgil, and the high way that he cut through that mighty hill of stone in one night, the whole length of an English mile.... From thence he came to Venice.... He wondered not a little at the fairness of Saint Mark's place, and the sumptuous church standing therein called Saint Mark's; how all the pavement was set with coloured stones, and all the rood or loft of the church double gilded over. Leaving this, he came to Padoa, beholding the manner of their academy, which is called the mother or nurse of Christendom; there he heard the doctors, and saw the most monuments in the town, entered his name into the university of the German nation, and wrote himself Doctor Faustus, the insatiable Speculator.... Well, forward he went to Rome, which lay, and doth yet lie, on the river Tybris, the which divideth the city in two parts: over the river are four great stone bridges, and upon the one bridge called Ponte S. Angelo is the castle of S. Angelo, wherein are so many great cast pieces as there are days in a year, and such pieces that will shoot seven bullets off with one fire.... Hard by this he visited the churchyard of S. Peter's, where he saw the pyramid that Julius Caesar brought out of Africa; it stood in Faustus his time leaning against the church wall of Saint Peter's, but now Papa Sixtus hath erected it in the middle of S. Peter's churchyard.... Other monuments he saw, too many to recite, but amongst the rest he was desirous to see the Pope's palace, and his manner of service at his table, wherefore he and his spirit made themselves invisible, and came into the Pope's court and privy chamber where he was; there saw he many servants attendant on his Holiness, with many a flattering sycophant carrying of his meat.... Faustus saw notwithstanding in that place those that were like to himself, proud, stout, wilful, gluttons, drunkards, whoremongers, breakers of wedlock, and followers of all manner of ungodly exercises: wherefore he said to his spirit, I thought I had been alone a hog, or pork of the devil's, but he must bear with me a little longer, for these hogs of Rome are already fattened, and fitted to make his roast-meat.... On a time the Pope would have a feast prepared for the Cardinal of Pavia, and for his first welcome the Cardinal was bidden to dinner: and as he sat at meat, the Pope would ever be blessing and crossing over his mouth. Faustus could suffer it no longer, but up with his fist and smote the Pope on the face, and withal he laughed that the whole house might hear him, yet none of them saw him nor knew where he was. The Pope persuaded his company that it was a damned soul, commanding a mass presently to be said for his delivery out of purgatory, which was done; the Pope sat still at meat, but when the latter mess came in to the Pope's board, Doctor Faustus laid hands thereon, saying: This is mine; and so he took both dish and meat and fled unto the Capitol or Campidoglio, calling his spirit unto him and said: Come, let us be merry, for thou must fetch me some wine, and the cup that the Pope drinks of.... His spirit, hearing this, departed towards the Pope's chamber, where he found them yet sitting and quaffing: wherefore he took from before the Pope the fairest piece of plate or drinking goblet, and a flagon of wine, and brought it to Faustus; but when the Pope and the rest of his crew perceived they were robbed, and knew not after what sort, they persuaded themselves that it was the damned soul that before had vexed the Pope so, and that smote him on the face, wherefore he sent commandment through all the whole city of Rome, that they should say mass in every church, and ring all the bells for to lay the walking spirit, and to curse him with bell, book, and candle, that so invisibly had misused the Pope's Holiness, with the Cardinal of Pavia, and the rest of their company.

Doctor Faustus, **IV.i.**

EFB, Chap. 29. The Emperor Carolus the fifth of that name was personally with the rest of his nobles and gentlemen at the town of Inszbruck where he kept his court, unto the which also Doctor Faustus resorted, and being there well known of divers nobles and gentlemen, he was invited into the court to meat, even in the presence of the Emperor: whom when the Emperor saw, he looked earnestly on him, thinking him by his looks to be some wonderful fellow, wherefore he asked one of his nobles whom he should be: who answered that he was called Doctor Faustus. Whereupon the Emperor held his peace until he had taken his repast, after which he called unto him Faustus, into the privy chamber, whither being come, he said unto him: Faustus, I have heard much of thee, that thou art excellent in the black art, and none like thee in mine empire, for men say that thou hast a familiar spirit with thee and that thou canst do what thou list: it is therefore (saith the Emperor) my request of thee that thou let me see a proof of thine experience, and I vow unto thee by the honour of mine imperial crown, none evil shall happen unto thee for so doing. Hereupon Doctor Faustus answered his Majesty, that upon those conditions he was ready in any thing that he could, to do his highness' commandment in what service he would appoint him. Well, then hear what I say (quoth the Emperor). Being once solitary in my house, I called to mind mine elders and ancestors, how it was possible for them to attain unto so great a degree of authority, yea so high, that we the successors of that line are never able to come near. As for example, the great and mighty monarch of the world Alexander magnus was such a lantern and spectacle to all his successors, as the chronicles makes mention of so great riches, conquering and subduing so many kingdoms, the which I and those that follow me (I fear) shall never be able to attain unto: wherefore, Faustus, my hearty desire is that thou wouldst vouchsafe to let me see that Alexander, and his paramour, the which was praised to be so fair; and I pray thee show me them in such sort that I may see their personages, shape, gesture and apparel, as they used in their life time, and that here before my face, to the end that I may say I have my long desire fulfilled, and to praise thee to be a famous man in thine art and experience. Doctor Faustus answered: My most excellent lord, I am ready to accomplish your request in all things, so far forth as I and my spirit are able to perform: yet your Majesty shall know that their dead bodies are not able substantially to be brought before you, but such spirits as have seen Alexander and his paramour alive shall appear unto you in manner and form as they both lived in their most flourishing time: and herewith I hope to please your imperial Majesty. Then Faustus went a little aside to speak to his spirit, but he returned again presently, saying: Now if it please your Majesty you shall see them, yet upon this condition that you demand no question of them, nor speak unto them, which the Emperor agreed unto. Wherewith Doctor Faustus opened the privy chamber door, where presently entered the great and mighty Emperor Alexander magnus, in all things to look upon as if he had been alive, in proportion a strong thick-set man, of a middle stature, black hair, and that both thick and curled head and beard, red cheeks, and a broad face, with eyes like a basilisk; he had on a complete harness burnished and graven, exceeding rich to look upon; and so passing towards the Emperor Carolus, he made low and reverent curtesie: whereat the Emperor Carolus would have stood up to receive and greet him with the like reverence, but Faustus took hold of him and would not permit him to do it. Shortly after Alexander made humble reverence and went out again, and coming to the door his paramour met him; she coming in, she made the Emperor likewise reverence; she was clothed in blue velvet, wrought and embroidered with pearl and gold; she was also excellent fair like milk and blood mixed, tall and slender, with a face round as an apple, and thus she passed certain times up and down the house, which the Emperor marking, said to himself: Now have I seen two persons which my heart hath long wished for to behold, and sure it cannot otherwise be, said he to himself, but that the spirits have changed themselves into these forms, and have not deceived me, calling to his mind the woman that raised the prophet Samuel: and for that the Emperor would be the more satisfied in the matter, he thought, I have heard say that behind her neck she had a great wart or wen, wherefore he took Faustus by the hand without any words, and went to see if it were also to be seen on her or not; but she perceiving that he came to her, bowed down her neck, where he saw a great wart, and hereupon she vanished, leaving the Emperor and the rest well contented.

EFB, Chap. 30. When Doctor Faustus had accomplished the Emperor's desire in all things as he was requested, he went forth into a gallery, and leaning over a rail to look into the privy garden, he saw many of the Emperor's courtiers walking and talking together, and casting his eyes now this way, now that way, he espied a knight leaning out at a window of the great hall, who was fast asleep (for in those days it was hot); but the person shall be nameless that slept, for he was a knight, although it was done to a little disgrace of the gentleman. It pleased Doctor Faustus, through the help of his spirit Mephostophiles, to firm upon his head as he slept an huge pair of hart's horns, and as the knight awaked thinking to pull in his head, he hit his horns against the glass, that the panes thereof flew about his ears. Think here how this good gentleman was vexed, for he could neither get backward nor forward: which when the Emperor heard all the courtiers laugh, and came forth to see what was happened, the Emperor also when he beheld the knight with so fair a head laughed heartily thereat, and was therewithal well pleased. At last Faustus made him quit of his horns again, but the knight perceived how they came, etc.

1616 text, IV.ii.

EFB, Chap. 31. Doctor Faustus took his leave of the emperor and the rest of the courtiers, at whose departure they were sorry, giving him many rewards and gifts: but being a league and a half from the city he came into a wood, where he beheld the knight that he had jested with at the court with other in harness, mounted on fair palfreys, and running with full charge towards Faustus, but he seeing their intent, ran towards the bushes, and before he came amongst the bushes he returned again, running as it were to meet them that chased him, whereupon suddenly all the bushes were turned into horsemen, which also ran to encounter with the knight and his company, and coming to them, they closed the knight and the rest, and told them that they must pay their ransome before they departed.

Whereupon the knight, seeing himself in such distress, besought Faustus to be good to them, which he denied not, but let them loose, yet he so charmed them that every one, knight and other, for the space of a whole month did wear a pair of goat's horns on their brows, and every palfrey a pair of ox horns on their head: and this was their penance appointed by Faustus, etc.

EFB, Chap. 52. Doctor Faustus travelled towards Eyszleben, and when he was nigh half the way, he espied seven horsemen, and the chief of them he knew to be the knight to whom he had played a jest in the Emperor's court...: and when the knight now saw that he had fit opportunity to be revenged of Faustus he ran upon him himself...: which when Doctor Faustus espied, he vanished away into the wood which was hard by them. But when the knight perceived that he was vanished away, he caused his men to stand still, where as they remained they heard all manner of warlike instruments of music, as drums, flutes, trumpets, and such like, and a certain troop of horsemen running towards them. Then they turned another way, and there also were assaulted on the same side: then another way, and yet they were freshly assaulted, so that which way soever they turned themselves, he was encountered.... The knight, that knew no other but that he was environed with an host of men (where indeed they were none other than devils), yielded: then Faustus took away his sword, his piece, and horse, with all the rest of his companions. And further he said unto him: Sir, the chief general of our army hath commanded to deal with you according to the law of arms; you shall depart in peace whither you please; and then he gave the knight an horse after the manner, and set him thereon. So he rode, the rest went on foot, until they came to their inn, where being alighted, his page rode on his horse to the water, and presently the horse vanished away, the page being almost sunk and drowned, but he escaped: and coming home, the knight perceived his page so bemired and on foot, asked where his horse was become. Who answered that he was vanished away: which when the knight heard, he said, Of a truth this is Faustus his doing, for he serveth me now as he did before at the court, only to make me a scorn and a laughing-stock.

Doctor Faustus, **IV.ii.**

EFB, Chap. 34. [In the previous chapter Faustus tricks a Jewish money-lender by offering him one of his legs as a surety for a loan. The usurer having thrown the leg away as useless, Faustus announces that he is ready to repay the money. Demanding either his own leg back or one of the usurer's in its place, he finally accepts a sum equal to the loan in return for his illusory dismemberment.] In like manner he served an horse-courser at a fair called Pheiffring, for Doctor Faustus through his cunning had gotten an excellent fair horse, whereupon he rid to the fair, where he had many chap-men that offered him money: lastly, he sold him for 40 dollars, willing him that bought him that in any wise he should not ride him over any water, but the horse-courser marvelled with himself that Faustus bade him ride him over no water. But (quoth he), I will prove, and forthwith he rid him into the river; presently the horse vanished from under him, and he sat on a bundle of straw, in so much that the man was almost drowned. The horse-courser knew well where he lay that had sold him his horse, wherefore he went angrily to his inn, where he found Doctor Faustus fast asleep, and snorting on a bed, but the horse-courser could no longer forbear him, took him by the leg and began to pull him off the bed; but he pulled him so, that he pulled his leg from his body, in so much that the horse-courser fell down backwards in the place, then began Doctor Faustus to cry with an open throat, He hath murdered me. Hereat the horse-courser was afraid, and gave the flight, thinking none other with himself, but that he had pulled his leg from his body; by this means Doctor Faustus kept his money.

1616 text, IV.v. 20-27.

EFB, Chap. 35. Doctor Faustus being in a town of Germany called Zwickaw, where he was accompanied with many Doctors and Masters, and going forth to walk after supper, they met with a clown that drove a load of hay. Good-even, good fellow, said Faustus to the clown, What shall I give thee to let me eat my belly full of hay? The clown thought with himself, What a mad man is this to eat hay, thought he with himself, thou wilt not eat much. They agreed for three farthings he should eat as much as he could: wherefore Doctor Faustus began to eat, and that so ravenously that all the rest of the company fell a-laughing, blinding so the poor clown, that he was sorry at his heart, for he seemed to have eaten more than the half of his hay, wherefore the clown began to speak him fair, for fear he should have eaten the other half also. Faustus made as though he had pity on the clown, and went his way. When the clown came in place where he would be, he had his hay again as he had before, a full load.

1616 text, IV.vi. 2-5.

EFB, Chap. 40. Doctor Faustus desired the Duke of Anholt to walk a little forth of the court with him, wherefore they went both together into the field, where Doctor Faustus through his skill had placed a mighty castle: which when the Duke saw, he wondered thereat, so did the Duchess, and all the beholders.... But as they were in their palace they looked towards the castle, and behold it was all in a flame of fire...and thus the castle burned and consumed away clean.

Doctor Faustus, **IV.iii.**

EFB, Chap. 39. Doctor Faustus on a time came to the Duke of Anholt, the which welcomed him very courteously; this was in the month of January, where sitting at the table, he perceived the Duchess to be with child, and forbearing himself until the meat was taken from the table, and that they brought in the banqueting dishes, said Doctor Faustus to the Duchess, Gracious lady, I have alway heard that the great-bellied women do always long for some dainties; I beseech therefore your Grace hide not your mind from me, but tell me what you desire to eat. She answered him: Doctor Faustus, now truly I will not hide from you what my heart doth most desire, namely, that if it were now harvest, I would eat my belly full of ripe grapes and other dainty fruit. Doctor Faustus answered hereupon, Gracious lady, this is a small thing for me to do, for I can do more than this; wherefore he took a plate, and made open one of the casements of the window, holding it forth, where incontinent he had his dish full of all manner of fruits, as red and white grapes, pears, and apples, the which came from out of strange countries; all these he presented the Duchess, saying: Madam, I pray you vouchsafe to taste of this dainty fruit, the which came from a far country, for there the summer is not yet ended. The Duchess thanked Faustus highly, and she fell to her fruit with full appetite. The Duke of Anholt notwithstanding could not withhold to ask Faustus with what reason there were such young fruit to be had at that time of the year. Doctor Faustus told him, May it please your Grace to understand that the year is divided into two circles over the whole world, that when with us it is winter, in the contrary circle it is notwithstanding summer, for in India and Saba there falleth or setteth the sun, so that it is so warm, that they have twice a year fruit: and, gracious lord, I have a swift spirit, the which can in the twinkling of an eye fulfil my desire in any thing, wherefore I sent him into those countries, who hath brought this fruit as you see: whereat the Duke was in great admiration.

1616 text, IV.vi. 100-109.

EFB, Chap. 37. Doctor Faustus went into an inn, wherein were many tables full of clowns, the which were tippling can after can of excellent wine, and to be short, they were all drunken; and as they sat, they so sung and hallowed that one could not hear a man speak for them. This angered Doctor Faustus, wherefore he said to those that had called him in, Mark, my masters, I will show you a merry jest. The clowns continuing still hallowing and singing, he so conjured them that their mouths stood as wide open as it was possible for them to hold them, and never a one of them was able to close his mouth again. By and by the noise was gone, the clowns notwithstanding looked earnestly one upon another, and wist not what was happened; wherefore one by one they went out, and so soon as they came without they were as well as ever they were: but none of them desired to go in any more.

Doctor Faustus, **Act V.i. 1-8.**

EFB, Chap. 56. Doctor Faustus was now in his 24 and last year, and he had a pretty stripling to his servant, the which had studied also at the University of Wittenberg: this youth was very well acquainted with his knaveries and sorceries, so that he was hated as well for his own knaveries, as also for his master's, for no man would give him entertainment into his service, because of his unhappiness, but Faustus. This Wagner was so well beloved with Faustus, that he used him as his son: for do what he would his master was always therewith well content. And when the time drew nigh that Faustus should end, he called unto him a notary and certain masters the which were his friends and often conversant with him, in whose presence he gave this Wagner his house and garden. Item, he gave him in ready money 1600 guilders. Item, a farm. Item, a gold chain, much plate, and other household stuff. This gave he all to his servant, and the rest of his time he meant to spend in inns and students' company, drinking and eating, with other jollity: and thus he finished his will for that time.

Doctor Faustus, **V.i.**

EFB, Chap. 45. The Sunday following came these students home to Doctor Faustus his own house, and brought their meat and drink with them: these men were right welcome guests unto Faustus, wherefore they all fell to drinking of wine smoothly: and being merry, they began some of them to talk of the beauty of women, and every one gave forth his verdict what he had seen and what he had heard. So one among the rest said, I never was so desirous of any thing in this world, as to have a sight (if it were possible) of fair Helena of Greece, for whom the worthy town of Troie was destroyed....

Doctor Faustus answered: For that you are all my friends and are so desirous to see that famous pearl of Greece, fair Helena..., I will therefore bring her into your presence personally, and in the same form of attire as she used to go when she was in her chiefest flowers and pleasantest prime of youth.... But (said Doctor Faustus) I charge you all that upon your perils you speak not a word, nor rise up from the table so long as she is in your presence. And so he went out of the hall, returning presently again, after whom immediately followed the fair and beautiful Helena, whose beauty was such that the students were all amazed to see her, esteeming her rather to be a heavenly than an earthly creature. This lady appeared before them in a most sumptuous gown of purple velvet, richly embroidered; her hair hanged down loose as fair as the beaten gold, and of such length that it reached down to her hams, with amorous coal-black eyes, a sweet and pleasant round face, her lips red as a cherry, her cheeks of rose all colour, her mouth small, her neck as white as the swan, tall and slender of personage; and in sum, there was not one imperfect part in her: she looked round about her with a rolling hawk's eye, a smiling and wanton countenance, which near hand inflamed the hearts of the students, but that they persuaded themselves she was a spirit, wherefore such fantasies passed away lightly with them: and thus fair Helena and Doctor Faustus went out again.... The students departed from Faustus' home every one to his house, but they were not able to sleep the whole night for thinking on the beauty of fair Helena. Wherefore a man may see that the devil blindeth and inflameth the heart with lust oftentimes, that men fall in love with harlots, nay even with furies, which afterward cannot lightly be removed.

EFB, Chap. 48. A good Christian, an honest and virtuous old man, a lover of the holy scriptures, who was neighbor unto Doctor Faustus, when he perceived that many students had their recourse in and out unto Doctor Faustus, he suspected his evil life, wherefore like a friend he invited Doctor Faustus to supper unto his house, unto the which he agreed; and having ended their banquet, the old man began with these words. My loving friend and neighbour Doctor Faustus, I have to desire of you a friendly and Christian request, beseeching you that you will vouchsafe not to be angry with me, but friendly resolve me in my doubt, and take my poor inviting in good part. To whom Doctor Faustus answered: My loving neighbour, I pray you say your mind. Then began the old patron to say: My good neighbour, you know in the beginning how that you have defied God, and all the host [of] heaven, and given your soul to the devil, wherewith you have incurred God's high displeasure, and are become from a Christian far worse than a heathen person: oh consider what you have done, it is not only the pleasure of the body, but the safety of the soul that you must have respect unto: of which if you be careless, then are you cast away, and shall remain in the anger of almighty God. But yet is it time enough, Doctor Faustus, if you repent and call unto the Lord for mercy, as we have example in the Acts of the Apostles, the eight Chap. of Simon in Samaria, who was led out of the way, affirming that he was *Simon homo sanctus*. This man was notwithstanding in the end converted, after that he had heard the sermon of Philip, for he was baptized, and saw his sins, and repented. Likewise I beseech you, good brother Doctor Faustus, let my rude sermon be unto you a conversion; and forget the filthy life that you have led; repent, ask mercy, and live. For Christ saith, *Come unto me all ye that are weary and heavy laden, and I will refresh you.* And in Ezechiel: *I desire not the death of a sinner, but rather that he convert and live.* Let my words, good brother Faustus, pierce into your adamant heart, and desire God for his son Christ his sake to forgive you. Wherefore have you so long lived in your devilish practices, knowing that in the Old and New Testament you are forbidden, and that men should not suffer any such to live, neither have any conversation with them, for it is an abomination unto the Lord; and that such persons have no part in the Kingdom of God? All this while Doctor Faustus heard him very attentively, and replied: Father, your persuasions like me wondrous well, and I thank you with all my heart for your good will and counsel, promising you so far as I may to follow your discipline: whereupon he took his leave. And being come home, he laid him very pensive on his bed, bethinking himself of the words of the good old man, and in a manner began to repent that he had given his soul to the devil, intending to deny all that he had promised unto Lucifer. Continuing in these cogitations, suddenly his spirit appeared unto him, clapping him upon the head, and wrung it as though he would have pulled the head from the shoulders, saying unto him: Thou knowest, Faustus, that thou hast given thyself body and soul unto my lord Lucifer, and hast vowed thyself an enemy unto God and unto all men; and now thou beginnest to harken to an old doting fool which persuadeth thee as it were unto God, when indeed it is too late, for that thou art the devil's, and he hath good power presently to fetch thee: wherefore he hath sent me unto thee, to tell thee that seeing thou hast sorrowed for what thou hast done, begin again and write another writing with thine own blood; if not, then will I tear thee all to pieces. Hereat Doctor Faustus was sore afraid, and said: My Mephostophiles, I will write again what thou wilt....

EFB, Chap. 49.   ...And presently upon the making of this letter, he became so great an enemy unto the poor old man that he sought his life by all means possible; but this godly man was strong in the holy Ghost, that he could not be vanquished by any means.... Thus doth God defend the hearts of all honest Christians that betake themselves under his tuition.

EFB, Chap. 55. To the end that this miserable Faustus might fill
the lust of his flesh, and live in all manner of voluptuous pleasures,
it came in his mind...in the 23 year past of his time, that he had a
great desire to lie with fair Helena of Greece, especially her whom
he had seen and showed unto the students of Wittenberg, wherefore
he called unto him his spirit Mephostophiles, commanding him to
bring him the fair Helena, which he did. Whereupon he fell in love
with her, and made her his common concubine and bedfellow, for
she was so beautiful and delightful a piece that he could not be one
hour from her, if he should therefore have suffered death, she had
so stolen away his heart....

Doctor Faustus, **V.ii.**

EFB, Chap. 63. *An Oration of Faustus to the students.* My trusty
and well-beloved friends, the cause why I have invited you into this
place is this: forasmuch as you have known me this many years, in
what manner of life I have lived, practising all manner of conjurations and wicked exercises, the which I have obtained through the
help of the devil, into whose devilish fellowship they have brought
me, the which use the like art and practice, urged by the detestable
provocation of my flesh, my stiff-necked and rebellious will, with my
filthy infernal thoughts, the which were ever before me, pricking me
forward so earnestly, that I must perforce have the consent of the
devil to aid me in my devices. And to the end I might the better
bring my purpose to pass, to have the devil's aid and furtherance,
which I never have wanted in mine actions, I have promised unto
him at the end and accomplishing of 24 years, both body and soul,
to do therewith at his pleasure: and this day, this dismal day, those
24 years are fully expired, for night beginning, my hour-glass is at
an end, the direful finishing whereof I carefully expect: for out of
all doubt this night he will fetch me, to whom I have given myself
in recompense of his service, both body and soul, and twice confirmed writings with my proper blood. Now have I called you, my
well-beloved lords, friends, brethren, and fellows, before that fatal
hour to take my friendly farewell, to the end that my departing may
not hereafter be hidden from you, beseeching you herewith, cour-
teous and loving lords and brethren, not to take in evil part any
thing done by me, but with friendly commendations to salute all my

friends and companions wheresoever, desiring both you and them, if ever I have trespassed against your minds in any thing, that you would all heartily forgive me: and as for those lewd practices the which this full 24 years I have followed, you shall hereafter find them in writing: and I beseech you, let this my lamentable end to the residue of your lives be a sufficient warning, that you have God always before your eyes, praying unto him that he would ever defend you from the temptation of the devil and all his false deceits, not falling altogether from God, as I wretched and ungodly damned creature have done, having denied and defied baptism, the sacraments of Christ's body, God himself, all heavenly powers, and earthly men; yea, I have denied such a God, that desireth not to have one lost. Neither let the evil fellowship of wicked companions mislead you as it hath done me: visit earnestly and oft the church, war and strive continually against the devil with a good and steadfast belief on God and Jesus Christ, and use your vocation in holiness. Lastly, to knit up my troubled oration, this is my friendly request, that you would to rest, and let nothing trouble you; also if you chance to hear any noise, or rumbling about the house, be not therewith afraid, for there shall no evil happen unto you; also I pray you arise not out of your beds. But above all things I entreat you, if you hereafter find my dead carcase, convey it unto the earth, for I die both a good and bad Christian: a good Christian, for that I am heartily sorry, and in my heart always pray for mercy, that my soul may be delivered; a bad Christian, for that I know the devil will have my body, and that would I willingly give him so he would leave my soul in quiet: wherefore I pray you that you would depart to bed, and so I wish you a quiet night, which unto me notwithstanding will be horrible and fearful.

This oration or declaration was made by Doctor Faustus, and that with a hearty and resolute mind, to the end he might not discomfort them: but the students wondered greatly thereat, that he was so blinded for knavery, conjuration, and such like foolish things to give his body and soul unto the devil: for they loved him entirely, and never suspected any such thing before he had opened his mind to them: wherefore one of them said unto him: Ah, friend Faustus, what have you done to conceal this matter so long from us? We would by the help of good divines, and the grace of God, have brought you out of this net, and have torn you out of the bondage and chains of Satan, whereas now we fear it is too late, to the utter ruin of your body and soul. Doctor Faustus answered, I durst never do it, although I often minded to settle myself unto godly people, to desire counsel and help, as once mine old neighbour counselled me, that I should follow his learning and leave all my conjurations, yet when I was minded to amend, and to follow that good man's counsel, then came the devil and would have had me away, as this night he is like to do, and said so soon as I turned again to God he would despatch me altogether. Thus, even thus (good gentlemen, and my dear friends), was I enthralled in that satanical band, all good desires drowned, all piety banished, all purpose of amendment utterly exiled, by the tyrannous threatenings of my deadly enemy. But when the students heard his words, they gave him counsel to do naught else but call upon God, desiring him for the love of his sweet son Jesus Christ's sake to have mercy upon him, teaching him this form of prayer: O God be merciful unto me, poor and miserable sinner, and enter not into judgment with me, for no flesh is able to stand before thee. Although, O Lord, I must leave my sinful body unto the devil, being by him deluded, yet thou in mercy mayest preserve my soul.

This they repeated unto him, yet it could take no hold, but even as Cain he also said his sins were greater than God was able to forgive; for all his thought was on his writing, he meant he had made it too filthy in writing it with his own blood. The students and the other that were there, when they had prayed for him, they wept, and so went forth, but Faustus tarried in the hall....

EFB, Chap. 59. This sorrowful time drawing near so troubled Doctor Faustus, that he began to write his mind...in manner as followeth.

Ah Faustus, thou sorrowful and woeful man, now must thou go to the damned company in unquenchable fire, whereas thou mightest have had the joyful immortality of the soul, the which thou now hast lost. Ah gross understanding and wilful will, what seizeth on my limbs other than a robbing of my life? Bewail with me my sound and healthful body, wit and soul, bewail with me my senses, for you have had your part and pleasure as well as I. Oh envy and disdain, how have you crept both at once into me, and now for your sakes I must suffer all these torments? Ah, whither is pity and mercy fled?

Upon what occasion hath heaven repaid me with this reward by sufferance to suffer me to perish? Wherefore was I created a man? The punishment that I see prepared for me of my self now must I suffer. Ah miserable wretch, there is nothing in this world to show me comfort: then woe is me, what helpeth my wailing?

EFB, Chap. 60. *Another complaint of Doctor Faustus.* Oh poor, woeful, and weary wretch: oh sorrowful soul of Faustus, now art thou in the number of the damned, for now must I wait for unmeasurable pains of death, yea far more lamentable than ever yet any creature hath suffered. Ah senseless, wilful and desperate forgetfulness! O cursed and unstable life! O blind and careless wretch, that so hast abused thy body, sense and soul! O foolish pleasure, into what a weary labyrinth hast thou brought me, blinding mine eyes in the clearest day? Ah weak heart! O troubled soul, where is become thy knowledge to comfort thee? O pitiful weariness! O desperate hope, now shall I never more be thought upon! Oh, care upon carelessness, and sorrows on heaps: Ah grievous pains that pierce my panting heart, whom is there now that can deliver me? Would God that I knew where to hide me, or into what place to creep or fly. Ah, woe, woe is me, be where I will, yet am I taken. Herewith poor Faustus was so sorrowfully troubled, that he could not speak or utter his mind any further.

EFB, Chap. 61. *How Doctor Faustus bewailed to think on hell....* Now thou Faustus, damned wretch, how happy wert thou if as an unreasonable beast thou mightest die without soul? So shouldest thou not feel any more doubts. But now the devil will take thee away both body and soul, and set thee in an unspeakable place of darkness.... Ah thou perpetual damned wretch, now art thou thrown into the everlasting fiery lake that never shall be quenched, there must I dwell in all manner of wailing, sorrow, misery, pain, torment, grief, howling, sighing, sobbing, blubbering, running of eyes, stinking at nose, gnashing of teeth, fear to the ears, horror to the conscience, and shaking both of hand and foot. Ah, that I could carry the heavens on my shoulders, so that there were time at last to quit me of this everlasting damnation!... Where is my hold? knowledge dare I not trust: and for a soul to God-wards that have I not, for I shame to speak unto him: if I do, no answer shall be made me, but he will hide his face from me, to the end that I should not behold the joys of the chosen. What mean I then to complain where no help is? No, I know no hope resteth in my groanings. I have desired that it should be so, and God hath said Amen to my misdoings: for now I must have shame to comfort me in my calamities.

1616 text, V.iii.

EFB, Chap. 63. It happened between twelve and one o'clock at midnight, there blew a mighty storm of wind against the house, as though it would have blown the foundation thereof out of his place. Hereupon the students began to fear, and got out of their beds, comforting one another, but they would not stir out of the chamber: and the host of the house ran out of doors, thinking the house would fall. The students lay near unto that hall wherein Doctor Faustus lay, and they heard a mighty noise and hissing, as if the hall had been full of snakes and adders: with that the door flew open wherein Doctor Faustus was, then he began to cry for help, saying: Murther, murther, but it came forth with half a voice hollowly; shortly after they heard him no more. But when it was day, the students, that had taken no rest that night, arose and went into the hall in the which they left Doctor Faustus, where notwithstanding they found no Faustus, but all the hall lay besprinkled with blood, his brains cleaving to the wall: for the devil had beaten him from one wall against another; in one corner lay his eyes, in another his teeth, a pitiful and fearful sight to behold. Then began the students to bewail and weep for him, and sought for his body in many places: lastly they came into the yard, where they found his body lying on the horse dung, most monstrously torn, and fearful to behold, for his head and all his joints were dashed in pieces.

The forenamed students and masters that were at his death, have obtained so much, that they buried him in the village where he was so grievously tormented. After the which, they returned to Wittenberg....

Doctor Faustus, **Epilogue.**

EFB, Chap. 63. And thus ended the whole history of Doctor Faustus his conjuration, and other acts that he did in his life; out of the which example every Christian may learn, but chiefly the stiff-necked and high-minded may thereby learn to fear God, and to be careful of their vocation, and to be at defiance with all devilish works, as God hath most precisely forbidden, to the end we should not invite the devil as a guest, nor give him place as that wicked Faustus hath done: for here we have a fearful example of his writing, promise, and end, that we may remember him: that we go not astray, but take God always before our eyes, to call alone upon him, and to honour him all the days of our life, with heart and hearty prayer, and with all our strength and soul to glorify his holy name, defying the devil and all his works, to the end we may remain with Christ in all endless joy: Amen, Amen, that wish I unto every Christian heart, and God's name to be glorified. Amen.

APPENDIX 3

Excerpts from Henricus Cornelius Agrippa, *De incertitudine et vanitate scientiarum et artium atque excellentia verbi dei declamatio* (1530), and *De occulta philosophia libri tres* (1533).

Henricus Cornelius Agrippa (1486-1535), whom Marlowe's Doctor Faustus aspires to emulate (I.i. 118-19), was a contemporary of the historical Doctor Faustus — with whose name his was frequently paired after the mid-sixteenth century by demonologists and polemicists against magic. Agrippa's *De occulta philosophia* is an encyclopaedic survey of magical beliefs and practices which also expounds a syncretic, magical form of Christianity: he finds in the emphasis of Hermetic, Cabalistic and Neoplatonic writings upon rebirth and deification a key to the saving message of the canonical scriptures. This book, which by implicitly challenging the uniqueness of the Judaeo-Christian tradition effectively decentres it, earned Agrippa the reputation of having been (as Jean Bodin wrote in 1581), "le plus grand Sorcier qui fut oncques de son aage" (fol. 219v).

His other major work, *De vanitate*, is a high-spirited attack upon all human arts and sciences, from logic to courtly place-seeking, and from whore-mongering to scholastic theology. Despite the evangelical posture which gives shape to its satire, and its rejection of the more obviously demonic magical practices, this book was suspected of having been intended as a kind of ground-clearing operation for the magical doctrines espoused in *De occulta philosophia*. Such suspicions could find support in the fact that Agrippa praises natural and celestial magic; moreover, as I argued in "Agrippa's Dilemma," *RQ* 41 (1988): 614-53, the same conflation of Christian and Hermetic notions of rebirth and deification that animates Book III of *De occulta philosophia* is also evident in *De vanitate*.

Jean Calvin in his *De scandalis* (1550) denounced Agrippa as an atheist and a Lucianic mocker of religious truths; and in 1584 André Thevet lamented that there was "no corner or secret of any discipline where he had not nosed about and there vomited some overflow of his mortal poison" (ii. fol. 544). While Agrippa claimed to be "professing divinity," he was thus believed to have done so only "in show" (*Doctor Faustus*, I.i. 3). The relationship between Agrippa's two major works seen by some sixteenth-century readers is arguably parodied by the pattern of Faustus's first soliloquy, in which a sophistical demolition of the orthodox academic disciplines, including theology, is succeeded by a rhapsodic praise of magic.

The connection between these works is complicated by the fact that Agrippa wrote an early version of *De occulta philosophia* in 1510, published *De vanitate* in 1530, and then in 1533 had printed a much expanded version of *De occulta philosophia*. The excerpts from *De occulta philosophia* are given in my own translation; the others are taken (with spelling and punctuation modernized, and with certain translator's errors amended) from James Sanford's translation, *Of the Vanitie and Uncertaintie of Artes and Sciences* (1569).

Of the Vanity

Of the Vanity, **Translator's Preface.**

...The author hereof walked in darkness, and together with his excellency of wit, he declareth in some places his blindness of understanding.... Some peradventure will object that it is impossible for so excellent a man to err and be deceived, who in all learnings (as appeareth) was conversant and well-exercised: unto whom may be said that which Tully writeth in the first of his *Offices*, where he saith: To be deceived, to slide, to err, and to be beguiled is man's property.... Socrates, who by the oracle of Apollo was judged the wisest of his age, confessed that he knew nothing at all, beside a certain slender discipline of love. If Socrates knew so few things, then cannot this author know all things, whose knowledge, though it were great, yet greatly he erred, and no marvel, for he gave his mind to unlawful arts, contrary to the laws of God and man. For it is said, and his works testify the same, that he exercised the art magic, and therein far excelled all other of his time. But in the end, his wicked knowledge was the cause of his miserable death: for as John Manlius, a German writer, doth record, when he was at the point of death he called to him a dog which went about with him, and spake to him with these words: *Abi a me perdita bestia, quae me perdidisti*: that is, Depart from me, thou wicked beast which hast destroyed me. So forthwith the dog, departing from him, cast himself headlong into a river; this dog was without doubt a devil of hell....

Of the Vanity, Author's Preface.

Will not this my enterprise (studious reader) seem unto thee valiant and adventurous, and almost comparable to the attempts of Hercules, to take up weapons against all that giant force of sciences and arts, and to challenge into the field all these most hardy hunters of arts and sciences?...to draw Cerberus bound in chains, to take away the golden apples of Hesperides, and many other noble adventures of this sort which were done by Hercules with great labors, and with no less danger, being of no less travail than peril to overcome these monsters of studies and schools. And I well perceive what a bloody battle I have to fight with them hand to hand, and how dangerous this fight will be, seeing that I am beset on every side with an army of so mighty enemies. O with how many engines will they assail me, and with how many shames and villainies will they load me?... The obstinate Logicianers will cast against me infinite darts of syllogisms; the long-tongued Sophisters, which wrest to every part their talk, with intricate snares of words, like a bridle, will stop my mouth.... The Musicians with their many tunes will [make] me a laughing-stock through the streets, and with jarring sounds and unpleasant ringing of pans, basins and dishes will trouble me more than they are wont at their weddings which be twice married...; the dancing player will make a tragedy of me upon his bawdy stage.... The vain worker in the art Perspective will engrave and depaint me more brutish and deformed than an ape, or Thersites; the wandering Cosmographers will banish me beyond Moscovie and the frozen sea; the Daedalean builder, with his most mighty engines, will privily undermine me, and compel me to wander in confused labyrinths.... The fatal Astrologers will threaten me to be hanged, and with the unstable turning of the heavens will forbid me paradise; the threatening Diviners will wish me all evil; the unreasonable Physiognomer will defame me for a cold man, and of small force in the act of venery.... The monstrous Gunner will cast against me the revenging flames of Jupiter, and the fire of lightning. The Interpreter of dark dreams will fear me with his horrible night sprites; the furious Prophet will deceive me with his doubtful oracle; the monstrous Magicians will transform me, as it were another Apuleius or Lucian, into an ass, yet not of gold, but perchance of dirt. The black Necromancer will persecute me with spirits and devils; the church-robbing Theurgist will offer my head to the crows, or perhaps to the jakes; the circumcised Cabalists will wish me their foreskin; the vain and foolish Juggler will make me appear either headless or without stones. The contentious Philosophers will tear me in pieces with most repugnant opinions; the juggling Pythagoreans will make me go into a dog, and a crocodile.... The politic Lawmaker will forbid me to bear office in the public weal; the voluptuous Prince will banish me the court; the ambitious Nobleman will put me out of the senate; the brainless people will exclaim on me in the streets.... The covetous Priests will excommunicate me; the Hooded Masquers and spiteful Hypocrites will rail against me out of the pulpit; the almighty Bishops will reserve my sins for everlasting fire.... The perbrake [i.e. spewing] Physicians will embrue me with urine and ordure, of the which the babbling Logicianer, disputing of sickness, will take from me a remedy in season; the rash Practicer, with a doubtful experiment, will put me in danger of death; the subtle old-beaten Physician, deferring the remedies, will prolong the sickness for his own avail.... The lofty Lawyers will accuse me of treason; the arrogant Canonists will excommunicate me with cruel cursings; the brawling Advocates will bring against me five hundred accusations.... The obstinate

Divine Sophistical Doctors will call me heretic, or compel me to worship their idols; our grim Masters will enforce me to recant....

Now, reader, thou perceivest through how many dangers I shall pass. Yet I hope easily to escape these assaults if thou, supporting the truth, and setting envy apart, shalt come with a gentle mind to the reading of these things. Beside this, I have the Word of God wherewith to defend myself, which boldly I will hold against these for a buckler and shield.... And I would have thee understand that I wrote not these things for hatred, for ambition, for deceit, or for error: neither a wicked desire, nor the arrogancy of a lewd mind hath moved me to write this, but the cause of all men, most just and righteous, because I see many [wax] proud in human learning and knowledge, that therefore they do despise and loathe the sacred and canonical scriptures of the holy Ghost as rude and rustical, because they have no ornaments of words, force of syllogisms, and affectate persuasions, nor the strange doctrine of the philosophers: but are simply grounded upon the operation of virtue, and upon bare faith.... We see other also, the which although they seem to themselves very godly, notwithstanding will prove and confirm the Laws with the decrees of philosophers, attributing more to them than to the holy prophets of God, or to the evangelists and apostles, they being as contrary to them as white is to black. Furthermore, in many, and almost in all places of study, a perverse custom and damnable use is grown, in that they bind with an oath the scholars which they receive to teach, never to speak against Aristotle, Boethius, Thomas, Albert, or against any other of their scholars, being accounted as a god, from whom if a man differ a finger's breadth in thought immediately they will call him heretic, a sinful person, an offender of godly ears, and worthy to be burned. These then so unadvised giants and enemies of the holy scriptures are to be assaulted, and their fortresses and castles ransacked; and to declare how great the blindness of men is, with so many sciences and arts, and with so many masters and authors, always to err from the knowledge of the truth: and how great a rashness and presumptuous arrogancy it is to prefer the schools of philosophers before the Church of Christ, and to set before, and make equivalent, the opinions of men with the Word of God. Finally, what a wicked tyranny it is, to bind the wits of students to certain appointed authors, and to take from scholars the liberty to search and trace out truth. All which things, sith they are so apparent that they cannot be denied, I must have pardon if to any I shall seem to have declaimed somewhat largely, and peradventure sharply, against any kind of learning, or against their professors.

Cap. 1 (Of sciences in general).

It is an ancient, and almost an agreeable and common opinion of all the philosophers, by the which they think that every science doth bring unto man some divinity, according to the capacity and value of them both, so that oftentimes, beyond the limits of humanity, they may be reckoned among the fellowship of the gods. From thence arose the divers and infinite commendations of sciences.... Notwithstanding I, being persuaded with other kind of reasons, am of opinion that there can chance to the life and salvation of our souls nothing more hurtful and pestilent than these arts and sciences...pardon me if herein I disagree from others, until I shall begin this mine opinion at every science by the order of the letters, not only with common arguments, and taken from the outward show of things, but with very strong reasons, and such as are sifted out of the inward bowels of things: not with any subtle eloquence of Demosthenes or Chrysippus (the which should be a shameful thing for me, professing divinity)...: for that a professor of the holy scripture ought to speak properly, and not eloquently, and to search out the verity of the matter, and not the garnishing of speech....

And that I may not suffer you to give ear in vain, I will now set before your eyes with what footing and tracing (as though with hounds) I have found out this my said opinion. If first I shall admonish you that all sciences be as well naught as good, and that they bring to us, above the limit of humanity, none other blessing of the deity but that perchance which that ancient serpent promised to our first parents, saying, *Ye shall be as gods, and shall know good and ill.* He shall then vaunt himself in this serpent which boasteth himself to have knowledge, as we read indeed that the heretics Ophiti did, which worshipped the serpent in their sacrifices, saying, That he hath brought the knowledge of virtue into paradise. With these agreeth the history of Plato that a certain spirit called Theutus, enemy to mankind, was the first deviser of sciences no less hurtful than profitable: as very wisely said Thamus, king of Egypt, reasoning of the inventors of sciences and letters.

...And so large is the liberty of the truth, and the largeness thereof so free, that it cannot be perceived with the speculations of any science, nor with any strait judgment of the senses, nor with any arguments of the art of logic, nor with any evident proof, with no syllogisms of demonstration, nor with any discourse of man's reason, but with faith only.... For every science hath in it some certain principles, which must be believed, and cannot by any means be declared: which if any will obstinately deny, the philosophers have not wherewith to dispute against him, and immediately they will say that there is no disputation against him which denieth the principles: or else will constrain him to flee unto some other things, without the limits of learning: As if any (say they) shall deny the fire is hot, let him be cast into the fire, and let him be demanded what he feeleth: so finally of philosophers they are made tormenters and hangmen, for they will by force compel us to confess that which they should teach by reason....

Cap. 7 (Of Logic).

...If therefore the principles of demonstration be very ill understood, and the circumstance shall not be admitted, certes hereof can be had none but very slender and uncertain knowledge: for we must believe things showed by certain weak principles, to the which we agree either for the forepassed authority of the wise, as it were to known limits, or else with experience we allow them by the senses. For every knowledge (as they say) hath his beginning of the senses, and the proof of true speeches (as Averroes saith) is that they agree with sensible things. And that thing is better known and truer whereupon most minds and senses do agree. Through the knowledge then of sensible things we are led by the hand to all such things that may be known by us. But sith that oftentimes all the senses are deceived, doubtless they cannot prove to us any certain experience. Furthermore, sith that the senses cannot attain to the intellectual nature, and the causes of the inferior things (of which their natures, effects, and properties or rather passions should be declared) by the consent of all men be altogether unknown to our senses, is it not manifest that the way of the truth is shut up from the senses?

Wherefore all these derivations and sciences which are fast rooted in the senses shall be uncertain, erroneous, and deceitful. What then is the profit of logic, and what fruit cometh of that learned demonstration, by principles and proofs, to the which we shall of necessity assent as it were to known limits?

Cap. 42 (Of Natural Magic).

Men think that natural magic is nothing else but a singular power of natural knowledges which therefore they call the greatest profoundness of natural philosophy, and absolute perfection thereof..., which with the aid of natural virtues, according to the mutual and convenient applying of them, doth publish works exceeding all the capacity of admiration: the which magic was much used of the Egyptians and of the Indians, where there was abundance of herbs, of stones, and other things thereunto belonging. They say...that the magicians were of this sort which went to worship Christ when he was born, visiting him with gifts, which the interpreters of the gospel do expound the philosophy of the Chaldees; such as were Hiarchus among the Brachmans, Thespion among the Gymnosophists, Buda among the Babylonians, Numa Pompilius among the Romans, Zamolxides among the Thracians, Abbaris among the Hyperboreans, Hermes among the Egyptians, Zoroastes son of Oromasus among the Persians. For the Indians, Ethiopians, Chaldeans, and Persians were very excellent in this magic....

Natural magic then is that which, having intentively beheld the forces of all natural things, and celestial, and with curious search sought out their order, doth in such sort publish abroad the hidden and secret powers of nature, coupling the inferior things with the qualities of the superior, as it were certain enticements, by a natural joining of them together, that thereof oftentimes do arise marvellous miracles, not so much by art as nature, whereunto this art doth proffer herself a servant when she worketh these things. For the magicians, as very diligent searchers of nature, bringing the things which be prepared by nature, applying and setting active things to passive, very oftentimes before the time by nature appointed do bring forth effects which of the common sort be accounted miracles...: as if a man in the month of March would cause roses to spring, and ripe grapes..., and greater things than these, as clouds, rain, thunder, beasts of divers sorts, and infinite transformations of things, of which kind Roger Bacon doth boast that he hath done many with pure and natural magic. Of the works thereof have written Zoroastes, Hermes, Evantes King of the Arabians.... But of the later writers few have written in natural magic, and they few things: as Albert, Arnold of Villanova, Raymond Lully, Bacon, Apponus, and the author of the book to Alphonsus published under the name of *Picatrix*, which notwithstanding intermeddleth much superstition with natural magic, which others have done also.

Cap. 43 (Of Mathematical Magic).

There be moreover other very prudent and adventurous searchers of nature which, without natural virtues, with the mathematical disciplines alone, the influences of the heavens being put thereto, do promise that they are able to bring forth things like to the works of nature, as bodies that go and speak, which for all that have not the virtues of the soul: as the wooden dove of Archytas was, which flew, and the image of Mercury that spake, and the brazen head forged by Albert the great, which as it is said did speak.... I suppose that is spoken of these skills, which Plato saith in the [tenth] book of his *Laws*: Men have an art, whereby they brought forth certain latter things, not partaking of the verity, and divinity, but made certain semblances much like to themselves: and the magicians, very presumptuous persons, have gone so far to do all things, especially with the favor of that ancient and terrible serpent the promiser of sciences, that like to him, as apes they endeavor to counterfeit God and nature.

Cap. 44 (Of Witching Magic).

...it is no doubt that magicians alone also with words and affections and other like things oftentimes do bring forth some marvellous effect not only in themselves, but also in strange things: all which operations they suppose to spread abroad upon other things the force engraffed in them and to draw these unto them...: and so by this orderly and linked composition of things Iamblichus, Proclus and Sinesius, according to the opinion of the magicians, do confirm that not only the natural and celestial gifts but the intellectual and heavenly also may be received from above: the which Proclus confesseth in the book *Of Sacrifice and Magic*; to wit, that by such consent of things magicians were wont to bind spirits. For some of them are fallen into so great a madness that they believe that with divers constellations of stars rightly observed by distance of time, and with a certain order of proportions, by the consent of heavenly sprites an image made may receive the sprite of life, and understanding, whereby he giveth answer to them that will demand any thing, and revealeth the secrets of hidden verity. Hereby it is manifest that this natural magic sometimes inclineth to Goecie and Theurgy; oftentimes it is entangled in the crafts and errors of the devils of hell.

Cap. 45 (Of Goecie and Necromancie).

The parts of ceremonial magic be Goecie and Theurgy. Goecie is grounded upon the intercourse of wicked sprites made with the rites of detestable curiosity, with unlawful conjurations, and with defensive prayers, banished and accursed by the decrees of all laws. Of this kind be they which at this day we call necromancers and enchanters...and at this day also there are books carried about with feigned titles under the names of Adam, Abel, Enoch, Abraham, Solomon..., which books yet do openly declare to him that doth subtly consider the order of their precepts, the usage of their ceremonies, their kind of words and characters, their order of construction, their foolish phrase, to contain nothing else but mere trifles and falsehood, and to be made in these latter times by men ignorant in ancient magic, most damnable artificers of damnation....

Cap. 46 (Of Theurgy).

Many think that Theurgy is not prohibited, as who saith it were governed by good angels, and by the divine power, whereas yet oftentimes under the name of God and the angels it is bound with wicked deceits of the devils, for not only with natural forces, but with certain solemnities and ceremonies also, we win and draw unto us heavenly things, and through them the divine virtues.... The greatest part of all ceremonies consisteth in keeping cleanliness, first of the mind, afterward of the body and of the things which are about the body.... Notwithstanding sometimes the unclean spirits and the deceiving powers do require also this cleanness, that they may be worshipped and adored for gods, and therefore we ought here to be very circumspect, whereof largely we have spoken in our books *Of hidden Philosophy* [i.e. *De occulta philosophia*]. But Porphyry, who doth much dispute of this theurgy or magic of things divine, doth finally conclude that with theurgical consecrations man's mind may be made apt to receive sprites and angels, and to see the gods, but that by this art there may any man come to God, he altogether denieth it....

Cap. 47 (Of Cabala).

...But as I doubt not that God hath revealed to Moses and other of the prophets many mysteries not to be disclosed to the ignorant people, which were covered under the bark of the words of the Law, so I know that this art Cabala, whereof the Hebrews do so much boast, and I with great labour have in time past searched out, to be nothing else but a mere agreement of superstition and a certain theurgical magic.... Therefore this Jewish Cabala is nothing else but a certain most pestilent superstition, wherewith at their will they do gather, divide, and transpose the words, names, and letters dispersed in the scripture, and making one of another do unbind the members of the truth.... From this Jewish heap of Cabalistic superstition proceeded (I suppose) the Ophites, the Gnostics, and Valentinian heretics...

Cap. 48 (Of Juggling).

But let us return to magic, whereof the juggler's skill is a part also; that is, illusions, which are only done according to the outward appearance: with these the magicians do show vain visions, and with juggling casts do play many miracles, and cause dreams.... By these things then which are already spoken, it is evident that magic is nothing else but a containing of idolatry, astrology, and superstitious physic. Of the magicians also is sprung in the Church a great rout of heretics, which as Iamnes and Iambres have rebelled against Moses, so they have resisted the apostolic truth [cf. 2 Tim. 3: 8]: the chief of these was Simon [the] Samaritan, who for this art had an image erected at Rome in the time of Claudius Caesar with this inscription: To Simon the holy God. His blasphemies be written at large by Clement, Eusebius, and Irenaeus. Out of this Simon, as out of a seed-plot of all heresies, have proceeded by many successions the monstrous Ophites, the filthy Gnostics, the wicked Valentinians, the Cerdonians, the Marcionists, the Montanians, and many other heretics, for gain and vain glory speaking lies against God, availing nor profiting men, but deceiving and bringing them to ruin and destruction; and they which believe in them shall be confounded in God's judgment. I being also a young man wrote of magical matters three books in a sufficient large volume, which I have entitled *Of hidden Philosophy*, in which books whatsoever was then done amiss through curious youth, now being more advised I will that it be recanted with this retractation, for I have in times past consumed very much time and substance in these vanities. At the length I got this profit thereby, that I know by what means I should discourage and dissuade others from this destruction. For all they that presume to divine and prophesy, not in the truth, not in the virtue of God, but in the elusion [i.e. deception] of devils, according to the operation of wicked sprites, and exercising deceits of idolatry, and showing illusions and vain visions, the which suddenly ceasing, they avaunt that they can work miracles...: all these, with Iamnes and Iambres and Simon Magus, shall be condemned to the pains of everlasting fire.

Cap. 55 (Of Politic Governance).

...But they which nowadays be called kings, emperors and princes suppose that they be born and created not for the people, for the citizens, for the common sort, for justice, but to defend and preserve the nobility: and do rule in such sort that they seem that the wealth of all the citizens is not committed to their custody, but given them to spoil and sack, taking all things from all men; and use their subjects according to their will and pleasure, and do abuse the authority given them from above towards their subjects....

Cap. 61 (Of the Magistrates of the Church).

...whosoever shall not be called by the spirit of God to the great office of God and to the apostolic dignity as Aaron was, and he that shall not enter through the gate which is Christ, but by some other place shall climb into the Church, through the window, through the favor of men, through voices bought, through the rule of princes, verily he is not the Vicar of Christ and the apostles, but a thief and a robber, the Vicar of Judas Iscariot and Simon the Samaritan...many such bishops and apostles have climbed up to the seat of Christ..., laying grievous burdens upon the shoulders of the people...not esteeming the true temple of God, and the lively images of Christ and the altars of the people's souls.... But do utterly neglect the weightiest and the best works of the gospel, of the law, and of Christian righteousness, judgment, mercy, and faith. They strain a gnat through their teeth and swallow down a camel, they stumble at a straw and leap over a block, blind guides, false and deceitful, the generation of vipers, scoured cups, whited sepulchres outwardly showing holiness in their mitres, in their caps, in their rachets, in their apparel, in their hoods: within they are full of filthiness, of hypocrisy, of iniquity; whore-hunters, dancers, stage players, bawds or whore-merchants, dicers, gluttons, drunkards, poisoners, which...have climbed and ascended not by the virtue of their merits, but either by filthy flattery, or by gifts, or by the favor of princes, or by force of arms to priesthoods, benefices, and bishoprics....

Cap 82 (Of Physic).

But now let us pass from warfare and nobility to Physic, which also is a certain art of manslaughter altogether servile, although it presume to pass under the title of philosophy, and above the knowledge of the law doth seek to have the next place to divinity, wherefore there is great contention between physicians and lawyers....

Cap. 83 (Of Physic, that consisteth in practice).

...Pindarus saith also that Esculapius, father of physic, was by Jupiter stricken with lightning for a due desert of covetousness, because wickedly and to the damage of the commonwealth he had practised physic. And if by any chance the diseased shall happily recover in their hands, they rejoice without measure; no man will be able to set forth the glory of so great a miracle. They will say that he hath raised Lazarus from death, that he gave him his life, that he is bound to thank them that he is alive: and by and by (attributing that to themselves, which belongeth only unto God), they avaunt that they have drawn him out of hell.... I put the case that the physicians know (and I would to God they knew) all the virtues and operations of the elements, roots, herbs, flowers, fruits, seeds, of living creatures also and minerals, and of all things which nature, the mother of them, hath brought forth; yet they cannot with all these virtues not only make man immortal, but which is less, not always cure him that is sick of every light disease....

Cap. 91 (Of the Law and Statutes).

...Behold now ye perceive how this knowledge of the law presumeth to bear sway over all other arts, and exerciseth tyranny, and how, preferring itself before all other disciplines as it were the first begotten of the gods, doth despise them as vile and vain, although it be altogether made of nothing else but of frail and very weak inventions and opinions of men, which things be of all other the weakest....

Cap. 97 (Of Scholastical Divinity).

Lastly it resteth to speak of divinity.... But let us speak first of scholastical divinity, which doctrine was first made by the Sorbonists of Paris, with a certain mixture of God's word and philosophical reasons, fashioned like two bodies, as if it were of the centaur's kind.... Hereupon scholastical divinity in the end by little and little was turned to sophisms, whilest that these divine sophisters of latter time and hucksters of God's word (which be not divines, except the title be bought) of so high a science they have made a certain logomachy, that is, an undiscreet altercation.... And in this manner...they have picked out very many apt questions to dispute upon divinity, in the which they, exercising their wit and consuming their time, have placed all the doctrine of divinity in them alone; against which if any will resist with the authority of the holy scriptures, forthwith he shall here say: The letter killeth, it is deadly, it is unprofitable.... Afterward they, having recourse to interpreting, to expounding, to glossing, and to syllogizing, do rather give it some other sense than the proper meaning of the letter.... Hereof it is come to pass that the high science of school divinity is not free from error and naughtiness, so many sects, so many heresies have the wicked hypocrites and hair-brained sophisters brought up: which, as Paul saith, preach Christ not for good will but for contention....

Cap. 101 (Of Masters of Arts).

...in the time past this was the superstition of the gentiles, which
with divine honors worshipped the inventors of things..., and placed
them in the number of their gods.... And this is that [dei]fication,
and no other, of sciences: which that ancient serpent, the shaper of
such gods, promised to our first parents, saying to them: Ye shall
be as gods, knowing the good and the evil.... It is better therefore
and more profitable to be idiots and know nothing, to believe by
faith and charity, and to become next unto God, than being lofty
and proud through the subtleties of sciences to fall into the possession of the serpent. So we read in the gospel how Christ was received
of idiots, of the rude people, and of the simple sort: who was con-
temptuously rejected, despised, and persecuted even to the death
by the high Priests, by the Lawyers, by the Scribes, by the Masters
and Rabbins. For this cause Christ himself also chose his apostles,
not Rabbins, not Scribes, not Masters, nor Priests, but unlearned
persons of the rude people, void well near of all knowledge, unskilful, and asses.

The Conclusion of the work.

Wherefore O ye asses, which are now with your children, under the
commandment of Christ by his apostles, the messengers and readers
of true wisdom in his holy gospel, be you loosed from the darkness
of the flesh and blood. If ye desire to attain to this divine and true
wisdom, not of the tree of the knowledge of good and ill, but of the
tree of life, [cast aside the sciences of men]...; now entering not into
the schools of philosophers and sophisters, but into your [own] selves, ye shall know all things: for the knowledge of all things is com-
pact in you, which (as the Academics confess) the holy scriptures
do so witness, because God created all things very good, that is to
say in the best degree wherein they might abide. Even as he then
hath created trees full of fruits, so also hath he created the souls as
reasonable trees full of forms and knowledges; but through the sin
of the first parent all things were [concealed], and oblivion the
mother of ignorance [entered] in. Set you then now aside, which
may, the veil of your understanding, [you] which are wrapped in the
darkness of ignorance. Cast out the drink of Lethe, you which have
made yourselves drunken with forgetfulness, await for the true light,

you which have suffered yourselves to be taken with unreasonable sleep; and forthwith when your face is discovered ye shall pass from the light to the light: for (as John saith) Ye are annointed by the holy Ghost, and have known all things; and again, Ye need not to be taught of any, because his annointing teacheth you all things.... O ye fools and wicked ones, which setting apart the gifts of the holy Ghost, endeavor to learn those things of faithless philosophers and masters of errors which ye ought to receive of God and the holy Ghost. Will you believe that we can get knowledge out of the ignorance of Socrates?... But descend into yourselves, you which are desirous of the truth, depart from the clouds of man's traditions, and cleave to the true light: behold, a voice from heaven, a voice that teacheth from above, and showeth you more clearly than the sun [that you are] your own enemies and prolong time to receive wisdom. Hear the oracle of Baruch: God is, [he says], and no other shall be esteemed with him; he hath found out all manner of learning, and hath given [it] to Jacob, his child, and Israel, his beloved, giving laws and commandments, and ordaining sacrifices; after this he was seen on the earth, and was conversant with men [cf. Baruch 3: 36-38]; that is to say, taking flesh, and with an open mouth teaching those things which under dark questions he hath taught in the Law and Prophets. And to the end that you may not think that these things be referred to divine things only, and not [also] to natural, hear what the wise man witnesseth of himself: It is He that hath given me the true knowledge of those things which are, that I might know the dispositions of the compass of the earth, the virtue of the elements, the beginning, consummation, middle, and revolutions of times, the course of the year, the dispositions of the stars, the natures of living creatures, the anger of beasts, the force of the winds, the thoughts of men, the differences of plants, the virtues of roots, and finally I have learned all the things which be hidden and unknown, for the Artificer of all things hath taught me wisdom [Wisdom of Solomon 7: 17-21]....

De occulta philosophia

De occulta philosophia, **Author's Preface.**

I do not doubt but that the title of our book of Occult philosophy, or of Magic, may by its rarity entice a large number to read it, among whom some twisted, feeble-minded people, and also many ill-disposed and hostile to my talents, will approach: these, in their rash ignorance taking the name of magic in the worse sense, will cry out, hardly having beheld the title, that I teach forbidden arts, sow the seed of heresy, am an offense to pious ears and to outstanding minds a stumbling block; that I am a sorcerer, a superstitious man, and a demoniac, because I am a magician. To these people I would reply that *magus* among learned men does not signify a sorcerer, nor a superstitious man, nor one possessed, but one who is a wise man, a priest, a prophet. The Sibyls were magicians; hence they prophesied most plainly of Christ. And indeed the Magi knew by the wonderful secrets of the world that Christ the author of the world itself was born, and were the first of all to come and worship him. And the name itself of magic was accepted by philosophers, extolled by theologians, and was also not displeasing to the gospel itself. Yet I believe those censors to be of such steadfast arrogance that they will forbid themselves the Sibyls and the holy magicians, and even the gospel itself, sooner than that the name of magic should be admitted into favor; to such a degree are they careful of their conscience, that neither Apollo, nor all the Muses, nor an angel from heaven would be able to deliver me from their curse. And I advise them now that they neither read, nor understand, nor remember our treatise, for it is harmful, it is poisonous, the gate of Acheron is in this book, it speaks stones: let them take heed lest it beat out their brains....

Book III, Dedicatory Epistle.

...The understanding of divine things purges the mind from errors and renders it divine, gives an infallible virtue to our works, and drives far away the deceits and hindrances of all evil demons. And at the same time it subjects them to our command, and even compels the good angels and the universal virtues of the world into our service; that is to say, the virtue of our works being drawn from the archetype himself, when we ascend to him all creatures necessarily must obey us, and all the choir of the heavenly beings follow us....

Book III, Chap. 1.

...We cannot obtain a firm and solid intellect (as Hermes says) otherwise than by integrity of life, by piety, and finally, by divine religion. For holy religion purges the intellect and renders it divine....

Book III, Chap. 3.

...now truly I will recount a mysterious, necessary and secret thing...which is the principle and complement and key of all magical operations: it is the dignification of man to this so very exalted virtue and power.... Indeed, the apprehension and power of all things inheres in our own selves. We are prevented, however, from having full use of these, through passions hindering us from our begetting, through deceptive imaginations and immoderate desires: which being expelled, divine knowledge and power suddenly arrive....

Book III, Chap. 6.

...Our mind, pure and divine, burning with religious love, adorned by hope, and directed by faith, placed in the height and summit of the human soul, attracts the truth, and suddenly comprehending, beholds in the divine truth itself, as though in a certain mirror of eternity, all the conditions, reasons, causes and sciences of things both natural and immortal.... Hence it comes to us, who are established in nature, sometimes to rule over nature, and to accomplish operations so wonderful, so sudden, and so difficult, whereby the spirits of the dead may obey, the stars be disordered, the divine powers compelled, and the elements enslaved: so men devoted to God, and elevated by these theological virtues, command the elements, drive away mists, summon winds, collect clouds into rain, cure diseases, raise the dead....

Book III, Chap. 44.

...The soul which is united to the mind is therefore called the soul standing and not falling: but not all men have obtained mind, because (as Hermes says) God the Father wanted to set it forth just as a contest and prize of souls. Those who, devoid of mind, despise this prize, being given over to bodily senses, are made like the irrational brutes, and share the same annihilation with them.... There is no work in the whole succession of the world so admirable, so excellent, so marvellous, that the human soul, embracing its image of divinity (which the magicians call the soul standing and not falling) cannot accomplish by its own virtue without any external assistance. The form, therefore, of all magical virtue is from man's soul standing, and not falling....

De occulta philosophia, **Appendix.**

[To the first edition of this book Agrippa appended chapters 41 to 48 of *De vanitate* — those chapters which deal with the various magical arts. The book therefore concludes with the following sentences, which I offer this time in my own translation.]

...At last I advanced to this, that I might know by what reasons it might be proper to dissuade others from this ruin. For all who presume to divine and to prophesy, not in the truth, nor in the power of God, but in the deception of demons, according to the operation of evil spirits, and by means of magical vanities, practising exorcisms, incantations, love-potions, conjurings, and other demoniacal works and idolatrous deceits, presenting short-lived deceptions and apparitions, boast that they work miracles: all these shall be destined, with Iannes and Mambres and Simon Magus, to be tortured by eternal fires.

APPENDIX 4

Excerpts from Jean Calvin, *The Institution of Christian Religion* trans. Thomas Norton (1561, rpt. 1587).

Jean Calvin (1509-1564), the most influential of the second-generation Protestant reformers and the great systematizer among sixteenth-century theologians, was a powerful presence in Elizabethan England. As A.D. Nuttall has remarked, the nearly one hundred English-language editions of his writings printed by 1640 far outnumber those of any other author (Calvin's close associate Théodore de Bèze stands in second place with fifty editions, followed by Luther and Bullinger with thirty-eight each.) Not until the early seventeenth century was Calvin's rate of publications in English overtaken — "and then it was by William Perkins and Henry Smith, both Calvinists" (Nuttall 1980: 21). Calvin's thought formed part of the dominant ideology of Elizabethan England, for although the Church of England retained an episcopal structure, its theology was strongly Calvinistic (Sinfield 12-14). This fact, Alan Sinfield observes, "has fascinating consequences for the study of literature of the period. It obliges us to entertain the thought, for instance, that Marlowe's Faustus is not damned because he is wicked, but wicked because he is damned" (14).

Calvin published the first edition of his most important work, the *Institutio christianae religionis*, in 1536. Revised and expanded texts were printed in 1539, 1543, 1545, 1550, 1553, 1554, and 1559, and French versions in 1541 and 1560. Thomas Norton's English translation of the final Latin version appeared in 1561, and was frequently reprinted; the selections which follow are taken from the edition of 1587.

Recent interpretations of Calvin's thought, among them William J. Bousma's very perceptive *John Calvin: A Six-*

teenth Century Portrait (1987), have tended to emphasize Calvin's affiliations with widely shared Christian traditions, both theological and humanist, and consequently to soften or obscure the distinctive turns in his arguments which are largely responsible for their persuasive power, and which made them seem to sixteenth-century readers either incontrovertible or highly disturbing—or both at once. The excerpts given here are chosen with a different end in mind. In highlighting the harshest aspects of Calvin's thought, they may help to suggest why, after six years of advanced theological study at Cambridge, Christopher Marlowe reacted with such violence against Christianity.

Calvin's starting point is a firm belief in the absolute sovereignty of God's will. He is, in many respects, a ruthlessly honest thinker. But whereas the thought of Luther or Pascal is dialectical in nature, Calvin's can more properly be described as equivocating. Dialectical thought, whether Platonic, scholastic, or post-Hegelian, requires the operation of at least two distinct terms. But because Calvin regards all actions and events, from Adam's fall to that of a sparrow, as being wholly determined by God's inscrutable will, and all categories and agents in creation as subsumed by that same will, a recurrent feature of his arguments is a reduction of all issues to the basic principle of the absolute monarchy of God. The dominant mode of his argumentation is thus, necessarily, equivocation—for when the reality of one term so wholly absorbs that of all others, an extended and serious discourse can only be constructed out of equivocations.

The most disturbing of Calvin's equivocations, and those of most relevance to *Doctor Faustus*, have to do with the relation between the divine will and human wills.

I. xvi. 3.

...there is not in creatures a wandering power, working or motion, but...they are governed by the secret counsel of God, so that nothing can chance but that which is decreed by him both witting and willing it to be.

I. xvi. 4.

...God doth so give heed to the government of the successes of all things, and...they all do so proceed from his determinate counsel, that nothing happeneth by chance.

I. xvi. 6.

...It is a fond madness that men will take upon themselves to do things without God, which cannot so much as speak but what he will.

I. xvii. 5.

The same men do unorderly and unadvisedly draw the chances of time past to the naked providence of God. For because upon it do hang all things whatsoever happen, therefore (say they) neither robberies nor adulteries nor manslaughters are committed without the will of God. Why then (say they) shall a thief be punished, for that he spoiled him whom the Lord's will was to punish with poverty? Why shall the murderer be punished which hath slain him whose life the Lord hath ended? If all such men do serve the will of God, why shall they be punished? But I deny that they serve the will of God. For we may not say, that he which is carried with an evil mind doth service unto God as commander of it, where indeed he doth but obey his own wicked lust. He obeyeth God, which being informed of his will doth labor to that end whereunto God's will calleth him. But whereby are we informed of his will, but by his word? Therefore in doing of things we must see that same will of God which he declareth in this word. God requireth of us only that which he commandeth. If we do anything against his commandment, it is not obedience but obstinacy and transgression. But unless he would [i.e., unless he willed it], we should not do it. I grant. But do we evil things to this end, to obey him? But he doth not command us to do them, but rather we run on headlong, not minding what he willeth, but so raging with the intemperance of our own lust, that of set purpose we bend our travail against him. And by these means in evil-doing we serve his just ordinance, because according to the infinite greatness of his wisdom he hath good skill to use evil instruments to do good. And see how foolish is their manner of arguing. They would have the doers unpunished for mischievous acts, because they are not committed but by the disposition of God.

I grant more: that thieves and murderers and other evil-doers are the instruments of God's providence, whom the Lord doth use to execute those judgments which he hath with himself determined. But I deny that their evil doings ought to have any excuse thereby. For why? Shall they either entangle God in the same wickedness with them, or shall they cover their naughtiness with his righteousness? They can do neither of both. Because they should not be able to excuse themselves, they are accused by their own conscience. And because they should not be able to blame God, they find all the evil in themselves, and in him nothing but a lawful use of their evilness. But he worketh by them. And whence, I pray you, cometh the stink in a dead carrion, which hath been both rotted and disclosed by the heat of the sun? All men do see that it is raised by the beams of the sun. Yet no man doth therefore say that the sunbeams do stink. So when there resteth in an evil man the matter and guiltiness of evil, what cause is there why it should be thought that God is any thing defiled with it, if he use their service at his pleasure? Away therefore with this doggish frowardness, which may indeed afar off bark at the justice of God, but cannot touch it.

I. xvii. 11.

...when [the saints] call to mind that the devil and all the rout of the wicked are so every way holden in by the hand of God as with a bridle, that they can neither conceive any mischief against us, nor go about it when they have conceived it, nor if they go never so much about it, can stir one finger to bring it to pass but so far as he shall suffer, yea, so far as he shall command, and that they are not only holden fast bound with fetters, but also compelled with bridle to do service: here have they abundantly wherewith to comfort themselves. For as it is the Lord's work to arm their fury and to turn and direct it whither it pleaseth him, so is it his work also to appoint a measure and end, that they do not after their own will licentiously triumph.

II. ii. 6-7.

...For I do much farther differ from the later Sophisters, even so much as they be farther gone from the ancient time. But yet somewhat, after such a sort as it is, we perceive by this division, after what manner they have given free will to man. For at length Lombard saith that we have not free will therefore, because we are alike able either to do or to think good and evil, but only that we are free from compulsion: which freedom is not hindered, although we be perverse and the bondmen of sin, and can do nothing but sin.

Therefore man shall be said to have free will after this sort, not because he hath a free choice as well of good as of evil, but because he doth evil by will, and not by compulsion. That is very well said: but to what purpose was it to garnish so small a matter with so proud a title? A goodly liberty forsooth, if man be not compelled to serve sin: so is he yet a willing servant that his will is holden fast bound with the fetters of sin. Truly I do abhor striving about words, wherewith the Church is vainly wearied, but I think that such words are with great religious carefulness to be taken heed of, which sound of any absurdity, especially where the error is hurtful. How few, I pray you, are there, which when they hear that free will is assigned to man, do not by and by conceive that he is lord both of his own mind and will, and that he is able of himself to turn himself to whether part he will?

II. iii. 5.

...Therefore [if] this, that it is of necessity that God do well, does not hinder the free will of God in doing well; if the devil, which cannot do but evil, yet willingly sinneth; who shall then say that a man doth therefore less willingly sin for this, that he is subject to [the] necessity of sinning?

II. iv. 1.

...The blinding of the wicked, and all the wicked deeds that follow thereupon, are called the works of Satan, of which yet the cause is not to be sought elsewhere than in the will of man, out of which ariseth the root of evil, wherein resteth the foundation of the kingdom of Satan, which is sin.

II. iv. 3.

The old writers...are sometime precisely [i.e. scrupulously] afraid simply to confess the truth, because they fear lest they should so open a window to wickedness, to speak irreverently of the works of God.... Augustine himself sometime was not free from the superstition, as where he saith that hardening and blinding pertain not to the work of God, but to his foreknowledge. But the phrases of Scripture allow not these subtleties.... It is oftentimes said that God blindeth and hardeneth the reprobate, that he turneth, boweth, and moveth their hearts, as I have elsewhere taught more at large. But of what manner that is, it is never expressed, if we flee to free foreknowledge or sufferance. Therefore we answer that it is done after two manners. For first, whereas when his light is taken away, there remaineth nothing but darkness and blindness: whereas when his spirit is taken away, our hearts wax hard and become stones: whereas when his direction ceaseth, they are wrested into crookedness. It is well said that he doth blind, harden and bow them from whom he taketh away the power to see, obey and do rightly. The second manner, which cometh near to the property [i.e. proper meaning] of the words, is that for the executing of his judgments by Satan, the minister of his wrath, he both appointeth their purposes to what end it pleaseth him, and stirreth up their wills, and strengtheneth their endeavors.

II. viii. 58-59

...In weighing of sins (saith Augustine) let us not bring false balances to weigh what we list and how we list at our own pleasure, saying: this is heavy, this is light. But let us bring God's balance out of the holy Scriptures, as out of the Lord's treasury, and let us therein weigh what is heavy: rather, let us not weigh, but reknowledge things already weighed by the Lord. But what saith the Scripture? Truly, when Paul saith that the reward of sin is death [Rom. 6: 23], he showeth that he knew not this stinking distinction [i.e. between venial and mortal sins]. Sith we are too much inclined to hypocrisy, this cherishment thereof ought not to have been added to flatter our slothful consciences.

I would to God they would consider what that saying of Christ meaneth: He that transgresseth of one of the least of these commandments, and teacheth men so, shall be counted none in the kingdom of heaven [Matt. 5: 19]. Are not they of that sort, when they dare so extenuate the transgression of the law, as if it were not worthy of death?... Is it a small matter with them, that God's majesty be offended in any thing? Moreover, if God hath declared his will in the law, whatsoever is contrary to the law displeaseth him. Will they imagine the wrath of God to be so disarmed, that punishment of death shall not forthwith follow upon them? And he himself hath pronounced it plainly, if they would rather find in their hearts to find in their hearts to hear his voice than to trouble the clear truth with their unsavory subtleties of argument. The soul (saith he) that sinneth, the same shall die [Ezek. 18: 4, 20]. Again, which I even now alleged: the reward of sin is death [Rom. 6: 23]. But albeit they grant it to be a sin, because they cannot deny it, yet they stand stiff in this, that it is no deadly sin. But sith they have hithertoo too much borne with their own madness, let them yet at length learn to wax wiser. But if they continue in their dotage, we will bid them farewell: and let the children of God learn this: that if all sin is deadly, because it is a rebellion against the will of God, which of necessity provoketh his wrath, because it is a breach of the law, upon which the judgement of God is pronounced without exception: and that the sins of the holy ones are venial and pardonable, not of their own nature, but because they obtain pardon by the mercy of God.

II. xvi. 2-3.

...God, which prevented us with his mercy, was our enemy until he was reconciled to us by Christ.... In a sum: because our mind can neither desirously enough take hold of life in the mercy of God, nor receive it with such thankfulness as we ought, but when it is before stricken and thrown down with the fear of the wrath of God and dread of eternal death, we are so taught by holy Scripture, that without Christ we may see God in manner wrathfully bent against us, and his hand armed to our destruction: and that we may embrace his goodwill and fatherly kindness no otherwise, but in Christ.

And although this be spoken according to the weakness of our capacity, yet it is not falsely said. For God, which is the highest righteousness, cannot love wickedness, which he seeth in us all.

Therefore we all have in us that which is worthy of the hatred of God.

III. iii. 10-11

...this image or shadow of faith, as it is of no value, so it is not worthy of the name of faith.... It is said that Simon Magus believed, which yet within a little after bewrayed his own unbelief. And whereas it is said that he believed, we do not understand it as some do, that he feigned a belief when he had none in his heart: but we rather think that, being overcome with the majesty of the Gospel, he had a certain faith, such as it was, and so acknowledged Christ to be the author of life and salvation that he willingly professed himself to be one of his...

I know that some think it hard that we assign faith to the reprobate, whereas Paul affirmeth faith to be the fruit of election [cf. 1 Thess. 1: 4-5]. Which doubt yet is easily dissolved: for though none receive the light of faith, nor do truly feel the effectual working of the Gospel, but that they are foreordained to salvation, yet experience showeth that the reprobate are sometime moved with the same feeling that the elect are, so that in their own judgement they nothing differ from the elect. Wherefore it is no absurdity that the apostle ascribeth to them the taste of the heavenly gifts [Heb. 6: 4-6], that Christ ascribeth to them faith for a time [Luke 8: 13]: not that they soundly perceive the spiritual force of grace and assured light of faith, but because the Lord, the more to condemn them and make them inexcusable, conveyeth himself into their minds so far forth as his goodness may be tasted without the spirit of adoption.

III. iii. 21.

...The Apostle also meaning to exclude apostates from hope of salvation, appointeth this reason, that it is impossible for them to be renewed unto repentance [Heb. 6: 4-6]: because God, in renewing them whom he will not have perish, showeth a token of his fatherly favour, and in a manner draweth them unto him with the beams of his cheerful and merry countenance: on the other side, with hardening them, he thundereth against the reprobate, whose wickedness is unpardonable. Which kind of vengeance the Apostle threateneth to wilful apostates, which when they depart from the faith of the gospel do make a scorn of God, reproachfully despise his grace, and defile and tread under feet the blood of Christ, yea as much as in them is they crucify him again. For he doth not (as some fondly rigorous men would have it) cut off hope of pardon from all wilful sins: but teacheth that apostasy is unworthy of all excuse: so that it is no marvel that God doth punish a contempt of himself so full of sacrilege, with unappeasable rigor.

III. iii. 22.

...This therefore is the spirit of blasphemy, when man's boldness of set purpose leapeth forth to reproach of the name of God. Which Paul signifieth when he saith that he obtained mercy because he had ignorantly committed those things through unbelief [1 Tim. 1: 13], for which otherwise he had been unworthy of God's favour. If ignorance joined with unbelief was the cause that he obtained pardon, thereupon followeth, that there is no place for pardon where knowledge is joined to unbelief.

III. iii. 24.

But whereas some do think it too hard, and too far from the tender mercifulness of God, that any are put away that flee to beseeching the Lord's mercy: that is easily answered. For he doth not say that pardon is denied them if they turn to the Lord: but he utterly denieth that they can rise unto repentance, because they are by the just judgment of God stricken with eternal blindness for their unthankfulness. And it maketh nothing to the contrary that afterward he applieth to this purpose the example of Esau, which in vain attempted with howling and weeping to recover his right of the first begotten [Heb. 12: 16-17]. And no more doth that threatening of the Prophet: When they cry, I will not hear [Zech. 7: 13]. For in such phrases of speech is meant neither the true conversion, nor calling upon God, but that carefulness of the wicked, wherewith being bound, they are compelled in extremity to look unto that which before they carelessly neglected, that there is no good thing for them but in the Lord's help. But this they do not so much call upon, as they mourn that it is taken from them. Therefore the Prophet meaneth nothing else by crying, and the Apostle nothing else by weeping, but that horrible torment which by desperation fretteth and vexeth the wicked. This it is good to mark diligently, for else God should disagree with himself, which crieth by the Prophet that he will be merciful so soon as the sinner turneth [Ezek. 18: 21-22]. And as I have already said, it is certain that the mind of man is not turned to better, but by God's grace preventing it. Also his promise concerning calling upon him will never deceive. But that blind torment wherewith the reprobate are diversely drawn when they see that they must needs seek God, that they may find remedy for their evils, and yet do flee from his presence, is unproperly called conversion and prayer.

III. xxiii. 3-4.

...if any man assail us with such words: why God hath from the beginning predestinate some to death, which when they were not, could not yet deserve the judgment of death, we instead of answer may again on our side ask of them, what they think that God oweth to man, if he will judge him by his own nature. In such sort as we be all corrupted with sin, we cannot but be hateful to God: and that not by tyrannous cruelty, but by most upright reason of justice. If all they whom the Lord doth predestinate to death are by the estate of nature subject to the judgment of death, of what injustice against themselves, I beseech you, may they complain? Let all the sons of Adam come: Let them strive and dispute with their creator, for that by his eternal providence they were before their generation condemned to everlasting misery. What shall they be able once to mutter against this defence, when God on the other side shall call them to reknowledging of themselves? If they be all taken out of a corrupt mass, it is no marvel if they be subject to damnation. Let them not therefore accuse God of injustice, if by his eternal judgment they be appointed to death, to which they themselves do feel, whether they will or no, that they are willingly led of their own nature. Whereby appeareth how wrongful is the desire of their murmuring, because they do of set purpose hide the cause of damnation which they are compelled to acknowledge in themselves, that the laying of the blame upon God may acquit them. But although I do a hundred times confess, as it is most true, that God is the author of it, yet they do not by and by wipe away the guiltiness which, being engraved in their consciences, from time with oft recourse presenteth itself to their eyes.

Again they except and say: were they not before predestinate by the ordinance of God to the same corruption which is now alleged for the cause of damnation? When therefore they perish in their corruption, they do nothing but suffer the punishment of that misery into which, by his predestination, Adam fell and drew his posterity headlong with him. Is not he therefore unjust, which doth so cruelly mock his creatures? I grant indeed that all the children of Adam fell by the will of God into that misery of state wherein they be now bound: and this is it that I said at the beginning, that at length we must always return to the determination of the will of God, the cause whereof is hidden in himself. But it followeth not by and by that God is subject to this slander. For we will with Paul answer them in this manner: O man, what art thou that contendest with God? Doth the thing formed say to him that formed it, Why hast thou formed me so? Hath not the potter power to make of the same lump one vessel to honor, and another to dishonor? [Rom. 9: 20-21].

III. xxiii. 7.

...It is a terrible decree, I grant: yet no man shall be able to deny, but that God foreknew what end man should have ere he created him, and therefore foreknew it because he had so ordained by his decree.

III. xxiii. 8.

Here they run to the distinction between will and permission, by which they will have it granted that the wicked do perish, God only permitting but not willing it. But why should we say that he permitteth it, but because he so willeth? Howbeit it is not likely that man by himself, by the only permission of God, without any his ordinance, brought destruction to himself: as though God appointed not of what condition he would have the chief of his creatures to be. I therefore will not doubt to confess simply with Augustine that the will of God is a necessity of things, and that what he willeth, it must of necessity come to pass: as those things shall truly come to pass which he hath foreseen.... Man therefore falleth, the providence of God so ordaining it: but he falleth by his own fault. The Lord had a little before pronounced that all the things which he had made were very good [Gen. 1: 31]. Whence therefore cometh that perverseness to man, to fall away from his God? Lest it should be thought to be of creation, the Lord with his commendation allowed [i.e. approved] that which came from himself. Therefore by his own evilness he corrupted the nature which he had received pure of the Lord, and by his fall he drew his whole posterity with him into destruction. Wherefore let us rather behold an evident cause of damnation in the corrupted nature of mankind, which is nearer to us, than search for a hidden and utterly incomprehensible cause thereof in the predestination of God.

III. xxiv. 12.

As the Lord by the effectualness of his calling toward the elect maketh perfect the salvation whereunto he had by eternal counsel appointed them, so he hath his judgments against the reprobate, whereby he executeth his counsel of them. Whom therefore he hath created unto the shame of life, and destruction of death, that they should be instruments of his wrath, and examples of his severity. From them, that they may come to their end, sometime he taketh away the power to hear his word, and sometime by the preaching of it he more blindeth and amazeth them.... He shall trouble himself in vain that shall here search for a cause higher than the secret and unsearchable counsel of God.

III. xxiv. 14.

...Whereas therefore the reprobate do not obey the word of God opened unto them, that shall be well imputed to the malice and perverseness of their heart, so that this be therewithal added: that they are therefore given into this perverseness because by the righteous but yet unsearchable judgment of God they are raised up to set forth his glory with their damnation.

Printed in Canada